THE BANDSMAN'S DAUGHTER

The Bandsman's Daughter

an autobiography by

Irene Thomas

M

ISBN 0 333 24195 9

First published 1979 by
MACMILLAN LONDON LIMITED
4 Little Essex Street London WC2R 3LF
and Basingstoke
Associated Companies in Delhi, Dublin,
Hong Kong, Johannesburg, Lagos, Melbourne,
New York, Singapore and Tokyo

Photoset and printed in Great Britain by
LOWE & BRYDONE PRINTERS LIMITED
Thetford, Norfolk

The poem on page 215,
'To His Wife by General Fu Wu',
is quoted from *Chinese Poems* by Arthur Waley,
by courtesy of Constable Publishers.

Contents

List of illustrations

(Unless stated otherwise, the illustrations are from the author's collection.)

To my husband Eddie
with all my love

CHAPTER ONE

Allegretto

IT IS CLASS, rather than sex, or money, or football, which is the great British secret obsession. You can be fiercely partisan about your local football team, you can be glumly earnest about sex, you can even take a morbid interest in money . . . work for it, gamble for it, strike for it, but you must not speak frankly about class. Politicians avoid the word, sociologists pretend it doesn't exist, or call it 'socio-economic strata', but anyone with a good ear and a fair amount of experience can tell a man's background, or class, after hearing his first few sentences.

I said 'a man's' because I think it is more difficult, or less usual, for a man to disguise his origins than it is for a woman. Women are naturally more perceptive, quicker to adapt, to imitate what they admire than men are, and have always been able to range up and down the social ladder fairly freely by marriage, liaison, luck or talent. Men generally rise by means of hard work, boldness and good fortune, and therefore have less time, and perhaps less need, to dissemble about their roots. Women, no matter how distinguished they may become, are still expected to display charm, a graceful manner, and a desire to please. If they do not, if they show disregard for the ancient idea that a woman must if possible look and sound agreeable, if they show any aggression or ill humour, they are treated with the mixture of contempt and fear that greeted the suffragettes and the noisier Women's Libbers of the nineteen sixties . . . the 'Oh-shut-up-and-go-home-you-silly-cow' response.

Almost all autobiographies, no matter what their authors may say, are written from a class standpoint, and the two most modish angles are the one where the author tells you that there were fourteen children in his family, and mother was a slut who pawned their shoes, and dad was a bully who beat up the whole household every Saturday night; and the other whose author was a member of a family of blue-blooded eccentrics. . . . Uncle Rollo slept in the stable with the horses, and Cousin Harriet had a close relationship with the second footman.

Very few people seem to admit to coming from my family's class, which I suppose could be described as Upper Working. It has no glamour. It causes no social problems. It pays its bills as they flutter through the letter-box, it rinses its empty milk-bottles, it still avoids hire-purchase whenever possible, it provides N.C.O.s in time of war and bank clerks and shop assistants in time of peace. The Middle Class, whose finer qualities it admires, is wary of it, and never writes television plays about it . . . no '*nostalgie de la boue*', you see. The Upper Class, whose standards it adapts to its own use, treats it with unpatronising respect. Carry on, sergeant.

There is a fine line which divides it from the Lower Middle, or 'Pooter' class. Lower Middle households could afford to employ domestic help, if only occasionally. Upper Working households could not easily do so.

My father was an archetype of the upper working class, or rather he became one, for he was born with no class at all. No parents, no home, no rank, no money, no name. His mother was described on her death certificate as a 'lady's companion'. In 1885 this meant someone who was a cut above the servants and yet not quite the social equal of the family. She seems to have come originally from Derbyshire, but had lived in Richmond, Surrey, with the same family for seventeen years. She was thirty-seven when my father was born, and to have an illegitimate child at all in those days was considered disgraceful, let alone to be no longer young when it happened. My father was born in a nursing-home in Upper Montagu Street, in Marylebone. Ten days later his mother died, of 'puerperal septicæmia, septic pneumonia and asthenia' the death certificate says (that lot would seem enough to kill anybody) and there is a blank space where it says 'Father's Name' on his birth certificate. If he knew who his father was, his deep sense of shame about his birth stopped him from telling anyone, ever. Most likely it may have been the son of the household. Apparently the only words my grandfather, whoever he was, ever said about my father, then ten days old, were: 'Take him away, I never want to see him again'. And he never did.

I suppose it was a miracle that my father escaped being sent straight to an orphanage, but two retired servants acted as foster-parents until he was fourteen, when he was sent into the army as a band-boy. The army, God bless it, didn't give a damn about his parentage, or lack of it. 'No father or mother, lad?' said the sergeant. 'No matter, the Army will be your father and mother.' And it was. It stuck a clarinet into his hands and said: 'You'll play that.' In many ways he was happy. He loved music, and the King's Royal Rifles (the old 60th) was a fashionable and honourable regiment. He travelled all over the world in the days when there was a lot of red on the map, and had the chance to develop his talents for games and athletics, and his skill as a marksman, which he began to show during the South African War. He admired the Boer people, and he was pleased to be told that his shooting was equal to theirs. Their method of training their sons to shoot straight was to send a boy out hunting with only one bullet in his rifle. If he missed he didn't eat, which concentrated the mind and steadied the hand wonderfully. The band-boys were encouraged to sing, too, but when their voices showed signs of breaking they would go out on to the veldt and shout and yell as loudly as they could . . . they thought it would make them into baritones more quickly.

There was a darker side to army life though. Apart from the danger of being killed by an enemy there was an even greater risk of being killed by cholera, typhus, enteric fever, malaria, yellow fever, typhoid and all the other horrors of the age before antibiotics. Then there would be the platoon bully-boy to throw a boot at your head if you knelt down to say your prayers at night. The cure for that seems to have been to finish praying and then hit him anyway.

Loathsome, too, was the sight of the poverty and distress in India, most of it due to the caste system and the selfishness and cruelty of some Indian rulers. One of the worst was said to have burned alive a polo-pony which had displeased him.

Like many soldiers before him my father found the country and the people fascinating and haunting, from the noise and smell of the bazaars of Peshawar and Lahore to the cool hill-stations like Simla and Darjeeling (old postcards show Simla as a kind of Guildford in the mountains). And he remembered the cold lakes of Kashmir and the barren bleakness of the Khyber Pass – in those days a place of glaring sinister light by day and nerve-twanging windy darkness by night. Being a bandsman ensured that he was part of most of the great ceremonial parades the Raj delighted in, and now, whenever I see the old film of King George V and Queen Mary at the great Durbar in Delhi in 1911, I know that on that vast parade-ground, under one of those white helmets, is my dad.

His term of service was over in 1913, and he became a civilian. It was typical of him that for some years before his discharge he would never take the afternoon sleep which was usual in the army, because he knew that it would not be possible in a civilian job, and he would have to stay awake all day, so he might as well get used to it He had his Army First Class Certificate of Education, he had been all over the world, and he was good-looking in a dark, serious fashion. In spite of his long years of soldiering he was as unlike the popular idea of a regular soldier as it is possible to be. He was almost completely teetotal, partly because he had seen so much drunkenness and the consequences of it, he had an iron self-control, never swore . . . 'Bust it!' was all he ever said even under the most extreme provocation – like dropping a hammer on his foot – and, for a man who had seen the gaudier sights of Port Said, Bombay, Cape Town and countless other places, he was remarkably shy of women. He had found a civilian job easily, and it was on an outing with one of his colleagues that he met my mother.

My mother was entirely different in temperament and upbringing from my father. His origins were completely unknown, her forebears could be traced back to 1350, or maybe earlier according to her Uncle Rufus. Her father was a blacksmith, one of a large family who lived in the Suffolk village of Grundisburgh. It's in *Akenfield* country, near where the Sutton Hoo treasure was found, and the people haven't changed much from the days when the Danes, their ancestors, rowed their longships up the misty inlets each bloodstained summer. They still have the same white, freckle-powdered skins, Baltic blue eyes lion-yellow hair and long bony faces. Grandad's family were half church and half chapel – he was one of the church half – and armed with a bible from the Rector he had set off to make his fortune in London, sometimes on foot and sometimes with a lift on a passing cart. He married a tiny energetic London girl, and took to keeping a pub. It was called The Hit or Miss, and it missed. So he found another, The Magpies, where Heathrow now sprawls. He wasn't a very good publican, The Magpies sold only ale and beer, and the local drinkers were farm labourers and field-hands from the flat, wintry market-gardens in the district. He would tell them not to drink so much and to take the money home to their wives – beer was all of a penny a pint then. So trade wasn't good, and he went back to being a blacksmith. His forge was in Croydon, and next to it was a wheelwright's shop where his son, my uncle, made the great cart-wheels of those days. When I was a tiny child I can remember being allowed to watch Grandad fitting an iron tyre around the edge of a wheel. It was thrilling to see the men lowering the wheel into water to shrink the hot iron on to the rim with a violent hiss of steam like the breath of demons. The forge was terrifying and fascinating, a cavern of red heat and black hammers, full of the reek of burning horn as some huge cart-horse's hoof was gripped between Grandad's knees while he fitted a new shoe the size of a dinner-plate. He wasn't the mighty Longfellow 'Village Blacksmith', but his arms and hands were immensely strong. He had great charm, and people smiled when they saw him approaching. He used to hang wood-shavings in my hair – 'to give you even more curls' he'd say. Even today, some of the iron railings and gates he made are still standing – those that escaped the wartime metal-melting. But horses were replaced by lorries and tractors, so he retired and he and Grandma came to live in the next street to us. I loved to visit his toolshed where he still kept some of his great hammers. He missed the forge, and the double-ring of hammer on anvil, but he took to growing vegetables, and fed me on brown bread and raw onions at tea-time in the shed on his allotment. And the odd raw carrot too, just pulled from the earth and cursorily dusted on his leather apron. When I'm scrupulously washing vegetables nowadays I wonder why we didn't drop dead through eating all that dirt. 'You gotta eat a peck afore you doy, thassa fact,' he'd say. He had a friend, old Mr Wigley, who used to sit on the bench with us at tea-time among the vegetables. I was six then, full of tales about school and its wonders, and Mr Wigley gave me a tin paintbox, bought out of his tiny pension. I've still got it, in memory of those lovely grubby onion-and-carrot afternoons.

My mother was Grandad's delight. She was fair and slender and elegant, and had a great talent for sewing. He had been so proud when she had been accepted as an apprentice at Gorringes, the big department store in Buckingham Palace Road. She sewed in an attic workroom with about twenty other girls, making gowns for society ladies, wedding dresses, court dresses, Ascot dresses. It must have been like the workshop in Charpentier's opera *Louise*. When a bride came in for a fitting of her satin-pearls-lace-and-chiffon wedding gown with its yards of flounced skirts and train, the workroom girls were at the mercy of her whims, and worse still, her mother's whims. If the ladies were kindly and reasonable the bride's dress would have a hair secretly sewn into the hem for luck, generally a long hair from my mother's head, as hers was blonde enough to be unnoticed against the white satin.

Sometimes girls were 'lent' to ladies in their own homes for special sewing jobs, say a dozen lawn nightgowns for a journey to India, or a set of plain cotton gowns for an accouchement, and a christening-robe too, maybe. Ladies ordered underwear in dozens then. My mother absorbed all the small graces of elegant living, and watched the parlourmaid lay the tables with the fine silver and glass. If you hadn't got silver fish-knives, she'd say, then you must use two forks to eat fish, never a steel knife. And ladies might keep their hats on at luncheon. Ideas above her station, perhaps, but she kept them all her life. 'To be poor and *look* poor are two dam' bad things' was her maxim.

Perhaps her craving for refinement kept her from marrying young like most of her friends. She sometimes helped in the bar during my grandad's landlording days, and hated every minute of it. Pubs were rough places then, and perhaps she thought that men, apart from her father and brother, were poor brutish creatures.

When she and my father were married in 1917 they were both thirty-three. His civilian life had been cut short by the 1914–18 war, and in 1915 he was back in the army again. Not this time in the world of exciting skirmishes, hot places and colourful parades, but in the dreadful icy mud of Flanders. His service could have been made slightly easier by his becoming a sniper – he was the battalion's best shot – but he refused. He thought it was somehow unethical to kill a selected man in cold blood. Also, he said wryly, snipers were generally eliminated as soon as possible by the enemy.

When the war was over he was billeted on a German family in Cologne, and after the tales of brutal soldiery I should think they found my quiet, polite, non-drinking father an ideal conqueror. They presented him with a bottle of real eau-de-Cologne for my mother. It was encased in a soft wicker-work cover, and she kept the empty bottle with its delicate orange-blossom scent for years afterwards, although she swore that when I was born the midwife stole most of it.

By the time I arrived my father had stopped occupying the Rhineland and had a job collecting money from gas-meters for the Brentford Gas Company. We lived in 'rooms' in Feltham for a few months, then we got our own house. It was in a fairly quiet road, and it was Detached. Detached houses were a cut above the terrace houses on the other side of the road, and if you stood sideways and edged yourself along our alley you could get to our back garden. The coalman's language was florid when he tried to carry sacks round to our coalshed. The house had an outside lavatory – a wooden bench with a hole in it . . . a great constipator in the cold weather, as nobody lingered. We had a bathroom too, but with only a cold tap, so hot water had to be carried upstairs in pails. Later my father's Gas Company connection got us a water-heater, but until then it was the tin bath in the kitchen for me, with hot water from the 'copper' in the corner.

For today's wives who have probably never seen one, a 'copper' was really a huge wash-bowl with a fire underneath, all built into a corner of the kitchen. A heavy round wooden lid covered it while the clothes were being boiled. Then followed a rinse in a zinc bath, then 'blueing' and starching and mangling and drying and ironing and airing. It was a horrid, dangerous, back-breaking system. Women were much tougher in those days, and if a woman had a large family she needed the strength of a mule. There was every excuse for giving up and becoming a slut, but not many did in our street. I was an only child, but it must still have been a constant struggle to keep me neat and tidy. Our road, quiet enough itself, and full of grimly clean families, was near the vast railway marshalling-yards, and the smuts floated over our washing with each heartbreaking breeze on Monday mornings. The yard worked all night, and I fell asleep to the clack-clink-tink-tink of trucks being shunted. I saw the yard from the train recently. It's a grass-grown wilderness now. All the towering lights and shiny rails are gone, and it has become part of Hounslow Heath again, as it was before ever the railways were built.

I wish I could say I remember being one year old, or two, or three, like Compton Mackenzie did, but I can't remember a thing until I was four, and had a blue velvet dress for my birthday, and shoes with tiny pearl buttons on the front. This frivolous delight in fine raiment has never left me. My mother's skill as a dressmaker made me the best-dressed child in our street, but she would never try to earn extra money by her needle. It was considered the man's job to provide for his family, and only when a husband was ill, or a drunkard, or disabled in some way was it fitting for a wife to 'take in sewing' or 'take in washing'. My mother would 'make' for friends, though, and would accept presents in return . . . sweets, plants for the garden, and so on. She made my grandad's thick flannel shirts, and my grandma's drawers, which really were plural . . . two separate lace-edged legs, gathered on to a drawstring at the waist. Old ladies in those days still wore ankle-length dresses and coats. Some of the old ladies in the next street, somewhat rougher than ours, wore men's caps, and canvas aprons. One even smoked a pipe.

In our own road there were unusual families. The Songis, whose father was Italian; the Denfords next door, noisy and good-natured Irish. Mrs Denford was an accomplished plate-smasher. Every morning two or three bits of crockery could be heard hitting the scullery flagstones, and later Mrs Denford's rosy face would appear to tell my mother cheerfully 'Ah well, if there wasn't any breakers there wouldn't be any makers'. The Colarossis were Italian too, and their father is immortal as long as Eros stays in Piccadilly Circus, for as a youth Mr Colarossi had been the model for Alfred Gilbert's charming statue. Years later a newspaper printed a picture of him – by then a respected family man – balancing on one leg and using his rolled-up umbrella as the famous bow.

But the most exotic clan of all were the Etoos. Billy Etoo and his sister Lily had a Japanese grandfather. I remember Lily as being the loveliest child I've ever seen, with black eyes and silky black hair. Every year at our school we had a May-Day celebration (nothing to do with working-class solidarity, or with watch-chained local politicians keening 'The Red Flag' through clenched teeth: it was simply an old-fashioned welcome to summer, with a maypole in the playground and a May Queen with a procession). My friend Annie was May Queen one year, and the teacher who organised the day had dressed her in the usual plain white dress, but with a cloak made of rose-covered chintz, and roses in her brown curly hair. Next year it was Lily Etoo's turn. The white dress was the same, but the cloak had mauve irises on it, and she carried irises in her arms and wore them in her crown. Fifty years later I can still remember how lovely she looked. Lily had straight hair though, which was not the ideal. Curls were the thing. My own hair was done up in 'rags' each night till my head looked like a small cauliflower covered with white Brussels sprouts. This achieved the floppy heavy ringlets every child wanted. Crusts had to be eaten up to induce curly hair . . . a cunning way of preventing waste.

I'm certain there were a lot more physically ugly people around in those days than there are now – but only physically. Although working-class life was very hard, and you would have to put up with it, or work harder to improve your lot, expressions on faces were not as sullen then, any newsreel film of 1920s and 1930s football crowds will show that. But there were many hunchbacks and dwarfs and mongols and children crippled with rickets or what is now called polio – we called it infantile paralysis then. Bad birthmarks were not treated as they would be nowadays, and of course there were many men who had been dreadfully disfigured by the 1914–18 war – not long over when I was a small child. For a man to be marred in that way was considered to be an honour, and boys who shouted after any cripple in the street would receive the flat of their parents' hands around their ears. Child guidance was only just rearing its dear muddled head among the upper middle class . . . it hadn't filtered down to us yet, and retribution for any insolence or misdemeanour was swift and sharp, administered by a parent or the local bobby. That didn't stop us staring at any strange face, though. One poor lady had half a nostril eaten away by what I now suppose to have been syphilis caught from her absent husband. She told everyone that she'd inhaled a tiny insect into her nose while smelling flowers. I don't think my mother was fooled, but I was always very careful about smelling flowers after that.

The streets were noisier then. Costers and rag-and-bone men yelling (they gave you a fern in a pot for any old iron or furniture), lavender-women really did wail the traditional 'Won'cher buyeee my sweet bloomin' lavender, sixteen bunches for a penneeeee.' The lamplighter came round on his bicycle on winter afternoons, and the muffin-man still tramped along ringing his little handbell, carrying on his head the great wooden tray of muffins covered with a white cloth.

The way our milk was delivered would give today's young mothers forty fits. The milkman had a pony and cart, and a big thirty-gallon churn. You took your own jug to the door, and he ladled out the pints of milk with a deep cylindrical metal scoop. I suppose lots of diseases were caught this way, bit it was the only way we knew until the wide-topped milk bottles began to clink onto the doorsteps, and you could pay once a week instead of every day. In those days we weren't on 'the main drainage' either. The cesspool cart came every few weeks, bringing with it the stink and noise of the pumping-engine.

The doorknocker sounded many times each day for hawkers, pedlars and gipsies selling clothes-pegs, mostly women with well-rehearsed toneless patter about 'what a lucky face you've got, lady, and you've got an old silk dress upstairs that you'll never wear again, and your little girl is musical, ain't she, and she'll go to America, and you'll live 'til you're ninety-four.' Strange chalk-marks were left on the pavements, a kind of shorthand to tell the next wave of pedlars what to expect . . . 'Not much here' or 'A soft touch here'.

I thought the gipsies were romantic, and I was at the age when most children need mystery in their lives, and long to be the long-lost sons of dukes, stolen by gipsies and adopted by their own humdrum parents. 'Have we got any pirates or gipsies in our family, grandma?' I said. 'Certainly not, miss.' (Grandma always called you 'miss' or 'milady' when she felt reproof was deserved.) 'Certainly not. We was always very respectable.' Grandma was a realist and a tough customer. Grandad was as soft as goose-feathers, and everybody knew it. Grandma was full of tart remarks like: 'Serves you right,' and 'No such word as can't.' She was a fine cook, though a slapdash one, and she had Cook's Luck, which is a rare gift. For instance, she once made a cake and forgot to put the sugar in. It had been in the oven half an hour, but she heaved it out and threw in the sugar, beat it up again and slammed it back in. It was perfect, but if anyone else had done that the cake would have been like a paving-stone. She gave me a doll's tea-set, and made me make small 'cakes' of mashed potato. When play was over I had to keep the grey sticky buns 'for tomorrow's dinner' she said. First lesson in home economics. Dinner was at midday for us. Tea was at six, and supper was what you had last thing, cocoa and biscuits.

In spite of being an only child I was never lonely, though sometimes solitary, which is pleasant even for a child, a fact that most people don't realise. I had my tabby cat, Tim, and plenty of small friends along the road, but playing in the street was frowned upon, partly from the upper-working-class snobbery about dirt and bad manners, and partly because heavy carts and horses rumbled through, and there was even the occasional motor-van. Carter Patterson, the carrier, had a great horse and van, and if you wanted to send a parcel you simply propped up a red-and-green card with 'CP' on it in your front window, and he called to fetch your package.

You could play in your own front or back garden though, and so you were always under the eye of some adult – parent or neighbour – even if your mother went out shopping. One of these days, planners will realise that this kind of housing is the only good way for young families to live. The most irritating part of that realisation will be when they tell us so.

When I was five my father thought it was time I was christened. I don't know why he waited so long. Usually babies were christened within a few weeks of birth, and my father was a fairly religious man. Anyway, I can remember standing on a stool by the font in our local church while the baptismal water trickled down my small snub nose.

My father got the name 'Irene' from a saints' almanac-card an old lady had given him while he was in France. June the twenty-eighth was St Irene's day. (Later I learned that this St Irene was a man, and a female saint who shares his feast-day was St Potamiaena, so I'm thankful not to have been christened Potamiaena instead. I was never called Irene, though. It was 'Reenie' inside the family, or 'Reen' to my schoolmates. Maybe I was christened in time to start school soon after my fifth birthday, for an unbaptised child would have been an oddity to the staff and pupils of Cardinal Road Mixed Infants.

Ever since I could remember sounds, grown-ups' conversation had buzzed and rumbled over my head. Half of it not understood, but the sounds had been there. I'm convinced that I learned my alphabet through my mother's discreet habit of spelling out letter by letter any tit-bits she didn't want me to hear. 'Mrs H. is having a B-A-B-Y,' she'd say. Curiosity is a great educator, and before I went into the Mixed Infants I knew the alphabet and could count up to a hundred.

My grandad made me a wooden pencil-box, and my mother took me to see the headmistress on that first day. Women teachers were all single then, and Miss Hutchins was an experienced headmistress who looked like a caricature of one. Tall, thin, with pince-nez and hair scraped back into a tiny bun. She put me into the Babies' class, and left me. I didn't cry, because I had always been told what school would be like. How many other children there'd be (there were fifty in the Babies' class), how long the day would be (no school dinners – we were all local children and we brought our own lunches or went home to dinner) and how many days a week it would last.

My teachers were a mixture of the traditional kind, like Miss Hutchins, and the New 'Flapper', like Miss Peacock, who had bobbed hair and wore 'floaty' voile dresses – the sleeves waved up and down when she beat time for us to sing 'The Keeper' and 'Early One Morning'. We learned music from big Tonic Sol-Fa scrolls hung on the blackboard. The classroom windows were high, near the ceiling, so you couldn't see out and had to attend to what was going on in the classroom. The door had a panel with a picture of 'Polly Put the Kettle On' in coloured glass. We learned sums with cardboard boxes full of small shells which we laid out in neat groups on the desk. I wasn't very good at sums, which disappointed my father a bit. He was a mathematical wizard himself, and used to checking great columns of figures when he paid the Gas Company's meter-money into local banks.

We learned writing on paper that had two blue lines for the small letters and red ones above and below for the capitals and loops. Miss Cousins had us reading and writing quite fluently by the time we were six, all except for one little boy who was a bit of a 'natural', and even he could write his name, tell the time and read words like In, Out, Left and Right. There had been no pre-school play-groups for us, so having to work did not come as a nasty shock as it must do to small children nowadays who have had two or more years of untrammelled playing with sand and swings and slides. Our day was short, half-past three was home-time, and most mothers met us at the gate for the first month or so. After that we skipped home on our own. No anxiety, everybody on our route knew us; there was very little traffic, and far fewer child-molesters than there seem to be now. Crime then was a sin, not some kind of illness, and sentences were short and savage, with 'Hard Labour' as the great deterrent. Even when a sentence had been served, the offender was better off if he moved away from the district. Memories were long and merciless.

Children seldom played truant. There were always a few boys who would rather fish for sticklebacks in the Longford River than go to school, but there was also the looming menace of the School Board Man. The School Board Man wore a flat cap, and bicycle-clips round his ankles, and carried a black note-book. When his old bicycle rattled over the bridge, small boys would disappear like disturbed minnows and huddle under the arch of the bridge in a muddy, panting mob, until Authority had passed. Often Authority's beady eye and licked pencil had noticed them anyway, and what with truancy, dirt, disobedience and general parental exasperation, a rough homecoming awaited the anglers. Teddy Soames was generally the chief truant. From the age of six Teddy knew he wanted to be a sailor, and saw no sense in school. When the headmistress came to call us in from the playground for afternoon school she always looked up to the roof where Teddy would be clinging to a drain-pipe like a small cheerful bat. 'Teddy, come down . . . what are you doing up there?' 'Climbin', miss. I wanna be a sailor and I'm practisin'.' He seems to have got his wish: one of the names on the local war memorial is Soames, Edward, Able Seaman. Teddy's sister Lucy was one of my Best Friends. Their father was a rag-and-bone man, and there was an enthralling rumour that their mother was a gipsy, and we were rather disappointed when she didn't wear big gold earrings and carry a tambourine. Their house made up for it, though. It was full of old tin baths, stuffed bears and broken iron bedsteads, and the outside walls were covered with coloured pebbles and shells arranged in patterns and stuck in cement. Local mothers must have got tired of the cry: 'Can we go up Lucy's house, mum?'

In spite of the happy blend of order and discovery at school, there was a darkness outside the school gates. The late twenties were a time of undeserved hardship for many working-class families, and children sometimes came to school with no socks or stockings, just broken lace-up boots on their feet, and torn jerseys and dirty necks. My mother clicked her tongue at this kind of slovenliness. In her eyes dirt was a fault, not an accident. Old jerseys, yes, but torn ones should have been mended, and necks scrubbed, even with cheap household soap. Some of the 'richer' mothers brought boxes of outgrown clothing to the headmistress, who discreetly distributed it among the most ragged children. Sometimes their parents simply sold the clothes – and not to buy food, either – and the children were as ill-clad as ever. There wasn't a lot of 'welfare' about in those days and there were some real tragedies; children often died of scarlet fever, diphtheria and tuberculosis ('consumption' to us), and minor diseases like ringworm and lice – nits – were very common. Nurse Duncan came round every week to look at our heads. She was a brawny Scotswoman who must have weighed thirteen stone. She wore a long brown gaberdine coat, and her great red hands pawed through our hair with eye-watering tugs. 'It beats me how y'r mither keeps this hair sae clean' she'd say to me. I thought of all the rain-water washing and fine-tooth combing and nightly brushing, and knew just how.

If Nurse Duncan found any puzzling health troubles the school doctor – a young lady whose cut-glass accent was the first I'd ever heard – would look at you and decide if you had to have Treatment. We dreaded Treatment. Usually it meant a long day sitting on benches in dim gas-lit corridors in the local hospital, and being snapped at by a nurse who was obviously determined that the meek were not going to inherit the earth while *she* was in charge of it. But the doctors themselves were usually kind, even though small operations were sometimes done without anæsthetic. I can remember, vividly, having a cyst removed from the corner of my eye in this way when I was eight. I was so astonished that I didn't move or cry, and so got a reputation for stoicism under fire, and a bar of milk chocolate from my father. It was soon after that day that one of my teachers discovered that I was very shortsighted, and I had to wear glasses. How she ever found time to notice this when she had forty-five other children to supervise is a mystery, but I expect she wondered why I was so keen to sit at the front . . . most children weren't.

I loved school, except for the games in the asphalt playground. I was a thin, timid child, and hopeless at everything except the ordinary drill. It was always called Swedish drill, so Sweden to us became a place where everybody swung their arms about a lot, another of those mysterious places like Thames Station, that we asked God every day to lead us not into. Why not, we wondered, where *was* Thames Station, and whatever went on there? But ordinary lessons were fascinating, and I even won a prize. I never really understood what it was for, but I trotted home with it (*The Merry Moments Annual* it was called) and had a bowl of glamorous tinned tomato soup for tea.

Not much fuss was made about tests and examinations then. If you were good at sums or composition, all right. If not, you were generally good at something else . . . sewing, running or singing. You could even win a prize for attendance. Nobody assumed that all children were or could be equally good at their lessons, and nobody was ever made to feel that they were better than other children if when they got to the Junior School they won the 'Scholarship', as the eleven-plus was called . . . they were simply different. That was how life was going to be, and we were going to have to get used to it, and face up to disappointments like not being able to do handstands or not winning the scholarship.

We all had our tiny consolations, though, like being given a part in the school play. One year it was *Snow White and the Seven Dwarfs*. Not the Disney version, Disney had hardly been heard of then. This Snow White was a home-made musical, with the words fitted to well-known tunes. I was Fairy Crocus, with a green bodice and a skirt made of yellow petals. My Best Friend was Fairy Rose, but in the excitement she wetted her pink knickers, and had to wear her ordinary navy-blue ones under her pink petals. I'm sure the National Theatre never has troubles like that.

One day my father was emptying the gas meter in a big music shop, and the manager showed him a fine upright piano which had been made for an exhibition. It had been in the shop for a year or more, and the legs were a bit chipped, so he let my father have it cheap. It was the ambition of every working-class family to own one of these things, and all our neighbours came to look at it. My dad had joined the local band, and his evenings were spent transposing clarinet music or copying parts, and he was determined that I should learn to play the piano. Lessons were expensive, a shilling for half an hour, but I went once a week to try to master the pieces in Smallwood's Pianoforte Tutor. It was hard at first – the keys are just as slippery and even farther apart when you're eight than when you're forty-eight. So I didn't want to practise until my mother threatened to sell the piano. That prodded me into action.

All these luxuries like piano lessons, and the material for the pretty dresses my mother made me, meant that there were things I wasn't going to have. A bicycle, for instance, but we all knew very early that we couldn't have everything.

Music meant a lot to me even when I was nine or ten. On Sunday afternoons we used to go to Richmond Park bandstand and see Dad playing the clarinet in the band . . . the *Zampa* overture, Strauss waltzes, selections from Gilbert and Sullivan, and evening hymns to end with. And every Saturday we went to the theatre or the music-hall. My father loved variety shows, and it didn't matter who was performing, we went to Richmond Theatre, or Kingston Empire, or the King's Theatre, Hammersmith. I was entranced at everything, especially at the man who brought two great boxes on to the stage and opened them up to show a 'Doll' in each one. The fair doll was in blue and the dark one in pink, and they came alive to dance and sing. It was the era of stage tableaux too, and lights were used to illuminate different parts of the stage while the cast made pictures illustrating heart-rending songs like '*Ora Pro Nobis*', all about an orphan dying in the snow on her mother's grave.

I didn't understand the comedians' jokes, which was just as well, but I remembered the songs and sang them loudly all the way home on the open-topped bus. Sometimes we walked down King Street, Hammersmith to see the shops. We walked in the road, of course, everybody walked down the middle of King Street on those evenings. Any cars would creep slowly along giving an apologetic toot to ask the crowds to part and let them through. If you tried it now you'd be a mangled heap in thirty seconds.

Every Saturday morning there were children's shows at our dear flea-infested Roxy cinema, and the chief attraction seemed to be the competition among small boys to see who could crawl under the seats towards the front, and get *behind* the screen to read the sub-titles *backwards*.

Even when parents could not afford the shilling or so for the 'pictures' there were lots of other things to do. Jam-jar fishing, swimming in the gravel-pits or the river, both horribly dangerous, I'm sure, dragging each other along in carts made out of orange-boxes, afternoons at the fair on our recreation-ground, reading, collecting leaves, drawing, watching the trains, or the aeroplanes at Hanworth Aerodrome. I suppose it all sounds very tame now, but it seemed to keep us from the self-induced boredom which is like a career for so many children today.

We had plenty to do at school, in fact more seemed to be expected of us every day. Winter Friday afternoons were the best, though. Lights on in the classroom while Miss Hindmarsh read us a story. *The Coral Island*, *Stories from the Operas* (lovely blood-and-thunder stuff for kids) *A Prisoner in the Caucasus*. Never mind if they contained long words, Miss Hindmarsh would explain them as she went along. And it was a nice change from the way the other days ended, with the ritual chanting of tables . . . 'Six nineza fifty-four seven nineza sixty-three', sitting bolt upright with your hands behind your backs. Miss Hindmarsh was a lot less dangerous than Mr Hirst, who prodded 'Fair Stood the Wind for France' into forty-six children, with a long map-pole for the ribs of those whose voices faltered. And it was 'Frannse', he insisted, not 'Frahnce'. He was homesick for Bradford, I think.

Little crazes swept the school at intervals. Once it was for 'folders' of thick paper, with a pocket inside where we kept picture-postcards, cut-out flowers off seed-packets, snapshots, newspaper cuttings, anything we thought was pretty. Then there were the tin boxes full of tiny glass beads and thin wire for making flowers with. And curtain-rings and darning-wool to make brooches. You wound the wool around the ring, then filled in the centre with French knots to make bunches of flowers, then presented the result to your astounded and delighted relations. The most mysterious fad of all was for old cotton-reels with four nails fixed into one end. With this gadget and some odd scraps of wool you could make a long, and so far as I can remember completely useless, woollen pipe.

Once a year we all gathered in the playground to have our class photograph taken. I still have one of them, a bit creased and dim now, but there we are, all forty-six of us in Class Two, agonisingly still for a few seconds until we were allowed to break away into our usual bubbling, twittering mass.

When we got to the top class of the Juniors it was time for us to take the Scholarship. If we passed in the top few we could have a free place at the County School about two miles away, though if our parents could afford it we'd still have to pay a part of the fees. As usual, little fuss was made about the actual examination, for we were expected to have worked hard, and if we didn't pass we could still go to the Senior School next door, and after a year or two there seemed to be some kind of second chance to try for the 'Grammar'. If you were clever with your hands instead of just with your head, you could go to the Technical School and study engineering or building and practical things like that. This system seems so eminently sensible that I can't think why it was ever changed. Any teacher who can't discover a child's chief interests and talents by the time it is eleven or twelve is not doing the job properly. Of course children change their minds later, but the *type* of gift a child has alters very little.

It was just about this time that my father got promotion, and the rise in pay that went with it. Three pounds a week! A fortune in our eyes. And he didn't have to ride that old bicycle in all weathers, he would be working indoors, in the office of the Gas, Light and Coke Company. Secretly, I was a tiny bit disappointed. I used to like his uniform with its lapel badge and peaked cap – from now on he'd be wearing ordinary clothes. And I liked to be able to shout 'Hallo daddy' when he sometimes rode by in the street.

I had by now won a free place at the grammar school, but the extra money would be a godsend, for even with my mother's talent for sewing, school uniform was going to be expensive. Up to then we'd worn cotton dresses in the summer, with huge hems to 'let down', and 'wellies' on our feet and woollen scarves crossed over our chests and pinned behind our coats in the winter. We weren't very chic, I'm afraid; there were no special clothes for children then.

I was sad at leaving my junior school friends and our teachers, but it was made clear to me that the teachers had done their best for me and I must do the rest myself. I had one small regret, and that was that I had never been our May Queen. That free place I had won was considered quite enough of a plum for me. One of the other little girls, who wasn't going to the grammar school, would have the glamorous cloak and crown, and be the Miss World of Cardinal Road Juniors.

From the first day at the grammar school I felt like a tiny piece of a great jigsaw puzzle that had been fitted exactly into its space. There were about four hundred pupils, thirty-five children in each form. 'Tommy' Adams, the headmaster, was a large, bald man in a navy-blue suit. He did little teaching – sixth-form German sometimes, for he had been to Heidelberg University as well as to Oxford – but the rest of his day seemed to be spent patrolling the corridors at a steady plod like a policeman on his beat. Any child who passed him would be expected to give, as it were, name, rank and number, and then talk with him as he walked. Talk in a clear voice, too, no mumbling. You could say whatever you liked, but could expect to be corrected.

The headmaster knew each child's name after the first few weeks, and the rest of the teaching staff were highly qualified and tough at the same time. There were no popularity stakes among the staff; they cared not a jot if you liked them as long as you respected them and worked hard for your own sake. As it happened, most of them were liked and admired just because they had never seemed to need adulation. The school must have been one of the first co-educational grammar schools, so there was a headmistress too. She was a grey-haired woman of great elegance, and she bullied us gently into maturity, and gave us what passed for sex-education lessons in those days. 'If any of you younger girls don't know what I'm talking about,' she'd say, 'then it doesn't apply to you, and you need not listen.' As many of us were physically mature at eleven or twelve there were very few who weren't listening. My own knowledge had been gained from the guarded language of the 'Answers to Correspondents' page of the *Lady's Companion*, a tuppenny magazine my mother read each week. But we were made to understand that our sexual development must take a bad second place to our education, and our primary purpose must be learning. There was a great deal of that to do. French, for a start. Our plump, pretty French teacher burst into the classroom on our second day at school, said to the nearest child: 'Fermez la porte, s'il vous plaît,' and we were off. No 'learning by discovery', no misty 'projects'. It was phonetics, grammar and chat, full speed, all the way up to Mérimée and Flaubert.

Latin, too, from a lady called Virginia Wilkins, with a civilised and cultivated mind. She had glasses, hair in a bun, grey *directoire* knickers under a navy serge skirt, grey lisle stockings, all the cartoon stuff, but with a gift for dropping jewels from that so-called 'dead' language into small hands and connecting them with art, history, music and twentieth-century life. A truly great teacher. Even though I can't remember more than a sentence or two of Latin now, the habit of order and the austere formality of it, like listening to Glück, can be rediscovered with delight.

The only subjects that caused me worry and sometimes tears were algebra and games. Algebra still looks pretty on paper, like a textile design, but is almost totally incomprehensible. Games were torture. All that hockey – bruises and running in the cold. Tennis – nervous hysteria and running in the heat. To a timid, short-sighted child there was only one solution. Commit some small crime for which the sentence would be Loss of Games . . .Extra French instead . . . lovely. In the end this ruse was unworkable, so I acted as ball-boy to the hearties, with relief and in comparative safety. But to be hopeless at games was to be despised, so I had to work doubly hard at my other small talents, like playing the piano, singing and acting. On speech-days some of us were expected to sing, and I loved accompanying other boys and girls when they practised their songs. I still do. I like being part of a team however small it is. My own voice was clear, straight and rather dull, but I bawled my way through 'God's Garden', 'A Brown Bird Singing' and so on, to moderate applause.

From the age of about thirteen I earned a few extra shillings each week as the pianist for a semi-professional concert-party. 'The Mayfairs', we called ourselves, and we travelled wherever there was a club or church hall to take us. Fred was the boss, and his wife Effie was the comedienne. She was an ex-music-hall performer, and fiercely puritanical where I was concerned. 'If you'd seen the things I've seen' she'd say darkly. I longed to ask her what these thing were, but I didn't dare, so after the show it was 'Three brown ales, three milk stouts, and a lemonade for the kid' and then straight home. For two years it was marvellous experience, but the late nights weren't very good for me, and when I had my hair bobbed I didn't look childish enough to be the Infant Phenomenon of the Keyboard any longer. So it was back to total concentration on school.

My father had bought a wireless with a loudspeaker instead of our old headphones-and-accumulators set. I listened avidly to everything. Plays, talks, music, Walford Davies, Geraldo and his Gaucho Tango Orchestra, Clapham and Dwyer, Henry Hall, A. J. Alan, and the marvellous, irreplaceable 'Children's Hour', with 'Toytown', Commander Stephen King-Hall, Romany and his dog Raq, and the Aunts and Uncles reading out the birthday names and telling children where to look for presents. 'In the greenhouse . . .', 'under the stairs . . .' If there were twins to name, the announcement would be followed by somebody singing: 'Hellooooo, twins' as a sort of extra greeting. In the evenings I heard whole operas, *Der Rosenkavalier* and *La Traviata*, and operettas like *Countess Maritza* and *Gipsy Love*. I suppose it was the B.B.C. as much as my school that educated me. All this acute listening compensated for the fact that when some of my schoolmates went to France and Spain on exchange visits I couldn't go because we couldn't afford it. I didn't resent this at all at the time, but I suppose the trips must have given my friends extra confidence.

My headmistress worked continuously to modify my suburban-Cockney accent, and the B.B.C. English I heard from the wireless helped to fortify my 'L' sounds, for it's the lack of 'L's, not the supposed dropped aitch, that gives that slipshod effect to a Londoner's speech. Up to that time I had happily said 'pensoo' for pencil, and 'meeook' for milk.

When I was fourteen, my Grandad fell ill with bronchitis, and for a week while my mother nursed him I was sent to live with my uncle and aunt. My uncle, once the wheelwright, now kept a general store in Coldharbour Lane, Brixton, and I helped serve behind the counter, which was great fun. The shop was tiny and dark, and smelled of Edwards' Desiccated Soup packets, and the cat slept on the half-open sacks of rice and oatmeal. Every time the door opened, the cardboard display signs with corn-plasters and hairgrips flapped against the window, and instead of the noise of the marshalling yard at night back home, I went to sleep to the sound of the clanging and grinding of trams, and the trains rattling over the railway bridge near the shop. Grandad died, and I missed him dreadfully. He was buried in our local cemetery, but I've always thought that his body should have been put on a longship and sent burning out to sea in the custom of his Danish ancestors.

Rudyard Kipling wrote at the beginning of his poem 'Lichtenberg': 'Smells are surer than sounds or sights to make the heartstrings crack', and for years afterwards the smell of dehydrated soup and vinegar reminded me of my uncle's shop, and of that day when I realised I'd never see Grandad again.

The next year at school was extra busy. It was preparation time for the Matriculation exam as the G.C.E. was called then. We'd moved house, too, from the little just-detached house to a newer just-detached house nearer the school. It cost £750, I remember. When the Matriculation results were announced – they were just pinned up on the school notice-board in those days, no private envelopes – I had done well, well enough to be almost certain of getting a State Scholarship to the University if I were to try. This would have been a triumph for the school, and you got your name painted in gilt letters on the honours board. But in my case there was an obstacle – money, or the lack of it. Scholarships were all very well, but university would mean another three years' dependence on my parents, and grants were not handed out, even to boys, with any enthusiasm at that time. My headmistress was bitterly disappointed. I think she believed that all her hard work in my case would be wasted. If she is still alive I can assure her that such a belief was unfounded, as I can remember the smallest thing she ever taught me, about English Literature or about manners, with gratitude and affection. To be quite honest, I was not too upset. University education seemed to lead to teaching, and I knew even then that I hadn't got the gifts of a good teacher, and to be less than good is to live a life of purgatory.

Of the careers I really wanted, music was not possible; to be a pianist, for instance, involves a very expensive training and someone has to keep you in what looks like idleness while you practise for those six or eight hours a day. The stage was, my father said, too precarious . . . all right as a side-line though. So it looked like something 'safe', like the Civil Service, until I got married, which happened to every girl who wasn't going to be a teacher or a nurse. I finally worked in the local Inland Revenue office. I liked the people, but not the work, which was mostly filing and putting forms in envelopes.

I did get married, too, when I was nineteen. My mother, with her shrewd East Anglian sense, told me I was making a mistake, but I took no notice. She was right, of course, but you couldn't tell young people anything then, any more than you can now; they know it won't apply in their case . . . they are, of course, Different. As Mark Twain said, when he was seventeen he thought his father was a fool. When he was twenty-one he was surprised how much the old man had learned in that time.

CHAPTER TWO

Allegro marziale

'My dear! . . . the *noise* . . . the *people*!'
(Guards officer after Dunkirk)

THE OUTBREAK of war in 1939 seemed a kind of relief. Ever since the Spanish Civil War there had been an uneasy calm – like the gap between seeing a lightning-flash and hearing the thunderclap. To ignorant young people like me it promised escape from a humdrum daily routine, and even some excitement. To our parents it must have seemed like Part Two of the 1914–18 war, with the same worries, the same irritations, the same propaganda – and in some cases the same leaders.

My father was one of the first to join the L.D.V. – Local Defence Volunteers – later called the Home Guard, an organisation made up of men who would be either too old, or too young, to be called up into the Forces. At first they had no uniforms – sometimes a hat filtered down the supply-chain, or a battledress jacket, or a pair of boots; but my father was very quickly issued with a rifle, a great heavy thing with a khaki webbing sling, which he kept propped up just inside the front door, all ready for the moment when we would hear the church bells ringing – the signal for invasion – and begin fighting, street by street, for our lives. The fact that he had lost none of his great skill as a marksman, even though he hadn't held a rifle for twenty years, was very gratifying, and must have consoled him a little for having to take up arms yet again. I still have one of his practice targets, with three of the five 'bulls' cutting into each other. My father was never the veterans' association type, never went to regimental reunions, never talked much about his army life – except that he would never drink from an enamel mug, or eat from an enamel plate. 'Reminds me of the army!', he'd say, but with a smile. For such a reserved, peaceable man the prospect of another war must have been acutely depressing, but he had a quietly stoical sense of duty, hence the rifle by the front door.

Far from bringing extra excitement to me and my contemporaries, the early months of the war seemed like the fading of a colour snapshot, leaving everything in blacks and greys. Everyone thought there would be air-raids at once, so all windows had to be blacked out at night with boards or thick curtains, and we stumbled about the unlit streets with torches dimmed with tissue-paper over the bulb.

As I was married and had a home of my own to run, even though my husband was away in the army, I was not to be drafted into any of the women's services like the A.T.S. or W.R.N.S., but could choose either Civil Defence or factory work. The National Fire Service was my choice, and for the next four years I wore the navy blue uniform with its red piping. They gave us a rather more exotic gas-mask, too, which made us feel a bit more important than ordinary civilians. My first posting was at a big fire station about two miles from my home, and I was part of White Watch, with three or four other girls. We learned how to take incoming fire-calls on the switchboard in the control-room, pass on the message in seconds, and how to get extra help if the fire proved difficult to put out, or threatened an ammunition-dump or arms factory. That, and keeping our overnight quarters – camp-beds and coal fires – tidy for Red Watch or Blue Watch when they relieved us on their next eight-hour shift, was about all the excitement we were going to get, it seemed.

The firemen we worked with were raffish, amiable characters, mostly ex-sailors, and with the sailor's salty language and cheerful irreverence. When the cleaning and polishing and drilling were over for the day we had some serious gambling-sessions of Housey-Housey – called Bingo nowadays – and a strange roulette-type game played by spinning the huge wheel of the escape ladder which is mounted on a fire-engine ('pump' to the Fire Service) and waiting for the numbers chalked on it to settle against an arrow stuck on the side of the vehicle. We had a piano in the rest-room, too, so I was soon busy running home-made concerts, primitive affairs with songs, clog-dances, recitations, jew's-harp-playing, concertina items and 'spoons'. It's one of my great regrets that I've never been able to master the art of playing the spoons. I feel every good Cockney should be able to play them, but alas I've no talent.

The first time the war seemed really menacing was one day when I met a boy who had been a couple of forms above me at school. He had been picked up from the Dunkirk beaches two days before, and was walking down our High Street on his way home. He was a weird sight, his battledress stained with sea-water, old plimsolls instead of boots, no forage cap, and all his kit gone except his knife and fork sticking out of his top pocket. He was still shaking, and stared past me as I chattered on about how good it was to see him and how pleased his parents would be. Maybe it was just as well that I didn't think of offering sympathy, he looked near to tears as it was.

Still the summer of 1940 drowsed on, enlivened only by Saturday night battles in the Town Hall Square between Canadian soldiers and British parachute troops. These were quite fierce at times, and no doubt excellent training for both sides.

But in September hundreds of Luftwaffe bombers began to attack London, and our lazy days were gone. As the days grew shorter the nights got grimmer, and we began to believe that we were truly fighting for our lives. Our heroes were the fighter pilots who made repeated attempts to beat off the invaders. We were encouraged to believe that carrots would improve our eyesight, and make us able to see in the dark, like night fighter pilots were supposed to be able to do. I can remember seeing a group of these young men walking along Oxford Street, with the crowds of shoppers making way for them. They wore dark glasses – reputedly so that their eyes would get used to darkness – and wore the top button of their jackets unfastened. I've never known the reason for that fashion, but it was their trademark. The names of fighter pilots, 'Cat's-Eyes' Cunningham, Stanford Tuck, 'Sailor' Malan, Neville Duke, were as familiar to us as the names of footballers are now, and it's strange to think that the morale of the whole country was raised more by this handful of mainly upper-middle-class youngsters, than by all the exhortations of politicians.

Looking back on the propaganda posters of the time I think they must have been devised by worthy chaps with ingenuous minds. The one that read 'Your Courage, Your Cheerfulness, Your Resolution will bring us Victory' took on a sour kind of class-hostility when read with the emphasis on the 'Your' and the 'Us'. One of the most familiar poster-characters was Billy Brown of London Town, always admonishing backsliders and lecturing the slothful. He could be seen rebuking a traveller in the tube train who was pulling at the trellis of sticky tape which covered the windows of trains in those days and saying: 'I trust you'll pardon my correction, that stuff is there for your protection!' Underneath, some passing wit had written: 'I thank you for your information – I want to see the bleedin' station!'

Other posters told us the nutritional value of whatever vegetable the government had too much of at any time – potatoes, carrots, swedes. But only those who have experienced Pilchard Pie for breakfast will have known one of the real horrors of war. This pilchard-and-potato pie was the invention of the elderly fireman who cooked our meals. He loved cooking, but the more hygienically-minded among us were always trying to replace him because he had the habit of sprinkling snuff along the hairs of his brawny tattoed arm, and then taking a long sideways sniff . . . while making pastry.

After some months of the cold and discomfort of the winter of 1940–41 we were again being showered with bombs, incendiary and high explosive, which made our night-shifts anything but dull. The Fire Service had some big vans called Control Units, a kind of fire station nerve-centre on wheels, and if a fire was big enough – 'conflagration' was the official term – this unit would be driven to the fire and used as an on-the-spot control room. Some of us worked in these vans, and luckily no one in our group was ever killed, although one brave, skinny Cockney girl won a medal for helping one of the firemen to hold a hose. When water comes hurtling out of the hose nozzle at 700 gallons per minute it takes two men to hold the head steady – our girl weighed about seven stone, including her steel helmet.

Those nights and days were a jumble of noise, darkness, jangling bells and the yellow glare of fires. Strange smells drifted in the smoke over the city – burning sugar and margarine, hot brick-dust and soot. In the mornings we picked our way through streets littered with hoses and broken glass, pieces of burnt paper fluttering down like black snow, and perhaps the roaring jet of a broken gas-main. We came to admire certain groups of people above all others; the Salvation Army, always ready with cups of tea and blankets – their little red-shield vans were first with help at every kind of disaster; the Women's Voluntary Service, splendid ladies whose courage and cheerfulness brightened the hideous nights, the police, the ambulance-drivers, and what were called the Heavy Rescue men, who dug out the people trapped under tons of rubble and broken masonry. There were moments of pure drama when the foreman of one of these gangs would call for absolute silence when he thought faint cries for help could be heard under the débris. These ten-second pauses were eerie, the only sound at first was the heavy breathing of the rescue squad and the cheep of sparrows. If there was a thin, desperate cry from the wreckage it was a joy to see the men's faces, streaked with soot and blood and dirt, light up with real pleasure at the prospect of digging out a fellow human being.

This determination was not only noticeable in the spectacular jobs like those of firemen, rescue squads and bomb-disposal men – whose icy, meticulous methods of work I still find extraordinary – but in the dull everyday existence of most women at that time, the housewives who sardonically made the best of the tiny food ration – two ounces of butter, one ounce of cheese each week. One egg a fortnight, with luck, and the truly awful dried egg powder. Spam (spiced ham), which came from America later in the war, was the butt of many jokes – one of the first was when Henry Kendall, in one of Alan Melville's biting revues at the Ambassadors Theatre, said to Hermione Gingold – I think it was in a sketch called 'Poison Ivy' – 'Will you have hot Spam or cold Spam' and the lady replied with gloomy resignation: 'I couldn't care less' – the first time *that* catch-phrase was heard. These revues, *Sweet & Low* in 1943, *Sweeter & Lower* in 1944 and *Sweetest & Lowest* in 1946, were topical, satirical and savagely funny. Who can forget La Gingold, as a Gaiety Girl, being propositioned by a Guards Officer in her dressing-room: 'Take those words out of your mouth, Major, you don't know where they've been;' and in the next sketch, with the rôles reversed, as a Wren officer importuning a simpering male ballet dancer in booming tones: 'I had the thrill of my life when I saw your Façade tonight.'

Besides the housewives who grimly made the best of everything, after hours spent standing in queues hoping to get some rarity like tomatoes or oranges, there were the unknown heroines in factories who worked until they fell asleep at their machines, and were then lifted off so that the next girl could take their place. Tiredness and fear were the enemies – it was hard not to feel tired if you were one of the 22,000 people who slept in rows on Underground platforms, and even on stationary escalators. Small wonder that occasional cracks showed in morale, caused by resentment and despair, and rumours persisted of 'stop-the-war' riots in some cities. We never believed any of them, though. It seemed impossible that anyone could think of surrender after all we were enduring. We were only thankful to survive each night, and twenty-four hours at a time was all we could cope with.

Life was not all blood and terror and worry, though. I had come through the worst of the blitz with nothing more disabling than a broken ear-drum, and I spent the last two years of the war as an instructor at the Women Officers' Training School in Hampstead. This was a very pleasant posting, in a huge house near the Heath, and during my time there I met people from many more walks of life than ever before. There was a W.R.N.S. training school a few streets away, and we often exchanged visits for concerts, tea-parties and lecture-films. In the evenings there would be an occasional concert by, literally, 'visiting firemen', for there were many famous musicians and writers in the Fire Service. One of the most civilised evenings was when Stephen Spender talked to us about poetry and led a discussion afterwards. It was gratifying to see how our cadets, by no means all intellectuals, showed how much they wanted to know about poetry, and on the next evening we listened to a string quartet playing Haydn, with the drawing-room windows open to the garden with its apple-blossom and wallflowers scenting the dusk. The war seemed a long way off, in spite of our uniforms.

All this culture didn't affect our juvenile tastes for the Good Life . . . or as good as could be managed in those austere days. Sometimes a group of us saved up enough money to have a meal in a restaurant – very daring, as who knows what we'd be eating. Snoek (a fish whose comical name led to nearly as many jokes as Spam), or horse steaks, whale-meat or – a real treat, this – venison. We went to the Cosmo at Swiss Cottage, and Kettner's, and Martinez and Boulestin's, and sometimes on to the Wellington Club in Knightsbridge, where a girl called Celia played cocktail-piano.

War-time teaches people many odd things; my days as an instructor were spent imparting to other people certain knowledge and skills we all hoped they'd never have to use. I had been shown, earlier in the war, how to make a Molotov cocktail by a veteran of the Spanish Civil War. This is a very chancy weapon – basically a bottle filled with petrol, and a piece of cloth as a fuse – and if it isn't made right it can do the maker more damage than the enemy. This warlike talent persuaded somebody who decided these matters that I was a fit person to lecture about bombs. So I had to, in spite of being one of the most physically timid people on earth. It was a bit more interesting than talking about 'The Ranks of the N.F.S.', or 'Methods of Communication', or 'How to organise emergency rations for 100 people'.

Sometimes I acted as, so to speak, 'straight man', or conjurer's assistant to a grizzled ex-sapper while he frightened us all to death with minor flashes and bangs. He had only one eye, which now I come to think of it was not surprising. We told our cadets all about the various kinds of bomb, from the five-hundred-pound high explosive – which, if it landed near you, would ensure that you would never receive any more birthday-cards – through the ordinary incendiary bomb, a neat cylinder about eighteen inches long, which could be dealt with by using a stirrup-pump (the roof of St Paul's Cathedral had been saved from these fire-raisers by a volunteer army of vergers, clergy and choirboys) and thence to more sophisticated creations like the phosphorus bomb ('Don't let it get wet – when it dries it'll start to burn on its own') and a particularly nasty thing – an anti-personnel 'butterfly' bomb, so called because of its two 'wings' which hooked it on to the tops of doors, or lamp-posts, or window-sills. It was only about the size of a large can of beans, but it acted as a kind of stationary hand-grenade, and any vibration – opening a door or window, say – would set it off. We heard that these bombs had almost paralysed a town in the North-East, because people were naturally afraid to go in or out of their houses for fear of setting off a 'butterfly'. For some reason they were never used much afterwards – perhaps they were too expensive or intricate to make.

But 'that one talent which is death to hide' – now, I'm happy to say, 'lodg'd with me useless', was discovered by the Guards sar'-major who taught us drill. Drill was supposed to give us a pride in our appearance, and also to teach us to obey commands instantly and automatically. I always hated it, but I saw the reason for it, and glumly made the best of it. All the drillee needs is concentration, and the driller's chief attribute is a good sense of timing and rhythm, as I found out when I became Sar'-Major's star pupil, when we all took turns at being instructor. Right turns, left turns, about turns, right wheel, left incline, you name it, I shouted it. The training-school parade ground rang to the sound of squads forming fours, marking time, dressing to the right, and so on. 'Dressing', for dewy-eyed youngsters among you, really means getting the line tidy before you start drilling . . . a bit difficult with girls. We had a plump, rosy girl out of the cookhouse who was hard to merge with the thinner girls – I'd go to the end of the rank and notice her rear end sticking out father than anybody else's. 'Dress forward a bit, Number Three,' I'd say, trying not to laugh, and she'd shuffle obediently into line with the rest. Then I'd look at the front of the rank and there she'd be again – farther forward than anybody else now. So we came to an arrangement; when I looked at the back of the rank she'd dress forward, and while I walked round to the front she'd shuffle back a bit.

All this caused great amusement among the people who lived in the houses overlooking the parade ground and watched us drilling every day. Heartless lot, we thought . . . they'd be jolly glad of a fine body of women like us to protect them from invasion, earthquake, fire or flood, wouldn't they?

At the end of one course I was to drill my squad, a mixed one of men and girls, in their final parade. We lined up, looking very stern and dedicated, like the people on the poster saying: 'Join the N.F.S.', and Sar'-Major inspected the ranks while I stood waiting to begin the drill. I saw him speak to the 'troops', but I was too far off to hear what he said. Words of encouragement, no doubt, I thought. Then he came back to me. 'Right, then', he said, 'They're all yours, girl.' Joyously I launched into a series of complicated instructions. The squad were doing fine . . . people came out of their houses to watch. Old men digging in the allotments at the side of the parade ground leaned on their spades, gazing admiringly at us. Puffed up with happy conceit I shouted on, showing off like mad. At last Sar'-Major said: 'That's it then, girl. Time's up.' The squad were now about twenty yards off, marching away from me. Ah well, it was over. 'Squad, HALT!' I yelled. Nothing happened. The line of smart navy-blue uniforms tramped farther and farther off. 'P'raps they carn 'ear yer,' said Sar'-Major . . . 'Shaht lahder.' 'HALT!!' I piped desperately. Still no response. I stared unbelievingly after them. They were on the allotments now, their shiny black boots chomping up and down amid the rotting cabbage stalks. The bystanders began to laugh. Mad with rage and shame I ran after my squad, hopping up and down and cheeping 'Halt, halt . . .' like an infuriated sparrow. Then I heard Sar'-Major's voice from behind me. 'Squad, halt!' he thundered. They stopped, discipline forgotten, men and girls stumbling about among the dead Brussels sprouts, holding on to each other and giggling. I looked back at Sar'-Major. He was leaning against the fence, his face buried on his arms, apparently crying . . . NO! the brute was laughing. I remembered his muttered remarks to the squad before they started, and the truth struck me . . . he'd *told* them to pretend they couldn't hear me. 'I suppose you think that's funny!' I shrieked. One of the old men on the allotments confirmed this. 'So it was, duck,' he cackled 'Better than Laurel'n'Ardy.'

The months dragged on into years, and even the most resilient of us began to realise that our youth was being drained away, and that those precious years of our late teens and early twenties would be lost for ever. Some of my old schoolmates would never come home again, and the faces that looked out from school photographs would be hidden for ever under the sea, or under desert sand or jungle earth. Some women who had lost husbands in the First World War lost sons in the second, and alongside numbing tragedies like that our day-to-day deprivations seemed contemptibly trivial. We did our best to keep up morale (now *there* was a nice new word for the papers to throw at us) by making the best of our appearance. Shoes were hard to get, and the ones we were reduced to wearing had wooden soles, sometimes hinged for easier movement. They made a distinctive 'clack-clack' noise, and were supremely uncomfortable. Silk stockings were only to be had from the flourishing Black Market. We were lectured at constantly about the Black Market. 'Unpatriotic', 'Frivolous', we were told. Well, maybe it was, but we reckoned that if some merchant seamen were willing to stuff their pockets with scent, lipsticks and silk stockings during Atlantic voyages where they would be bombed, torpedoed, burnt or frozen, and then could earn a lot of extra money from selling the luxuries at home, then all we could say would be 'Good luck to them'. But these windfalls were seldom met with, and most of the time we simply painted our legs with liquid make-up to look like stockings. The more artistic and conscientious girls even drew a seam (all real stockings had seams then) up the back of their legs with an eyebrow pencil. Dresses were quite pretty. You couldn't have very many, clothing was only obtainable with clothing coupons – although you could buy those if you knew where to ask – but the fact that material was scarce made manufacturers design simple dresses, and a useful skirt could be made by unpicking the seams of an old pair of trousers and joining the pieces up again. And if you could get a few scraps of the silk used for making parachutes you could make some really decadent-feeling underwear. Strictly illegal, though! The shoulder-bag made its first appearance then; developed, I suppose, by the necessity of having to carry your gas-mask everywhere in the early days of the war. (To make sure the Civil Defence and Fire Service always carried theirs, we had a small gas-chamber at the training-school, where four or five cadets at a time were shut in, wearing their gas-masks while the room filled up with gas. After a while they were told to remove their masks for five or six seconds, and then they were let out. It was only tear-gas, but the effect was salutary – we carried our gas-masks.)

In the early months of 1944 I caught bronchitis quite badly, and by the time I got better I was considered not to be fit enough to stay in the N.F.S. I was sorry to leave my friends and comrades, and all the mixture of tedium and excitement each day had brought, and the unusual places I'd been to during my time with the service – up the great grain-silo on the Isle of Dogs, for instance, where you could see the City, dusty and shattered, below you like a tactical model of a battlefield; and on one of the fire-boats on the Thames which were hardly ever driven at full power because the wash slammed the barges against the banks – with consequent lurid shouts from the bargees. So I handed in my uniform and went off to work as a supply teacher in a school in West London. I had no qualifications, but schools were short of staff, and provided you could stand you were in.

Teaching small children must be one of the world's hardest jobs. Our school was fairly new, in an area where most families worked in the bleak, misty fields of cabbages and cauliflowers and in the nearby factories. I was given a class of eight-year-olds, and right from the first day I knew I hadn't got that special gift that makes a good teacher – that ability to let a class have fun and then recall them to the business of learning, at a snap of the fingers. My class just had fun, no matter how I snapped my fingers. There were forty of them, ranging from very poor to poor, and you didn't have to be a genius as a teacher to be able to tell which children were going to make their lives better and which weren't. There were the two or three very bright ones – one small boy let me use the answers to his sums to mark the rest of the class – he was never wrong. Then there were the plodders, who took a while to catch on, but once encouraged would persevere. The boisterous ones (jump on them as soon as they start being a nuisance and then give them something physical to do, like giving out the text-books and cleaning the blackboard) would not be really happy until playtime, but there was no real harm in them. There were always one or two that you knew would grow up into criminals, and there would be nothing anyone could do to prevent it. Or else, if they were astute enough to stay on the right side of the law, they could become business men – after all, there is a certain disregard for other people's feelings which can be common to both classes.

One does not so much *teach* in those circumstances, as keep the children from actually killing each other. The only lessons they really enjoyed, I think, were singing, and acting 'plays', and listening to me reading stories . . . punctuated at intervals by cries of 'Please miss, 'e 'it me!' 'Please miss, I never!' They took a fiendish glee in telling me lurid details of misfortunes, like: 'Albert's dad 'ad 'is finger cut right orf by a saw, miss . . . 'anging by a fread of skin, it was, miss.' And then waiting to see if I'd blench.

One day when we were all going to morning school we found we couldn't cross the main road to the school gates. Mile upon mile of huge camouflaged lorries, tanks, personnel-carriers, armoured cars, guns, and jeeps went screaming along towards the south. The noise was thunderous, and houses and shops by the roadside shook, cups and plates tinkled on kitchen shelves. Wave upon wave of bombers roared overhead, and people came running out of their houses to see the awesome sight. Grown-ups and children jumped up and down on the pavement waving and yelling 'Good luck, good luck, God bless you' to the men in the great convoy. They couldn't hear us, of course, but they waved back. Nobody had to tell us what it was all about. It was the sixth of June, 1944, and ever since the early hours of that morning Allied forces had been landing on the Normandy beaches. When at last we got into the classroom I wrote the date on the blackboard. 'Remember this day', I said. Not much learning was done that day, what with the noise and the excitement, so we played games, and sang, and fixed up our poster of Lord Louis Mountbatten – one of a series depicting all the Allied commanders. I never found out who had designed these, but they were superb 'Boy's Own Paper' pictures, with, in our case, Lord Louis all gold braid and blue eyes, with battleships in line ahead steaming along over his shoulder.

When the end of the war came, nearly a year later, it was as though a household had been through a cataclysmic disaster, like a fire or a flood, and had trudged back home to assess the damage. Apart from the anguish of these who had lost people they loved, the devastation was appalling. Irreplaceable streets which had made London a miracle of fascinating, shabby elegance, had been reduced to a few mounds of dusty brick and blackened beams. Paternoster Row, with its bookshops, each with a swinging sign outside, was gone, and so were some of the lovely streets of eighteenth-century houses in the West End. I remember one house where only the staircase remained, curving superbly upward into the rainy sky, the wrought iron wheat-ears on the banisters vibrating to the rattle of passing traffic. All the fine

Georgian and Victorian railings had been torn out of walls and balconies, to be melted down as scrap-iron, we were told. *Were* they, I wonder – or were they just thrown somewhere to rust? The streets were never the same when those railings had gone, even thirty years afterwards my eye still misses that black-lace border that every terrace used to have.

Acres of small houses were gone, too; mean courts and alleys where on hot nights before the war people sat on wooden chairs out in the street and chatted with neighbours – partly to be cooler, and partly to avoid the activities of the 'Norfolk Howards' indoors. Norfolk Howard is the Cockney for bed-bug, after the chap who had his name changed from Bugg to Norfolk Howard. These creatures were the legacy of a hundred years of squalor, and generations of housewives had been defeated by their breeding habits. There were good reasons for being rather glad those houses had gone, and at first, when they were replaced by rows of little hutch-like prefabricated houses, many people were well pleased. The 'prefabs' at least let you live in some privacy, not bundled up with your in-laws, and they had tiny gardens too. Now these have gone in their turn, replaced by twenty-storey lumps of concrete, full of lonely people, and surrounded by windy acres of bleak scrubby grass covered with broken bottles and empty plastic ice-cream pots. These ant-heaps are often named after a local councillor or busybody, but he seldom actually lives in one! The architect is generally happily installed in a Queen Anne house in Buckinghamshire. It was all done in the name of the people, of course, or what the well-meaning middle class thought 'the people' should have, whereas if the truth be known, it's the middle class who probably have the right temperament to live contentedly in tower-blocks, and don't mind solitude. Working-class people, most of them, hate it, and would much rather live in streets with mother, or sister, or auntie a few doors *along*, not above, or below. If only the rows of tiny houses had been rebuilt as they were before, with improved drainage and plumbing, what miseries we would have been spared. Much noise was made by starry-eyed planners about how class barriers would all be swept away after the war; 'the war made us more democratic'. Alas, nonsense. 'People talked to each other in air-raid shelters, queues for food and so on' we were told, and some people even reminded us that 'The Colonel's Lady an' Judy O'Grady are sisters under their skins'. Well, the Colonel's Lady and Judy O'Grady *were* sisters, simply because each was loyal to the Army, and each had the same aim, to survive, and to help her man survive too. When their men were finally discharged I doubt if the Colonel's Lady or Judy O'Grady ever encountered each other again, let alone lived next door to each other in what sociologists love to call 'a social mix'. But their intense respect for each other remained, and so did the mutual respect of the two classes for some years after the war, until each became infected with the disease of the other. The working class gradually adopted the ruthless and greedy attitudes that in past centuries had made the upper class upper; and the upper class, out of a sense of guilt maybe, lowered its standards to what it thought would mollify the working class. In the words of Arthur Hopcraft it 'threw away its Little Lord Fauntleroy suit when it discovered dungarees'. The comradeship of Mrs O'Grady and the Colonel's Lady only lasts when they have a loyalty to what they consider honourable and worthy of their devotion. One cannot feel the same allegiance, in peacetime, to the House of Commons.

One of the strangest, and most pleasant, surprises after the war was the growth of the rose-bay willow-herb on the ruins; heaven knows where the seeds blew from, but in a few weeks the piles of broken masonry were covered in mauvish-pink flowers . . . and did I really see grass growing up between the paving-stones on Southwark Bridge? London seems to me now like a once-great actress, past her prime, raddled, shrill and dirty, her style and flair gone; but there are some April mornings full of daffodils and almond blossom and Portland stone, and autumn evenings scented with woodsmoke and roasting chestnuts, when I can hear her old voice, strong and clear, and love her for what she used to be.

By that time I had saved a few pounds – after all, what was there to spend it on in 1945? – and I decided that I'd use it to pay for some singing lessons. How pleasant it would be to have been trained for something, I thought, instead of just picking things up as I went along. So I found Gladys Palmer, a well-known opera and concert mezzo-soprano, and she did her very best to train my not-very-interesting 'straight' voice. She taught me more than singing, though. It was my first encounter with the better-class musical world, with echoes of all the charming stage-productions of the thirties, and I drank it all in greedily, along with Miss Palmer's china tea, in her lovely drawing-room with its grand piano and framed photographs, an oasis of civilisation after the desert years. As a small child, watching singers and actresses on the stage of the Kingston Empire, and listening to them on the wireless, I had always longed to be like them. Most actresses in those days had very 'upper-class' voices, and mine would never be that, but at least I could sing a bit, and I bawled my way happily through the arias in the contralto operatic repertoire, my worst vocal excesses gently curbed by Miss Palmer. Singing was never easy for me – it's a very physical activity, and I hadn't got much strength – but I sang in tune, and gained confidence all the time, and developed an even stronger love for opera than I'd had as a child, when my family and friends used to make jokes about my 'singing at Covent Garden one of these days'.

One of these days, it all came true.

CHAPTER THREE

Cabbages and Rings

DURING THE WAR the Royal Opera House, Covent Garden, had been used as a dance-hall. Pallid G.I.s – all Americans seemed to us to be the colour of putty – danced to Glenn Miller tunes, with girls in dresses that had sharp-pointed shoulders, and hairstyles that sported a 'pompadour' in front and a snood (a kind of coarse hair-net) at the back.

But now the dance-floor had gone, with all those tons of dead chewing-gum, and like a duchess who for six years had devoted herself to war-work the building got out its red velvet and white-and-gold paint, all ready to return to its proper station in life.

The Sadler's Wells (now the Royal) Ballet had kept the cultural lamp in the window for the war years, but in October 1946 a new permanent opera company was to be formed, and all the operas were to be sung in English. Auditions for the chorus were held all over the country. 'Why don't you try?' said my singing teacher. 'If you get in it'll be good experience for you.'

The audition was bewildering. I'd never been on such a vast stage before, or seen such a huge auditorium. Not that I could see much. The footlights blazed in my face and the rest of the house was in darkness. 'What are you going to sing?' somebody called. I named an eighteenth-century Italian song. 'What?' said the voice. I repeated the title, in even more peculiar Italian it seemed, because the voice was silent for a few seconds. Then it said: 'Oh, all right, go ahead.' I piped away desperately for a few minutes. I felt I was furlongs away from the pianist, I couldn't even hear him properly. Half-way through my song the voice said 'Thank you.' Oh well, I thought, that's it, then, it's no use. Four weeks later a chorus contract arrived for me to sign . . . 'to sing, perform and act as required'. For the sum of eight pounds per week. A fortune! And at Covent Garden. Forty-eight weeks of the year. I felt as though somebody has just given me all the flowers and silks and scents in the world.

The singers who were finally chosen met for the first time in the Crush Bar of the Opera House one autumn morning. If you've ever tried to get a drink during the interval at Covent Garden you know how the Crush Bar got its name. It's an impressive room, all crimson carpet, cream walls, glittering chandeliers and little red velvet-and-gilt chairs. We sat in rows, seventy of us, all ages, shapes and sizes. That's the great difference between an opera chorus and the chorus of any other musical show. In opera you're all supposed to be different people – peasants, soldiers, citizens, courtiers – so you can be any age, any type, as long as you can sing.

Some of us had been working in musical shows for years; some of us were amateurs. A good many of the men were just out of the forces. One was lame, one scarred by burns, and all of us were poorly dressed. I was wearing a coat my mother had made me out of an army blanket. We didn't look very well fed, either, rationing was very severe then. But joy and hope made us animated, and we listened intently when the General Administrator made his elegant speech of welcome. ('Who's that, then?' 'Name of David Webster . . . Sold socks in Liverpool.' '*Socks?*' 'Sshhh!'). He introduced our chorus-master, Douglas Robinson, a chubby Yorkshireman with a military moustache and glasses; an odd mixture of shyness and absolute confidence, with a fine sardonic humour and, as it later proved, a flair for training choruses amounting to a kind of genius.

There was a time when the words 'opera chorus' conjured up a picture of crowds of solid-looking people dressed in terracotta cloaks, all standing in rows behind the principal singers, never moving except to raise one arm on the last chord. In this new company things were going to be different.

The first opera we would be seen in was to be Purcell's *The Fairy Queen*, a late seventeenth-century mixture of Shakespeare and pantomime. We would not appear on the stage, but in two-tier boxes at each side, in William-and-Mary costumes.

When we began to rehearse with Douglas Robinson the music looked fairly easy, but from the first notes we sang we were made to realise that this chorus-singing was going to be hard work. For a start every word was going to be heard. With seventy people this means that every consonant at the beginning of a line must sound a fraction of a second before the first vowel-sound, which must be exactly on the beat; and every vowel-sound at the beginning of a word – an 'a' or an 'e' for example – must start with a 'glottal stop', not the the best kind of training for a solo singer, which we all hoped we were going to be one day. Still, even though we thought it would ruin our voices we tried it, and it was really very gratifying, after a few weeks, to see people's heads jerk up in astonishment and pleasure when we began to sing.

Some of us had never taken part in any professional performance before, and to those people the final *Fairy Queen* rehearsals must have been an eye-opener. Robert Helpmann and Margaret Rawlings were Oberon and Titania in this jumble of opera and ballet and Shakespeare, and there were *pas de deux* from stars of the Sadler's Wells Ballet like Margot Fonteyn and Michael Somes, and an enchanting girl called Moira Shearer. I meet Moira Shearer occasionally nowadays, and she looks hardly older than she did then. She seems to me to be an example of a complete human being, physically lovely, full of character, a happy wife and mother with many interests outside her home but with her heart inside it, and never for an instant regretting leaving the ballet on her marriage to Ludovic Kennedy. To see her in *The Fairy Queen*, all red curls and knots of ribbon, dancing round the plump Welsh tenor who sang 'If love's a sweet passion, Why does it torment?' was a joy. She gave the flimsy little song a mixture of romance and mischievous humour which was exactly what it needed. The conductor of this pleasant hotch-potch was Constant Lambert, a thoroughly nice man, but cursed with an addiction to drink. But no matter how drunk he might be, during *The Fairy Queen* he was always completely in charge, and we grew fonder of him at each performance. It was touching to see tears in his eyes when Margot Fonteyn danced as the Spirit of the Air. Our respect for his great talent was mixed with regret for his weakness, which in the end destroyed his health.

The sets and costumes for *The Fairy Queen* were by Michael Ayrton. Twenty years later, on a *Round Britain Quiz* recording, I met him again. 'I wore one of your costumes once,' I told him. 'Of course,' he said, 'I remember.' This was typical of him – he couldn't possibly have remembered me, but he didn't want to hurt my feelings. I was just going to say 'It was only a chorus costume,' but I thought he might be embarrassed at finding his kindly deception discovered, so I didn't.

Our days were spent in rehearsing, three hours in the morning and three in the afternoon. If we had a performance at night we just did the three hours in the morning. This left the afternoon free. Sometimes we went to matinées at nearby theatres – our Equity cards got us in free – and sometimes we had classes in make-up, movement and costume.

All kinds of make-up. Black eyes, bruises, squints, Chinese faces, Egyptian faces, the days were long past when an old operatic tenor used to smear on a burnt-cork moustache and beard and declaim: 'Where is the stage, and what is the opera?' We were energetic, eager and busy, no wonder we were happy.

The chorus rehearsed in the girls' dressing-room at the top of the building, up four noisy flights of concrete stairs. There was no proper chorus rehearsal-room. We sat in a clutter of make-up boxes, crinoline frames, wigs, mirrors, shoes and dress-rails with Robbie and the pianist wedged into a corner. But we didn't mind the discomfort. After all, it was to be the start of stardom. We didn't know it then, but the musical director's creed was the same as for continental opera choruses; the chorus was to be a career in itself, and only in very exceptional cases would a chorus singer ever become a principal. The technique is quite different. A really good chorus singer must somehow subdue his or her personality in many ways to the demands of the composer, the conductor and the producer, and absolute obedience is required from each member of the chorus during a performance, otherwise the big set-pieces are a mess. Being a good chorus singer is like being one of the Tiller Girls; precision is the chief virtue. It has always puzzled me that chorus singing is not better taught in colleges of music. After all, very few young singers will ever make a good living as solo performers. We began to forge a company spirit. Choruses can do this, simply because they are a majority, and they are permanent, like the orchestra, whereas principal singers come and go. We got to know each other; friendships and romances began. Florence and Jim got married, and we sang them the Wedding Chorus from *The Fairy Queen*. Ann was whisked off to sing for Benjamin Britten in a new opera.

Our first real stage appearance was in Bizet's *Carmen*, as Spanish factory-girls and soldiers. Our shoes hurt a bit, being new, our wigs were hot, and our costumes prickly, but we were actually *acting* at last, and we thought we were jolly good. The critics, while they praised the sound we made, said we weren't abandoned enough . . . too English, they said. The Welsh boys took this very hard. There were a lot of them, especially tenors, as in most opera companies. (In fact Sadler's Wells was once known as Sadler's Welsh.) The conductor was our permanent musical director, Karl Rankl. He was an Austrian, a fine conductor, fanatical about accuracy, discipline and order – all the Teutonic characteristics of the traditional German conductor, and yet he was a refugee from the tyrannies of Europe, later becoming a very welcome British citizen. The story of the day his naturalisation papers arrived was told with great glee He was said to have opened the envelope and shouted to his wife: 'Liebchen, we are British!' Madame Rankl was thereafter known as the British Liebchen. Though he had a nice sense of fun our more bizarre customs must have bewildered the poor man, and the orchestra, who had immense respect for his ability, once shocked him profoundly. He raised his arms to begin rehearsing the prelude to *Carmen* and when he brought them down for the first beat the orchestra played an entirely different overture. 'What is this, what is this?' he yelled, and had to be taken to recover in a seat in the stalls, where the orchestra manager explained to him that it was April 1st, and er . . . the English custom was . . . er . . . to play jokes on their friends. Dr Rankl, totally nonplussed, pretended to be amused, but I think he always kept an almanac at home after that, to warn him of any lurking prank-days.

Carmen is a very long opera. The pubs are shut by the time you've got your make-up off and changed to go home – very trying! Opera-singers then – and now for all I know – drank a good deal. It's thirsty work, and Covent Garden was rich in pubs, open at six in the morning for the market workers – The Grapes, The Enterprise, The Lamb and Flag and The Nag's Head just opposite the stage door. We rehearsed in the upstairs room of The Nag's Head occasionally, and got to know Wally Pack, the landlord, and his wife. The Nag's Head then was not the fashionable tavern it has become now. No framed playbills on the walls, and no elegant fittings. But it had more character then, I think. Wally Pack had been a famous boxer in his youth, but he was now very lame, and so when a troublesome customer (few, in those days) had to be dealt with, Wally knew that because his feet were no longer fast he was only going to be able to land one punch, and that would have to be the good one. So he developed the habit of idly twisting the rose in his lapel at these times, and from Wally's lapel to the miscreant's nose was only ten inches or so.

Mrs Pack was our confidante, proxy auntie, message-taker and friend. She devised a potent reviver for the low-spirited, christened

Pack's Pick-Me-Up, a Guinness with a glass of port in it. Two of those, and even post-war austerity looked a brighter shade of grey.

Food rationing was still very severe . . . for those who kept strictly to the regulations, that is. We had the feeling that some rosy-cheeked politicians might have been quite surprised to see what the official ration of food for one person was. But you could buy meals out, off the ration, and we did. In Floral Street there was a tiny café run by a cheerful chap who spoke the sort of fractured English opera-singers are used to hearing. The place was always full of blue smoke from the great pans of chips he cooked, so it was called Smokey Joe's, or simply Smokey's. We could get fried steaks there, lean and tender and juicy. I'm sure now that they must have been horse-meat, but as long as we didn't know we didn't care. It was warm in the caff and the tea was good, so what if we did come out smelling of cooking-oil? The principals and the music staff, some of them foreign, went there too. They probably thought all English restaurants were like that.

All this was in the days before the Covent Garden district became a mass of fashionable 'workshops'. It was all strictly business then, either music or vegetables. When we arrived at the theatre, most of the market business would be over, and only a few lorries left marooned among the crushed cabbage stalks and broken carrots. Iron gates covered the warehouse fronts, but behind these reigned the Cats. Covent Garden cats were unlike any others, a feline Mafia, followers of the Vagabond King Cat, Apaches all. Great torn-eared toms, baleful queens, even the kittens were delinquents. At first I used to put a hand through the bars and say 'Hello, pussy-cat' to the two emerald eyes gleaming in the dark shop. One of the porters yelled: 'Don't touch 'er, don't touch 'er, she'll 'ave yer 'and orf!' and showed me his hand, laid open from wrist to thumb that very morning by that same pussy-cat. Cat-worshipper as I am, I left those specimens alone, and apart from growling respectfully at each other, we never made contact. Dogs never ventured into Covent Garden, they had more sense. The only dog recognised by everyone was the tiny dachshund belonging to the man who ran the Opera House's publicity, who was almost a caricature of an Englishman. Tall, bony, always wearing a British Warm and a bowler, and I never heard him say more than two sentences. In rainy weather he would hail a taxi to send the dog to the opera-house while he walked there himself through the wet. He was an Olympian figure to us, and it was rumoured that he never read anything except the Court Circular.

The porters took a fatherly interest in us, bellowing morning greetings, whistling approval of any new clothes we might have, and commenting on the singing they heard daily from the chorus-room windows. 'Bloody lovely, innit.' Even our dressers came in for raucous comment and exhortation, no matter how old they were. An interesting difference used to be noticeable when any Cockney man addressed an older woman. If he called her 'Ma' it meant that she appeared to him to be respectable, comely and good-natured. But if he called her 'Auntie' it meant that she was a blue-nosed old maid, and likely to remain so . . . still a crime in those days.

During the savage winter of 1947 we were glad to spend our days in the theatre, for the fuel shortage meant that our homes were freezing. I shared a tiny flat in Notting Hill Gate with one of the sopranos, and the old lady who lived in the flat above us fell ill and wouldn't go to hospital. She was one of the old school . . . polite, reserved and kindly, and quite adamant in her refusal to be moved. When we finally persuaded her to go it was too late, and she died, as neatly and gracefully as she had lived.

Every performance of *Carmen* was like a Mediterranean holiday to us in that winter, the lights had to be strong to represent the sun of Seville, and the warmth from them soothed our perished bones. The 'Smoking Chorus' in Carmen must have been torture for the audience. Absolutely NO SMOKING for them, and there were all the girls on the stage puffing away at illicit fags. Dog-ends were collected after the scene by the prop-boy, and the legend was that he re-rolled them and sold them. The stage manager used to make a point of not wishing us luck on first nights. 'You don't need luck, darlin's, you've got *talent*.' But luck deserted our Don José, a cheerful, strapping lad from New Zealand. After Carmen's contrived escape from him in Act 1, she gave him a playful shove – she was a hefty girl – and his *toupée* fell off. He played the last few minutes sporting a shiny bald head.

When the new production of Mozart's *The Magic Flute* was to be cast two singers were imported from Germany. Some newspapers were incensed at this, it was 1947, the war had only been over two years, and apart from the killing it felt to us as though the war was still on, what with the cold, the rationing, and, in Stafford Cripps, a Chancellor who seemed the bleakest character since Peter the Hermit. But most of us thought that having to learn all their rôles in English might be punishment enough, and we found that Hans Hotter, who sang the Speaker, was an amalgam of all the old German virtues of rectitude, politeness and learning. The soprano who was to sing Pamina was a pale blonde, with a sweet expression and a charming face very wide at the cheekbones (which I've noticed is a facial characteristic of many first-class singers). She was pleasant to us, and we eagerly waited for an orchestral rehearsal when we would first hear her sing. Most of us had never heard anything like it before. Her voice had a marvellous pearly quality like an audible rainbow, and a haunting melancholy under that wonderful silvery sound. Her technique was formidable, and in spite of her fragile appearance she must have been physically stronger than she seemed. Those shimmering tones and that lovely face are still with her today, and I'm always enchanted by the singing of Elisabeth Schwarzkopf.

In *The Magic Flute* – called by some Covent Garden porters the 'Dodgy Whistle' – there are three small parts, sometimes sung by boys, the Three Genii, or Boys, or Spirits. Soprano, second soprano and alto. My flatmate, Valerie, and I were chosen to sing the second soprano and alto parts with one of the principal sopranos as First Boy. ('Flatmate' is an ominous description of an opera-singer, but Valerie never sang flat in her life.)

Ensemble singing was, and is, one of my great delights. I think I must have sung in every kind of operatic ensemble from a duet (one of the two bridesmaids in *The Marriage of Figaro*) through trios, quartets, quintets, right up to the sixteen-girl 'Madrigal' in *Boris Godunov*. I love the feeling of being responsible for a harmony part, especially if it's a fairly difficult one, and yet being part of a team. The sets and costumes for the *Flute* were by Oliver Messel, in his most opulent fairy-tale style, a mixture of Ancient Egypt and Crete, with a touch of the Inigo Joneses. Our make-up was eerie, too. Long green, white and black eye-lines, slanting up, ballet-style. Oliver Messel drew us a sketch of what he wanted our eyes to look like. We asked him to leave it with us, but he wouldn't – we didn't realise how famous he was, and how much a simple sketch like that might be worth, we just thought he was a small, handsome artist.

The Three Boys were to be little leaf-covered woodland things, and we had the exotic experience of wearing our tights while one of the scenic artists painted leaves in outline all over our legs. These tights were not like the easy stretchy ones of today. They were solid cotton, and could only be kept really smooth by rolling the waistband over and twisting a penny – an old penny – into each side. After a three-hour opera this became agonising. I still sometimes feel as though I've got holes in my sides. During the opera Tamino (the same balding New Zealander as in *Carmen*, this time with a hat like an upturned lily-of-the-valley on his head) plays the flute, and thus attracts the forest animals to listen to his music. These small animals were children from one of the theatre schools, and one of them – a deer, I think – was Millicent Martin, nowadays one of our cleverest and most versatile stars of revues and musicals.

It was thrilling and terrifying to hear the music that introduces the charming little trios Mozart wrote for the Three Boys. The auditorium was just a dark haze, and all we could see through the blue-white glare of the spotlight was the conductor's white shirt-cuffs waving up and down. Covent Garden is acoustically perfect except for one 'dead' spot near the front of the stage, and the smallest voice, properly produced, will carry to the gallery. So we piped away, loving every minute, and ignoring the stabbing of those pennies in our ribs, and the head-dresses cutting into our skulls, and the icy draught blowing from the wings. Later on in the season Adèle Leigh, now the wife of the Austrian ambassador, became our First Boy. Apart from the tiny rôle of the page in *Rigoletto* I think it was her first Covent Garden part. Adèle was fun; she had been evacuated to America during the war – her mother ran a dress-shop there – and the arrival of one of Adèle's American parcels was a real crowd-puller. One memorable day she got a pair of real nylon tights, white ones, to wear when she sang Barbarina in *The Marriage of Figaro*. As she unwrapped them we might have been seeing the Grail in *Parsifal*. Nylon stockings were available on the flourishing black market in those days, but nylon *tights* . . . well!

We three dressed in one of the ground-floor dressing-rooms on *Flute* nights, and the Sadler's Wells Ballet minor principals used it on ballet nights. Their company was well established, and ours was very new and they could have despised us as newcomers but they were delightful girls, and that ground-floor room was like a cage of tropical birds; full of chatter, scent and giggling, with the occasional trophy like Adèle's tights, and a ballerina's new feathered hat, bought by the current boy-friend, shown off amid shrieks of approval. How the *corps de ballet* ever danced in those days is a miracle; singing was tiring enough, but dancing must have been even worse, what with the cold, the grim conditions outside the theatre, and the iron discipline inside, and the dancer's eternal woes like strained muscles, sore toes and exhaustion. I once saw a letter in a newspaper from a young man who said his ideal girl must have 'the feet of a ballerina' . . . had he ever *seen* a ballerina's feet, I wonder?

The story of *The Magic Flute* is highly contradictory. The Three Boys work for the Queen of the Night at the beginning of the opera. At the end they are servants of Sarastro who opposes her, proper little Vicars of Bray. We once performed a shortened version of the *Flute* at a special matinee for children. Goodness knows what they made of the tale, which is a fine old mixture of allegory and pantomime.

Unlike the charming *Flute* most opera stories are real X-certificate, full-frontal stuff, full of disasters like assassination, incest, rape, torture and just plain murder. You name it, they sing about it. If you took phrases like 'O horror!', ''Tis death!', 'O Heaven!' and 'Thou traitor!' out of the libretto of every opera, there wouldn't be an awful lot left. As one wit has observed 'Opera is when a guy gets stabbed, instead of bleeding, he sings.' The end of every performance sees the stage strewn with dead or dying dukes, counts, princes and princesses lying about on the hard boards, huge, heavily-breathing piles of velvet, like great coloured bumble-bees. And operatic heroines would be the despair of those resourceful ladies who write the answers to readers in magazines. I can imagine them being very stern with a certain Cio-Cio-San of Nagasaki . . . 'Don't depend on this American sailor you say you've met, these whirlwind romances are notoriously unreliable, and since you are only fifteen I think you are too young for a permanent relationship . . . Isn't there a good youth-club in Nagasaki?' To Azucena, Spain, 'Oh dear, what an unfortunate little slip-up that was, throwing the wrong baby on to the bonfire like that, but you really must put the past behind you and not brood so much.' And to Mimi, Paris: 'You really *must* see your doctor about that cough.'

All those doom-laden stories could cast a blight on the people who actually sing the stuff, you might think. Not a bit of it. To begin with, to be an opera-singer at all you need the lungs of a bull and the constitution of an ox, for singing is a very physical thing. It's not only in what one might call the 'louder' operas that you need vitality, weight and strength; those long elegant melodies of Mozart are not for weaklings, either.

Tempers often fray, and a first-class operatic row has to be heard to be believed. None of your tight-lipped, South-Kensington scratchiness either, oh dear no. The best kind of contests are between two similar voices, for instance two sopranos of equal weight and notoriety. Better still, between an international quartet, soprano, contralto, tenor and baritone. Generally the contralto and tenor back out first. The reason for this may be that contraltos are usually good-natured ladies, fond of knitting and used to, as it were, playing second fiddle, and tenors are often vain and fearful that all the shouting will damage their voices. This leaves the stage clear – literally – for the soprano and baritone. If they are of different nationalities it's even better, for when their English fails they just carry on in Italian, Czech, Spanish or Serbo-Croat. If the conductor can be goaded into joining in, then the awe-struck spectators – chorus, stage-hands, rehearsal pianists and orchestral players – can expect even more delights, with helpful linguists on the musical staff translating the more obscure insults for everybody else. But a couple of hours later there they all are, in some nearby café, eating huge steaks and laughing and kissing each other.

Not only singers have rows. There used to be a notice in the wings at one of the most elegant theatres in Brussels forbidding the stage-hands to discuss politics during a performance.

Maybe the lurid melodrama of the stories makes opera-singers louder and more highly-coloured than, say, straight actors, although many of today's stars seem to be trying to look like the girl next door, which I think is a pity. Happily some of them still keep up the bobby-dazzling tradition . . . diamonds . . . furs . . . vast hats, tiny dogs, secretaries, maids, hairdressers, husbands and/or lovers clearing the way or trailing behind Madame in a cloud of her expensive scent. So don't be misled by Madame's achingly lovely singing. She probably has the strength of a front-row rugger forward, and the bargaining power of an Armenian carpet salesman. That voice is the product of years of work from which many a heavyweight boxer would shrink.

After *The Magic Flute* new productions followed each other fast. We rehearsed new work in the mornings and sang the repertory at night. The next production was Massenet's *Manon*, and the producer was Frederick Ashton. The production was like him, elegant, charming and classy. We loved working for him, he had a marvellous sense of the ridiculous, and provided you worked hard he was good-tempered. It was during *Manon* that I became one of the chorus 'representatives' – a sort of shop-steward – to talk to the management and music staff about any grievances we had. There weren't many at that time. Meetings were held in the conductor's room before the performance, with the 'reps' already in their eighteenth-century costumes. I can thoroughly recommend this to the T.U.C. Satin breeches and tricorne hats would lend a lot of tone to the Annual Conference.

Manon remains one of my favourite shows. It's almost a musical – not really heavy enough for what most people think of as grand opera. Heddle Nash was the hero in the first performances, and later Walter Midgley sang the rôle of Des Grieux. Both were admirable, but I preferred Midgley's silvery, French-style tenor. The famous Mr Nash was a dear; affable and entirely unaffected. The cut-glass accent he sang lyrics in was rather different from his everyday speech. After one morning's rehearsals when he was cast as David in *The Mastersingers* he announced to us: 'I'm goin' to do a recording this afternoon. *Real* music. . . . 'Andel!' He was reputed to have said to Sir John Barbirolli after a particularly splendid performance of *The Dream of Gerontius*: 'Spot on, eh, Guv'nor?'

Our *Rosenkavalier* was an intriguing event. Joan Cross, the distinguished soprano, was to produce it, and the first thing she did was to sit us all down on the floor while she told us the story of the opera. This was so logical and sensible that I wondered why nobody else, with one exception, ever did it. *Rosenkavalier* is marvellously erotic music, even though the real X-certificate bit takes place before the curtain rises. The Prelude is always assumed to be a sound-picture of what's supposed to be going on behind that three-ton velvet curtain. This production was enchanting, all pink and white and green and silver, like wading through roses while drinking iced champagne. When Robbie told us what characters we would assume mine were: Act One, Maidservant. Act Two, Servant, and there were speculations about what must have happened in the interval. The part of the still-lovely Marschallin, who gives up her younger lover to a girl of his own age, was sung by Doris Dorée, an American who had once been a dancer on Broadway. Not a romantic voice perhaps, but extremely efficient, and with perfect diction. She was a fine musician, too, which is not all that usual among opera-singers, even today. During a power failure the curtain had to be lowered while Miss Dorée was alone on the stage, but when it went up again twenty minutes later she picked up the fairly complicated vocal line with complete accuracy.

Our most technically difficult opera from the chorus point of view must have been Benjamin Britten's *Peter Grimes*, with musical time-signatures like 7/4 and 15/8 and so on – more like a Rugby score really, but it was a fascinating new style and I loved every bar of it. The whole opera was to be blessed with one of the finest producers the stage, musical or 'legit', has ever known, Tyrone Guthrie. There were actors who would walk miles barefoot over broken glass just to say one line in a play produced by this man, and after he had introduced himself to us we knew why. He looked like a slightly dotty retired colonel, tall, thin, and pale-eyed, and he spoke in whole literate sentences in a rather 'spitty' voice. It was rumoured that he lived in a house full of kittens and old socks. He knew every note, every bar of the complicated score of *Peter Grimes* as well as any conductor. He treated everyone in the cast with absolute impartiality. If you were five minutes late your ears would be shrivelled by the polar blast of his displeasure, and so would be the ears of the grandest international singer for the same crime. He was riotously funny, utterly efficient, and completely in control. Order and discipline reigned, which in an opera-house where there can be up to two hundred singers and orchestra in one production, is vital, and a godsend to everybody. It was a tough, happy production, and needed only one thing to make it perfect. Fog. The last act of *Grimes* needs special lighting effects to simulate a thick sea-fog. This was not easy to achieve, and 'Tony' Guthrie tried all the technical tricks he knew, but he wasn't quite satisfied with the result. But on the first night there occurred one of the last genuine London pea-soupers. It crept into every house, office, church and theatre, and the stage of the Garden was veiled in a greyish-yellow haze.

We took *Grimes* to Paris, to the Opéra, and to the lovely Théâtre Royale de La Monnaie in Brussels. The Paris Opéra was magnificent . . . for the audience, like a *nouveau riche* Vatican. Backstage was just as vast, but Spartan. In our huge echoing dressing-room there was a sort of grey granite horse-trough which was our only vessel for washing off the grime (if you'll forgive the pun) and stone-cold water, and no plug in the trough. Still, Paris was worth a mess, and the champagne the Opéra staff gave us at the welcoming reception was delicious. We'd never tasted anything like it. We staggered happily over the great polished floors, laughing and practising our dreadful French on the poor harmless 'Frogs'. Nobody went to bed much before three in the morning, no matter what or who the attraction thereto. We wandered about Paris, to Les Halles – which was still in the heart of the city then – and along the river. Dior's New Look was just filtering down to the likes of us from the cloud-capped heights of *haute couture*, and we revelled in the full calf-length skirts and tiny waists. I bought a huge black straw hat, and was promptly made to pay duty on it by the British Customs. Heigh-ho, home again.

One of the Garden's most ambitious and expensive productions was to be Mussorgsky's *Boris Godunov*. The producer was that same Peter Brook who had blown the one breath of criticism on our first efforts when the new company was formed. He was only twenty-five then, a Boy Genius if ever there was one, but I don't think he had much experience of opera, or singers, and the prospect of directing a huge chorus (extra singers were used in *Boris* making the chorus in the Coronation Scene up to about two hundred people) must have been daunting. But he tried, hard, and it was probably not his fault that at times we didn't get on. He had an irritating habit of beginning to clap his hands when he wanted us to stop a rehearsal, but never quite completing the clap. This drove everbody mad, because it looked like indecision, and the one thing a huge operatic production must have is a producer who is completely decisive. Stopping a rehearsal is like halting the Aldershot Tattoo in full blast. Peter Brook has since proved to be a dedicated and highly talented producer of plays, but directing an opera is much more complicated. If you hold up a full rehearsal you have to regain the concentration of a ninety-piece orchestra as well as your two hundred singers before you can go on. Voices and legs get tired, too. The *Boris* revolution scene was quite violent, and after a few hours of heavy singing and running around the huge stage waving old Lee-Enfield rifles – real ones – above our heads, and kicking Russian nobles to death we'd had enough. But we were grateful to him for including the seldom-performed 'Polish Scenes' in the production. These scenes aren't really necessary to the plot, but they are very glamorous and charming, a relief from all the dark doorways and flickering torches of the rest of the opera. One of his happier ideas was the scene in the snow outside a Polish castle with shadows of dancers inside the lighted windows. The Polish nobles pushed their ladies around in little sledges, and pushed them off the stage when the two juvenile leads began a love-duet. One of our sopranos got deserted by her sledge-pusher and was left centre stage, with the two principals glaring balefully at her. With great aplomb Mabel gazed into the wings, and as if in answer to a call from off-stage she scrambled out of the sledge, scooping up a 'snowball' as she ran, and throwing it off-stage and galloping after it. Mabel was lucky in love, too. She had a boy-friend who was a chef . . . oh bliss in those hungry days . . .

and he sent her packets of heart-shaped biscuits with 'I love Mabel' on them in pink icing.

After the production of *Boris* was over Peter Brook was exhausted, we were told. We were genuinely sorry, for I think we gave him a bad time. Later he produced the almost producer-proof *La Bohème*, a much smaller undertaking than *Boris*, and made a very good job of it, although he seemed to lose that bitter-sweet essence, like the scent of chrysanthemums, that *La Bohème* should distil. Maybe he was too young. But the lovely and fascinating Schwarzkopf was Mimi, and even though the chorus has nothing to do in the last act we would all stay behind just to watch her death-bed scene.

La Traviata promised to be a real treat. Schwarzkopf was to be Marguerite, and the producer was to be our beloved, terrifying Tyrone Guthrie. Once again he knew every single note of the whole opera, had all the major moves in his head and stuck to them, and bullied and convulsed us into the mid-nineteenth-century demi-monde of Paris . . . 'don't stand around like that, dear people, you look like Penberthy's window.' Anyone who remembers the old Penberthy's in Oxford Street, its windows full of pink corsets arranged in rows with the occasional pair of serviceable grey knickers like an exclamation-mark, will know just how we looked! *Traviata* is a great favourite with choruses, it's one of the few operas where no designer can make you look awful, because all the women are supposed to be high-class Parisian tarts, and all the men rich and sophisticated. The designer, Sophie Fedorovitch, had a real flair for the period, and a glorious sense of colour, ranging from the spring-like yellow, orange and white of Act One, through the decadent magenta-and-black of the Act Three party, to the grey desolation of Act Four. Once again nobody went home until Schwarzkopf had 'died'. Fedorovitch even had the girls taught how to walk in the vast crinolines of the 1860s. I wince now whenever I see an actress lift the skirt by one of the hoops . . . the proper way is to press the hoop inwards towards your knees and glide.

Another 'upper-class' opera for the chorus is *Rigoletto*. The women don't sing at all in it, but they appear, dancing with the courtiers in the opening scene, while the dissolute Duke of Mantua sings about his conquests, and his toady, the hunchback Rigoletto, torments and mocks an outraged father who is brave enough to accuse the Duke of seducing his daughter. The production was in English, and we were using an old translation which was almost unsingable. For example,

The Duke's opening lines were translated as:

> Soon 'twill be time my intentions were concluded
> With yon fair maid of humble antecedents.

Try *that* wearing a tight ruff and keeping one eye on the conductor!

Some translations of opera libretti seem to have been written by naïve maiden aunts using a 'postilion-struck-by-lightning' phrasebook. Our comrades and friendly rivals, the Sadler's Wells chorus, had most of the luck in these matters though. During Tatiana's birthday-party waltz in *Eugene Onegin* they were able to sing heartily: 'BALLS in the COUN-try are QUITE a sens-SA-tion' Lovely stuff, especially when it's what the translator, serves him right, wrote. Like the moment in *Faust* when Marguerite declines the grand gentleman's help because she says she is: 'Not a lady, not a beauty'. Some Marguerites never sang a truer word.

But sometimes the chorus, tanked up with ale after some pre-performance celebration, invented its own translations. In the Kermesse scene an acute listener could have heard a good half of the chorus bawling: 'Up with 'er petticoat, down with 'er drawers, I'll show you my thing if you'll show me yours'. Well . . . a Kermesse is supposed to be uninhibited.

The best we could offer at Covent Garden was the passionate utterance of Escamillo the toreador when he first meets Carmen . . . 'When I face the bull, that name I will breathe', and that same character's complaint when Don José has taken a pot-shot at him: 'Just an inch lower down and I should have been short' . . . at least that's what it sounded like in our imported Italian Escamillo's English. But we were easily amused in those days, it was the original era of the 'Knock, knock' jokes. Our favourite was 'Knock, knock'. 'Who's there?' 'Euripides' . . . 'Euripides who?' 'Euripides drawers, you buy me some more.' All the classical stuff, notice.

And all this time, just down the street at Drury Lane Theatre, there was *Oklahoma!* with marvellously intelligible home-grown American lyrics. Even when the original words of some opera libretti are English they are often quite difficult to sing and therefore difficult for the audience to hear. *Peter Grimes* is not easy to understand, even from singers with good diction. For instance, after the prelude, the first line the chorus sings is: 'O hang at open doors the net, the cork, while squalid sea-dames at their mending work'. *The Consul* and *The Telephone* by Gian Carlo Menotti are examples of good colloquial speech fitted to music and ironically one of the best opera translations is Dent's *The Magic Flute*, where the words don't really matter all that much except as a means of 'colouring' the divine notes. *The Marriage of Figaro* is another example of a good English translation, and it is undoubtedly one of the supremely singable operas. Full of real people of all ages and types; a flimsily silly story full of hidden heartbreak like the sharp tang of southernwood. My small straight voice got me the part of one of the two bridesmaids, who carol the pretty little duet of thanks to the Count who has relinquished his *droit du seigneur*, and now peevishly wishes he hadn't. Schwarzkopf was Susanna, and sang the part as though it had been specially written for her, particularly the aria *'Deh vieni, non tardar'* towards the end of the opera when Susanna, tired of all the intrigues and plots of the Mad Day, is at last alone in the garden at night, and reflects that it is, after all, the day of her marriage to her delightful young husband, even though he isn't nearly as clever as she is. Everything about youth and love and hope is contained in the last phrases of that soliloquy.

Valerie and I got two more small rôles – non-singing ones – in that glorious, preposterous, old-fashioned romp *Il Trovatore*. We were cast as the two ladies-in-waiting who lead the heroine gently away after she has been struck all of a heap by her lover's intention to run off from their wedding and rescue his mother from being burned as a witch by the wicked count who is really his own brother . . . (Well, I did say it was preposterous.) We gloated a bit at first, for it's traditionally the two best-looking girls in the chorus who get cast in that scene, but we knew that it was really because we were the only two who'd fit into the costumes without them having to be altered. They were two of Covent Garden's very oldest and most beautiful dresses, works of art from the early 1900s, with velvet and silver *appliqué* embroidery on grey silk. I expect they fell to pieces long ago, they were very fragile even then, but they were a joy to wear. *Trovatore* is a feast for those who love a rip-roaring tune on every page of the score, and blood-and-thunder choruses, gipsies' curses, attacks on convents and so on, with the principal singers lined up facing the footlights and singing full blast, and no new-fangled nonsense about subtle inner meanings.

Valerie and I made a 'corner' in Speechless Handmaidens. Nothing to do with our voices – we were still chirruping happily away with Adèle Leigh on *Flute* nights, but whenever a heroine had to be consoled, or a train carried, or a cloak put on a queen's shoulders there we were, handmaidening away like mad. One of our Great Train jobs was in the finale of *Turandot* when we and six ballet girls carried the two vast trains made of metallic gold leaves for the Princess and her bridegroom. *Turandot* has always been one of my favourite operas, partly for its glittering orchestral score, full of pseudo-Chinese effects with harp, celeste and flute over muted strings, and one genuine, pretty Chinese tune sung by a chorus of children. It was also our chance to work with the great Eva Turner, whose enormously strong soprano could make the lights at the back of the gallery flicker. She was a fine combination of cosmopolitan experience and earthy Lancashire sense. Walter Midgley – a Yorkshireman – was her Prince, and the red rose and the white fought an amicable battle for the audience's attention . . . it was a draw, with honours even; Turner's power and Midgley's style brought the blood-boltered folk-tale to glorious *fortissimo* life.

It was our first experience of the Fainting Guardsman Effect, too. In the last century Queen Victoria had been annoyed with what she considered the slovenly bearing of the 'supers' who made up the companies of soldiers in the various operatic triumph scenes, coronations and so on. So she decreed that a company of real-life guardsmen should take part in operas calling for the military presence. And in *Turandot* there they were, perhaps descendants of the originals, dressed as Chinese war-lords and much tormented by the chorus and ballet girls, fresh-faced lads who bore the huge noise nobly. But their contribution called for a lot of standing about on steps holding spears, and on hot nights at least one of them would collapse like a slow-motion chimney-demolition on film, and two or three Chinese peasants in the singing chorus would stagger offstage with the body. If it was nearly curtain-time they'd just let him lie there. *Aida* was another great chance for guardsmen to faint, and I think they envied their handsomest comrade – he could at least sit down, for he was chosen to represent the god Phta, enthroned twenty feet above the stage in the Consecration scene. His only complaint was that he had to be smothered in gold paint and sit stonily still. *Aida* is heavy work for the chorus, and what with all the 'blacking-up' (or 'browning-up') to look as anciently Egyptian as possible, and the long trumpets blasting into your ear on the stage in the Triumph scene it's uncomfortable, too, but the music is splendid.

One of our finest soloists was a continental soprano with a mass of magnificent hair. But that wasn't what she was vain about. She thought that her *legs* were marvellous, and insisted that the skirt of her costume was slit up to the thigh. Her dresser, a respectable Scotswoman, used to hide in corners sewing up the seam before each performance, but Madame could be observed backstage diligently unpicking the seam with a nailfile, and exposing her over-sumptuous thigh. Years later somebody was alleged to have tried to murder her by pouring chloroform on the white fur rug by her bed as she slept. Perhaps it was an enraged costume-designer. Another principal soprano, a rosy Rubens-type Belgian, called forth the comment from the stage manager that: 'from behind she looks like two cats fighting in a sack.'

Wagner's music is better than it sounds, said Mark Twain, and I agree with him. There are some wonderful moments, but there are some *mauvias quarts d' heure* too. *'Die Meistersinger von Nürnberg'* is a monumental work full of argument about how to write music – instead of just getting on with it, like Verdi did. If you are in the chorus there's a great gap just after the opening chorale in the church. So you can either sit in the dressing-room gossiping and lengthening your eyelashes with blobs of hot-black (a dying art nowadays . . . and it always was a futile and painful hobby) or you can get dressed, go over to the pub, and come back hours later, in time to take part in the last act. But some of the thinner girls in the chorus were cast as Apprentices, together with eight men, which meant that during the whole of the interminable debate about the rules of song-writing carried on by the Masters of the various guilds, the apprentices are forced to sit on benches on the stage, apparently listening attentively to their betters. During all the eye-rolling and nods of approval our attention could stray beyond the footlights and into the first few rows of the stalls, where many a tired business man – or maybe black market millionaire, who knows – it was the era of spivs and drones – could be seen with his head sunk on to his white shirt-front until roused by a sharp dig from the elbow of the fur-stoled lady next to him. But through all the endless wrangling on the stage (*endlische melodie* Wagner called it, and he was right!) no such backsliding was visible in the royal box at the prompt side of the stage. Only the occasional sparkle of diamonds as the occupants breathed. What stamina the royals had . . . but who knows, perhaps they *liked* Wagner.

Incidentally, I've never understood why the royal box was there, only half the stage could ever have been seen from that angle. But there was a delightful little drawing-room behind it – surely a godsend during the intervals. Nowadays on gala nights royalty sees the performance from the centre back of the house, much more sensible.

The sets used in *Die Meistersinger* had been designed years before by Rex Whistler. The stage-hands loved them because they were beautifully made and therefore easy to move about. Even the cataclysmic scene-change from Hans Sachs' cobbler-shop to the meadow outside Nuremberg never took more than two-and-a-half minutes. It couldn't . . . there are only two-and-a-half minutes' music for it to happen in. We were always half hoping that some luckless chap in a flat cap and khaki overalls would be caught running into the wings as the curtain went up – a time-traveller in sixteenth-century Germany – trapped in the onrush of all those Nurembergers with their banners and rosettes.

That scene-change can be quite dangerous, with tons of heavy scenery rolling about the stage, so we had to wait by the curtain for the stage manager's signal to move, and then *run*. The extra chorus we used in *Aida* and *Boris* took part in that last act, and our guardsmen contributed one or two of their famous faints. All hands were mustered to stand in the wings giving cues to the various Guild processions to start moving. One dear soul – a stagecraft teacher – was discovered giving his cues from the score of *Rigoletto*. It seemed to work, though.

The rehearsals for that colossal finale, when all the townsfolk assemble for the song contest, had been hilarious. The producer was an amiable Austrian who had been a radio sports-commentator. We liked him immensely but his English was almost non-existent. When he wanted crowd noises he'd yell: 'Now iss laughing and talking otherwise we have dead,' and to clear a space for the entrance of a procession: 'Now iss forming a gap and bringing it in.'

How the stage and the sets ever stood up to the weight of all those hundreds of people is a mystery, and a tribute to the men who built them, and by the time the Prize Song was due we were all glad to stand and listen after all that singing and cheering. The tenor who sang it was a huge, good-natured Icelander, none of the more colourful costumes was big enough for him, nothing except an enormous grey velvet number, and as he always stood with his toes turned out he was nicknamed Willie the Whale, after the great grey character in Disney's cartoon about opera.

Peter Brook was by this time our Director of Productions, and one of his most refreshing ideas was to let two members of the chorus have a night off to watch the performances, opera or ballet, from the stalls. Only one snag . . . we had to write a 'critique' for him to read. When my turn came to watch *Die Meistersinger* I was astonished to see that the noisy street fight in Act Two was over so soon. To us it seemed to go on for ever. It takes place at night outside Pogner's house, and during the complicated shouting of the various warring guilds and their apprentices you could easily lose your place in the music. If this happened you had to wait until you heard the basses bellow: 'WAX-BOILERS!' then you knew where you were. The scenery of that opera was full of small eye-level holes made by Robbie so that he could relay a beat to the chorus when they couldn't see the conductor. Nowadays it's all done by closed-circuit television, and I imagine all the hazard has gone out of it.

It was during the rehearsals of the finale that the Great Chorus Rebellion occurred. The translation of the last chorus went: 'Honour your German masters, If you would shun disasters' and we refused to sing that, on the grounds that we'd just wasted six years fighting them. Totally illogical, I know, some of the German singers we were on stage with at that very moment were admired and respected by all of us, but there we stood, in sullen, silent rows until the producer and conductor had a conference and changed the words to: 'Honour your *noble* masters'.

Like Pelion upon Ossa, Wagner followed Wagner. After the Cow-and-Gate prettiness of *Die Meistersinger* it was back to Teutonic mists and myths for us, made mistier by the fact that The Ring and *Tristan* were to be sung in German, as most of the principal singers would be German. If the Welsh members of the chorus forgot their German they simply continued in either tonic sol-fa or Welsh. The Ring, in which, thank heaven, there's nothing for the women's chorus to do, goes on literally for days, and really is a most immoral tale, full of incest and adultery. David Franklin pointed out that every single character in it is a child of Wotan except Hunding, the part he was singing. Our chief delight was to watch the men's chorus all dressed up in fur rugs and with horned helmets, standing on a mountain-top thumping their spears three times in approval of whatever windy daftness was being sung by the chief characters. There would always be one renegade who'd raise his spear for a fourth thump, realise his mistake in time, and craftily lower the spear without making a sound.

At the end of that first post-war *Götterdämmerung* there was a technical miracle worth watching, when the great castle falls in ruins and is engulfed by floods. Great lumps of 'masonry' hurtled to the stage and the 'waters' rose. 'I'd like to do that once more' said the producer

. . . and every huge broken pillar rose up again to make the castle whole, just like running a film of a falling building backwards. I expect that scenery has gone to make firewood long since, but it was a technical triumph. The stage machinery that worked the 'ruins' was in the charge of Mr Ballard, a trim elderly gentleman with a white moustache, who always wore a stiff butterfly collar with his black suit and bowler hat, and whose favourite operatic crime-story was his account of how Grace Moore, the American 'operatic' film-star of the thirties, had asked for *microphones* to be used in Covent Garden.

When rehearsals of *Tristan* were in progress we were allowed to go down to the stalls to listen to the orchestral run-through. The auditorium was partly in darkness, except for the orchestra pit and a light over a music-stand in one of the lower side boxes. Somebody was sitting there, a well-built woman in a black Persian lamb coat. Occasionally there was a wink of light from the diamond earrings she wore, but otherwise we couldn't see her face. Then she began to sing, and the effect was shattering. The voice was like a great golden sunset. It rang round the auditorium, cut through the orchestral sound, and hit both yours ears like a blow from an angel's wings. The singer was Kirsten Flagstad, and to my mind there has never been another like her. She was heroically built, with the physical strength and stamina of a yak. She had a very pretty face, with brilliant blue eyes and a cheerfully regal disposition. Anyone who heard her singing the *Liebestod* might imagine that after the curtain came down she would fade quietly away into a Celtic twilight of mist and tears. But there she'd be at a party, peacefully drinking stout, and rummaging in her great black handbag to find what is called in Scandinavia 'Grandma's Boasting-Book', full of photographs of children and grandchildren. When the management gave us a slap-up all-night party (I forget what it was for, but it was a splendid romp) one of the ballet boys did a tap-dance, three of us sang a 'comic' song I'd written, Margot Fonteyn worked the main spotlight in the roof, and in the early hours of the morning Madame Flagstad sang songs by Grieg. During that treat a fight broke out at the back of the stalls between the staff and some hefty gate-crashers, but through all the bar-room brawling Flagstad sang imperturbably on. A monumental lady, and when she sang Isolde you forgot the big middle-aged woman on the stage, and saw only a girl crazed with love, stumbling up a cliff-path to where her lover is dying on a makeshift stretcher in the courtyard of a bleak castle. Her Tristan was a German tenor Fritz Seider who towered above even her, and it was rumoured that he wore a corset. We thoroughly approved of him because in the first act during the ship-board scene he passed the time on the curtained-off prow of the ship by doing card-tricks for the chorus of sailors.

About once a year the whole company went on tour to any city with a theatre large enough to take us. Whatever time of year it was the weather always seemed to be cold, and some of the train journeys could take as long as eight hours in that post-war turmoil. We played cards with the orchestra – pontoon, with a suitcase-top as a table . . . third-class rail didn't run to tables in those days. And hoped our digs would be good.

Stephen Leacock, in his essay on 'Boarding-house Geometry', describes a landlady as: 'A parallelogram, that is, an oblong angular figure, which cannot be described, but which is equal to anything'. The landladies I knew then certainly were.

After a long, cold journey on a winter Sunday night it's a comfort if you know that your digs are going to be good. At Mrs P's, for instance, it didn't matter after all that your shoes were wearing thin, and that you knew that you were never going to be a star. As soon as you saw the inside of Mrs P's neat little house in Liverpool nothing seemed so bad. I say the inside, because the outside was grim. Mrs P lived in one of those districts they write heavily sociological television plays about. The nights were full of shouts and running feet, and blood and broken glass on the pavement next morning.

After a week of Mrs P's suppers of brown bread fried in pork dripping, and ham and sausages and cups of strong Lancashire tea – with perhaps a drop of something in it if she thought you looked a bit poorly, it was a nasty shock to meet Mrs M. in the next town. Mrs M. was a gaunt woman with hair like corrugated iron, and a voice that could cut steel girders. As the taxi-driver carried our bags into her front hall (taxi-drivers did that in those days) all she'd said was: 'Mind t'wallpaper!' But she proved kind and honest, and full of weird, Goonlike proverbs like: 'A rolling rissole gathers no gravy,' delivered with a perfectly straight face.

The addresses of really good theatrical digs are jealously guarded by actors, and only passed on to close friends. In strange towns the 'Equity' book – a list of lodgings compiled by the Actors' union – was always useful. From that book we got to know Mrs Cardiff whose house was full of roses . . . on the wallpaper, the bedspreads, the carpets and the china. Mrs C was a fortune-telling addict. The cards, the tea-leaves, the ouija-board . . . you name it, she'd foretell your future with it.

Mrs Birmingham was a mine of information about matters surgical, operations and weird folk-remedies for all diseases. You didn't complain of a sore throat in her hearing . . . she'd have a scarf round your neck in no time, and be trotting you round the local gasworks.

Lodging with Mrs Manchester was like living on the stage in one of those plays about volatile Jewish families. Nobody ever seemed to go to bed, they were up to all hours, laughing, singing, quarrelling, banging doors and shouting. The food was marvellous, but I think she gave our bacon ration to the cat.

Most theatrical digs tend to be either warm and grubby, or cold and clean. Mrs McThing managed to be cold and mucky – and expensive, too. The McThing herself was a slovenly blonde with a Come-Dancing hairstyle like yellow concrete. She searched our cases while we were at the theatre, too, we knew that, because we'd wound a hair round the lock and it was broken. And two pairs of our precious nylon stockings – akin to diamonds in those days – were gone. So we had to use that time-honoured theatrical remedy for a really bad landlady. You go to the fishmonger and get a kipper, and you nail it to the underside of the table, where it will fester and throb for weeks . . . maybe months . . . until eventually Mrs McThing's neighbours cry out for the sanitary inspector to come and find the evil smell. And serve her right, too.

Every time I go through Crewe station I think of all those towns – and somehow Crewe still looks like a bombed monastery.

The chorus did its own tour of Wales. The girls wore new grey-and-red dresses, and we all sang choruses from the repertory, and some special ones. We also learned the Welsh National Anthem in Welsh . . . always useful. One of our pianists was George Malcolm, the famous harpsichordist. He was a rare character, besides being a fine musician. We were awe-struck at the way George re-tuned the organ at a cinema in Cardiff, and left a polite note for the regular organist telling him what he'd done. 'Dear Sir, your organ is now a quarter of a tone sharp. Yours etc. G. Malcolm,' What nerve and style.

It was on this tour that I got the only chance I'd ever have to sing the part of Maddalena in the last act quartet from *Rigoletto* when the contralto soloist fell ill. The operatic world remained unmoved.

One of our most outlandish productions was a fruit-salad affair called *The Pilgrim's Progress*. Not the Vaughan Williams opera, but a mixture of words and music, from Bach to the best of British Gluck and Bach again, linking the Bunyan story. The conductor was Sir Malcolm Sargent, who shook hands with me by mistake at a rehearsal when I was sitting in for the pianist who had gone to the lavatory. (There was a story about Sir Malcolm Sargent which I think is the very peak of one-upmanship. To a radio interviewer who came to talk to him at his home he mentioned that he'd had a kind note from the Queen Mother. 'Just a minute' he said, rustling through some letters, 'I'll find it for you . . . oh no, not that one . . . that's from the Queen . . . ah, here it is.' Follow *that*!)

The producer was Ralph Reader who ran the Scout 'Gang Shows'. He was a pleasant chap, very hard-working and experienced. His highest accolade was to say 'Chickety-snitch, boys and girls' when we'd pleased him. Odd to hear Bach thus described. Lots of famous actors played the speaking parts . . . Jack Hawkins, Barry Jones, Robert Speaight and Frank Pettingell, with Apollyon played by Hugh Miller . . . odd that the nicest man in the cast should play the Evil One. At one of the performances we had an audience consisting entirely of clergymen. Two thousand white dog-collars gleamed in the dark, and the bar profits slumped alarmingly.

We did some broadcasting, too. Robbie formed a group of sixteen singers to perform Elizabethan madrigals. We called ourselves the 'Garvent' Singers. Better than 'Coden' Singers, I suppose.

But, during the three years I was a member of the company I had come to realise that, much as I loved it, opera was not for me. My voice was not good enough for an operatic career, too small and too 'straight'; I wasn't physically strong enough, and I lacked that one quality a good singer must have – complete single-mindedness. Too many other things could distract me from the course of a career.

The outside world looked inviting, with the rumours of higher pay, so I decided to leave, and to try my luck in the commercial music world. I thought I would miss the opera, and I did in many ways. I missed the Opera House itself, with those rather homely cream-painted backstage corridors and cramped dressing-rooms. I missed the music – nothing is ever as violent and glamorous again. I missed the extravagant costumes and the glitter and colour of the audience on gala nights. I missed Joe, the stage-door keeper, and the market, and the Nag's Head and Smokey's. But I'd had three years of working for the very best conductors and producers of that time; I knew the scores of about twenty operas, and I'd made good friends. I didn't miss the smell of greasepaint – greasepaint was beginning to be passé by then and the new make-ups came out of pots. In fact, it's not the smell of greasepaint you miss, it's the smell of the size that the scene-painters use. In the years that followed there were times when I wished I was back and part of a company again, but you can't go back once you've moved on.

Three things still give me that rare crawling tingle of the scalp and backbone . . . the overture to *Rigoletto* with its crescendo of repeated octaves . . . the beginning of *The Magic Flute* which I heard so often over the Tannoy when we were dressing for our Three Boys roles . . . and the memory of a murky winter afternoon when Robbie had said at the end of a chorus rehearsal: 'If you ladies care to stay for a few minutes you may like to hear what the gentlemen have been practising in their separate sessions' . . . and we first heard the splendour of the Prisoners' Chorus from Beethoven's *Fidelio*.

The chorus today is different from the chorus then. Their voices are every bit as good, but the old attack and enthusiasm are sometimes missing. The times are different, maybe that's it. We were young, and thankful just to be alive, and looking forward to a world we thought could only get better. Even in grim post-war London optimism coloured our outlook just as the rose-bay willow-herb covered the ruins of the city. The willow-herb has gone, and most of the ruins, but I've still got my *Rigoletto* earrings, and the other Speechless Handmaiden is still one of my dearest friends.

CHAPTER FOUR

Alla zingarese

THERE NOW followed the period in my life which I can only describe as a mess, very much like the life-style of the characters in *Scènes de la Vie de Bohème*. Now those conditions may be fine on the operatic stage, and with Puccini's music too, but in real life they are not nearly as attractive. By this time I was divorced, and living with Eddie, who has now been my husband for nearly thirty years. We had a dark, graceless furnished flat in West Kensington – the unfashionable end – owned by a woman who was a dead ringer for the witch in *Hansel and Gretel*.

'Living together', when I was a child, was a phrase used by grown-ups in tones half of outrage, half of envy. In those unpermissive days it was a state to be avoided, by women anyway, except where one or other partner was irrevocably tied to a former spouse by religion, or insanity, or just sheer bloody-mindedness. Among working-class people another drawback was the expense of such a mode of living. Looking back on it, I think those proletarian moralists were more than half right. It *is* a rather unsatisfactory set-up, particularly for women, with all the disadvantages of marriage and none of the advantages. In these clinical times, when everybody is so frank and fearless about matters of morality ('Frank and Fearless' have always sounded to me like a music-hall act . . . fast deteriorating into 'Tedious and Tasteless') it's quite fashionable to sneer at the 'piece of paper' – the marriage certificate – but that piece of paper can be the bond that does not break in those times of trouble – or just plain disenchantment – which no partnership can escape. If you are married, the sheer inconvenience of a divorce may make you try to improve your marriage. If you are not married, you can simply give up and run away, and your character will be the weaker for it. I must make it clear that I don't think that rather bleak philosophy applies in cases of physical or mental brutality – I'm talking about ordinary civilised people.

Such an arrangement is not nearly as easy as it looks, even now, and in the late 1940s and early 1950s it was further complicated by booby-traps like ration-books and identity cards with different surnames.

Eddie Thomas and I had met while we were both in the opera company, and we have loved each other through good times, bad times, and very bad times, ever since. He is Welsh, one of the short, dark, Silurian South Welsh – the ones who wear the Number 10 jersey in every Rugby team. He was the eleventh in a family of twelve children. Their father was a miner born in Ohio, the son of emigrants who later returned to the Rhondda, a man of immense charm, and considerable learning, but with a great weakness for drink – a financial handicap for the twelve children, and a positive tragedy for their mother. She was, by all accounts, as near to a saint as any woman can ever be, kindly, hardworking, and a living demonstration of Christianity against dreadful odds. She loved her enormous family dearly, but she died, worn out with work and poverty, when Eddie was six. Her husband survived for many years afterwards, and when he died he had the sort of funeral you see in old films about Welsh miners – scores of singing men following the coffin to the rainy graveyard. At his wife's funeral there had not been as much singing, but I think there may have been more tears. Most of the eight boys had an enormous capacity for hard work, and nearly all of them won scholarships to university – it was either the university or the pit in those days, a choice which concentrated the mind wonderfully. The youngest boy, Gwyn, became a novelist, playwright and broadcaster. Of the four sisters, the one I knew best was Minnie. She had inherited her father's charm and her mother's generosity, and to visit her tiny terraced house under the awesome fiery mountain-side was like putting numbed hands into warm furry gloves. Minnie loved company, and laughter, and singing, and her Chapel, and baking bilberry pie, and keeping her house neat. In spite of her strong Noncomformist beliefs, she uttered not a word of censure about Eddie and me, her dark eyes smiled on us equally, and the warmth of her welcome was the same as for her more conventional relatives. She is dead now, and the world is a poorer place.

When their mother died, the oldest sister took charge of the family, putting off her own marriage until the youngest boy was safely into

Oxford. Such a sense of family duty would be very rare nowadays, I feel. With such a huge family it was not surprising that the youngest ones found it difficult to get a word in edgeways. Gwyn says they were in their teens before they realised that the older ones might have been speaking Welsh.

Eddie had always loved singing, and when he left university and began teaching he still worked hard on his voice. He won two scholarships – one to Dartington Hall, and one to the Webber-Douglas School – but that was in the few months before the war, and for the next six years he was in the army, in North Africa and Italy, and apart from some Forces broadcasting his musical career came to a stop. When the war was over, he joined the Glyndebourne chorus, and sang small parts at the Edinburgh Festival, then joined the Covent Garden company later. Although his voice was outstandingly good – a sweet bass-baritone – his physique was against an operatic career. Being a 'Number 10 jersey' size is not the best height for the czars-and-kings-and-high-priests rôles that basses generally get. 'What we need', he said, 'are shorter operas – for shorter people.'

When we left the Garden he did a good many broadcasts of the early-morning-recital type, but you can't live long on those. We found it was not easy to find jobs where we could be together, although each of us could have taken work in different parts of the country. This determination not to be parted led to the kind of living that Rodolfo, Mimi and their friends sang about – but we were older – one war older, and the bohemian life grew more and more difficult. Many of our friends were in the same position, particularly some of Eddie's former army comrades, so we spent most of our time with them in bars, and pubs and hotels. I don't think there's a single pub from Hammersmith to Hyde Park Corner that I didn't get to know – too well.

All the men reminded me of sixteenth or seventeenth-century characters – the sort of men who never really feel at home anywhere after a war. When the Thirty Years War was over the taverns and ale-houses must have been full of them. One of the most endearing of our friends was Henry. Henry was the son of a wealthy family, kindly, elegant and aimless. He could not bear being alone, so each day he sat in the same bar, and whenever he felt the draught caused by the door opening to admit a new customer he'd put money on the counter – without looking round to see for whom he was going to buy the drink. He had a chic and lovely girl friend, and we idled away hours and days either in bars or in Henry's flat, talking and drinking. Another of our friends, a Welsh ex-paratrooper, even *kept* a bar in a big block of flats. More talk, more drinking, more time-wasting . . . even the occasional meal.

It was about this time when we discovered that there was a moderate living to be made simply by making music in pubs. This was before every pub had a juke-box, and there was usually a piano in the better establishments. I played, and Eddie sang. Our pay was mostly liquid, but there were a few meals as well. Even when the pubs closed, landlords often continued the party with a few of their friends late into the night, and although the music was always melancholy – maudlin, perhaps, and never loud, there'd soon be a disapproving hair-curlered, dressing-gowned wife looking round the door and reminding her landlord husband sharply that it was two o'clock, or three o'clock in the morning. I knew just how these women felt, but I've always noticed that men's appetite for soft, sentimental music is unlimited. There were even private parties where we sang and played and were rewarded with money, and meals, and sometimes – best of all – friendship. Tom and Bertha, who kept a butcher's shop in Soho, often saved us from real hunger by the present of a rabbit or some liver.

Singing duets together would have been the answer to our problems, but good duettists were nearly always baritone and soprano. Bass-baritone and mezzo (as I was) never have the cutting edge that is needed. Eddie had a job as a kind of vocal demonstrator for a man who specialised in teaching film stars to sing for their rôles in musicals, and I eked out a tiny living playing for dancing-classes, and even for children's talent-contests. The iron fortitude of the judges at these affairs always amazed me, after all, there must be a limit to the number of times you can stand hearing *The Pixie March* played on the violin by eight-year-olds. There's no limit though, to the grotesque talents of the young. There's always a fourteen-year-old who'll play the *William Tell* overture on his teeth with a pencil, and a hefty ten-year-old in satin shorts aping the gestures of grown-up performers, who'll follow 'The Good Ship Lollipop' with a floor-shaking tap-dance. Most performers brought no music with them – it's quite usual to be asked to play: 'the quick bit in the Rachmaninov concerto'. The way to call the bluff is to ask: 'Which Rachmaninov concerto?' Ten-to-one they'll settle for 'Tiptoe Through the Tulips'. It's the *mothers* of dancing-class and talent-contest children you must watch if you want to see nature red in tooth and claw. On the whole I was glad to get back to playing pub-piano. At least there I could be surprised – the most unlikely people turn out to have immortal singings in them. That quiet, grey man sipping his half of mild ale in a dim corner of the bar may prove, towards closing-time, to be a fine, ear-splitting tenor.

By this time La Vie de Bohème was beginning to be tedious. I had sold what small pieces of jewellery I had, and there's nothing like doing that to make you feel really poor. Only one jeweller was polite, and I was probably cheated through being too timid to argue about the prices. We grew expert at making cigarettes out of the ends of other cigarettes, and at smoking the ends of *those* right down to the last half-inch by holding them on the point of a pin, and our shoes were often reinforced with several thicknesses of brown paper to keep out the wet. We could have given up smoking – but then we would have needed more food. No doubt about it, we would have to change our life-style, but to what? I was the right size and shape for modelling, but in those days all the *haute couture* jobs went to upper-middle-class girls, and all the rest got were corset catalogues. I was a bit too old for the Windmill Theatre – twenty-five was their upper age limit – and the singing jobs I was offered would have meant a lot of touring in the provinces. I'd seen enough of old 'tourers' at auditions. There was one dear old soul who turned up at every West End audition for years. She'd march to centre-stage, lift her skirt to her thighs and shout: 'AND I have a beautiful soprano voice!' Brave, but doomed. And I could remember other performers whose careers never got better however long they toured; one veteran comedian-acrobat in particular, who towards the end of his act used to do a handstand balanced on the back of a chair. Then, upside-down, he'd turn his poor old beetroot-coloured face towards the audience and croak, *apropos* nothing: 'Aren't plooms cheap today?' No future in that – even if I could do hand-stands. But at least in theatrical companies you can always raise a few bob by simply taking a suitcase of odds and ends – scraps of material, ribbon, aprons, buttons, clothes – and selling them for small sums. Our funds were nonexistent by this time. I had even passed the test to become a G.P.O. telephonist on the Continental exchange, but you needed five shillings for the certificate, and I hadn't got the money if we were to pay our rent and eat too. Eddie was offered a Glyndebourne chorus contract, but wouldn't accept it without me, and by this time I was not really capable of singing any more. I had fallen ill with a kind of anæmia, and had to spend a short time in hospital. Eddie decided that this kind of life must end. He had thought of going back to Covent

Garden, or even of rejoining the Army, but both would have meant a kind of separation for us. So he went back to teaching, at first on a supply basis, for various London schools. At least the money was enough to live on, but so wayward is municipal bureaucracy that it was three months before his first pay cheque arrived.

One icy January morning we were married in Fulham Register Office. My mother and father came to the wedding – my father always liked Eddie, even though he did not approve of our living together. Dear Henry was a witness, and gave me my only wedding present, a pressure-cooker. I still use the bottom part as a preserving pan for jam-making. I wore my old black 'New Look' coat, because it was warm and looked good – luckily full skirts were still fashionable – and we all went to lunch in a small French restaurant

Soon after that, we were able to get the rent of our flat halved by the local rent tribunal, but the atmosphere emanating from our landlady afterwards was less than cordial, so we tried to find another place to live. In those days it was even more difficult than it is now, so many buildings had been destroyed and not yet rebuilt after the war. But one of our pub acquaintances knew of a woman who had a place to let. She came into the pub about an hour later, and said we could see the flat, 'but it isn't very nice'. It wasn't, either. It was on the ground floor, ten feet by ten, with a kitchen that had been the scullery of the old house – and still had the 'copper' in the corner. It had no bathroom, and an outside lavatory with dry-rot fungus growing out of the walls. But it was self-contained, cheap, and she was a kind and generous woman. She even bought an old piano for ten pounds at an auction and put it in our room because she liked to hear us singing. She was a fey character; she'd been educated at Cheltenham Ladies' College, and I could never imagine how she became mixed up in the landlady business, except that she had made two rather unsatisfactory and costly marriages. I came home one day to find her standing on the windowsill outside, dressed in an elegant pale grey suit, painting our window-frame with some rust-coloured paint she'd found in the shed. 'Eeek!' I shrieked, 'You'll ruin that suit, get down!' So I got up there myself, and we chatted away in the warm sunshine like two old codgers on a park bench. We lived in that flat for six years. It was infested with dry rot, mice, beetles and spiders, but I can remember being happy and feeling at home as I had seldom felt before. To keep the mice down we got a cat, a lovely black half-Persian. We called her Twm – Welsh for Tom – before we knew she was female. We loved her dearly, but one night she went away and never came back. Cat-thieves had been infesting the district, and I couldn't bear to think of her being caught by them, but I think that's what happened to her. Our next Twm – a tabby-and-white tyrant with a dominating personality and a whole vocabulary of different vocal sounds – owned us for the next fifteen years. He saw the mice off, warned us of any strangers approaching, and comforted us with his presence in grim times. He was a doughty fighter, and a great one for getting stuck up trees until there was a sufficiently large audience of people tweeting 'Puss, puss, Twm, Twm', and waving plates of food, and wobbling up ladders towards him . . . then he'd walk disdainfully down on his own. Once he came home with a broken leg. I was distracted because he'd crept into the coalshed and wouldn't come out, but the vet left some tablets for us to give him when we could entice him out again. On the fifth day he tottered out, his white fur filthy, and began to eat and wash himself. Ever afterwards he limped a bit, but he stayed at home much more than before, and became a real house-cat. To this day I miss his round furry face with its gooseberry-green eyes, and his cat-talk, and his calming presence.

Eddie still worked hard at his singing, and gave a few recitals on what is now Radio 4, and would pace up and down doing breathing exercises and dangling a piece of string behind him for Twm to play with while I sat by the fire reading and reading and reading. I read everything – history, biography, novels, travel books, guide-books, maps, poetry, essays – everything our local library had. It was cheap, no strenuous exercise was involved, and I had always been curious about almost everything. One of the only connections we kept with our life in the theatre was the entertainment world's newspaper *The Stage*. I read it from cover to cover, and sometimes heard of our old friends in its columns – or heard nothing, which was worse. Sometimes I'd read the advertisements, too. 'Cat wanted for panto. Must have own skin.' 'Kardomah, Fills the stage with flags.' 'Girls wanted for cabaret in Beirut.' 'Singers required for Maple Leaf Choir.' Who were *they*, I wondered, and rang the number they had given. They were a newly-formed vocal group, run by an accountant, Fred G. Fred was a very fine musician, and absolutely dedicated to his spare-time work as a choir-trainer. I was auditioned with about twenty other hopefuls in a room above a pub in Marylebone. Part of the audition was a sight-reading test – the alto line in a part-song by E. J. Moeran – not the easiest music to sing at sight. Sight-reading tests are nearly always obscure pieces of music that the candidates only have a thousand-to-one chance of ever having seen before. A collection of them would make a bizarre musical show.

I can't remember ever having *tried* to learn to read music at sight. I'd always been able to play piano music – simplifying the left hand, usually! – at sight, but singing is a different matter, you have to make the notes yourself, and pitch the intervals, and read the words as well, all at once. Robbie had run a series of sight-reading classes for us at Covent Garden, and even though I could sight-read anyway I always went to them, you can never know too much about your job, and sight-reading needs constant practice.

Fred G. chose me for a smaller group which had been formed from the Maple Leaf Choir, and we made a demonstration disc to send to prospective producers. There were eight men and four girls in this smaller group, and we sang Fred's arrangements of the popular songs of that day; 'Little White Cloud', 'El Cumbanchero', 'Something to Sing About'. Eventually we were booked to provide the vocal backing for *The Sleeping Beauty on Ice* at the Empire Pool, Wembley. We were paid eight pounds ten shillings a week, good money in those days . . . but there were thirteen shows a week, two each day – three on Saturdays. Ice-show dubbing is a strange profession. Ice-rinks are usually vast, echoing places, and skaters had neither enough breath, nor voice, to attempt dialogue. So the singing and speaking was done by actors and singers who worked in a kind of wooden shed on stilts above the arena with the conductor and the orchestra, and microphones to relay the music and speech to the audience. When you are dubbing speech for skaters you rehearse the dialogue to correspond with set gestures the skater will make. Skater bows: 'Your Highness!' Skater throws right arm to side: 'I have seen the Princess.' Skater puts hands on either side of face: 'She is the most beautiful princess in the world!' Then perhaps a song follows, and here the skater generally follows the music. A lot can go wrong with all this, skaters can fall, or stumble, and this will delay the dialogue cues. One enchanting American girl, called Gloria Nord, was so prone to falls that the stage-hands used to run a nightly sweepstake on the number of times she'd hit the ice. She was much tougher than she looked, though, a tiny blonde with a glittering smile and great personality. I think we were as delighted as she was when the company were chosen to take part in a Command Performance. The small ice-rink specially built in the theatre ensured that at least she didn't have so far to fall. Ice is extremely hard, and, towards the end of a show, bumpy, jagged and dangerous. A sequin or a flower dropped from a skater's costume can freeze to it and form an unexpected hazard. Some star skaters seem to like a film of water on the ice, and anybody who has seen a skater's calf sliced an inch deep by somebody else's blade will admit that principal skaters are entitled to their whims about the surface of the ice.

The principals are generally skating champions who have turned professional. (The delightful Daphne Walker was one.) Most of the chorus men are either dancers who can skate a bit, or, for the more strenuous battle scenes, ice-hockey players between seasons. These lads are generally good-natured Canadians, amiable fellows, but not likely ever to win the Nobel Prize for literature. One of our singers met a boy skater in the street: 'Hullo, Mike, haven't seen you in the ice-shows lately, what've you been doing?' 'Ice-hockey.' 'Oh, more remunerative, is it?' . . . 'No, ice-hockey.'

One rather worrying aspect of ice-shows used to be the way the lights were lowered, or changed to ultra-violet, for special, often beautiful, effects. The skating chorus runs on to the ice using the same entrances as the audience use to get to their seats, and I was sure that one day some luckless man returning from the gents would get swept on to the ice with the great rush and slither about among all the glittering blades and floating draperies like an overturned tortoise among birds of paradise.

Skaters were not on the ice for more than a few minutes at a time, but for the actors and musicians in the 'box' ice-shows were a test of endurance. A one-bar electric fire was placed near the conductor's feet, but the rest of us wore coats, gloves, scarves and fleece-lined boots, and waited for the spot near the end of each show, just before the finale, when 'speciality' acts would be keeping the audience amused for about twenty minutes, and we could all go to the canteen, except for the drummer, who had to provide bangs, drum-rolls and cymbal-crashes for acrobatic troupes and clowns.

The Empire Pool canteen was excellent, and a warm haven for us all between the three Saturday shows. The leading actor was 'Jimmie' Grant Anderson, a vivid character with a mischievous sense of humour and vast experience. Jimmie actually *owned* a small theatre in south-west London, and regaled us with accounts of the weekly shows. 'Mexican dance troupe this week . . . the devils, they're *cooking* in the dressing-rooms!' Or 'Carl Rosa Opera this week – marvellous! . . . the bars are coining money every night!' Jimmie loved Shakespeare, and if you caught him in a happy mood, could give you the whole of the Tent Scene from *Julius Caesar* . . . both parts at once. His politics were true-blue Tory, which conflicted with those of one of the speciality acts, a young man called Jackie who performed incredible balancing feats on a kind of table above the ice, culminating in a specacular 'fall' as the table tilted over. He and Jimmie argued fiercely in the canteen, and each session would end with Jimmie shouting: 'Oh go and do your act in the Kremlin, then!' at the grinning Jackie. The marvellous Frediani family of acrobats were our friends, too. They were 'pure' acrobats – in other words they used no apparatus of any kind. Papa Frediani ruled all the boys with a firm hand, and their disciplined upbringing had made them into delightful companions. Even though their native language was Spanish (we were all *gringos* to them!) they teased and joked in English . . . 'Anybody wanna date with our sister? Pretty girl, don't smoke, don't drink, never been out with a boy.' As various masculine ears pricked up: 'Only one snag – she only eighteen months old!' They were a typical circus family, close-knit, well-mannered, and obedient and respectful to their parents. This may sound archaically old-fashioned, but it certainly produces delightful children. After all, unless trapeze children, for instance, obey their parents instantly, someone can end up with a broken back. Circus people are traditionally careful about their daughters' welfare, too, and this watchfulness extends to any young girl even temporarily in their care. I knew an eighteen-year-old soprano who worked each night at a famous circus, providing 'ethereal music' for a high-wire act, and each night the circus proprietor sent her home in his own pale blue Jaguar, right to her parents' door.

Jimmie couldn't resist a quip at the expense of the Fredianis, though. Every night as they bounced out of the arena, panting and sweating, he'd say with mock despair: 'Here they are again, too damn' lazy to learn a comic song.' Even though the speciality acts had nothing to do with the pantomime story we always watched them with admiration, and marvelled at their complete dedication to their work. I was reminded of the great Rastelli, perhaps the most famous juggler of all time – he travelled all over the world, but never saw any of it. Just his hotel room and the circus or theatre, because he was always either practising or performing.

These were a few really excellent singers among the dubbers in these ice-shows, and I could never understand how they could bear their comparative anonymity. They seemed happy enough – the work was very regular and the money was fair, and perhaps they didn't have that ninety per cent of luck which must always go with ten per cent of talent for real success. Two of our own group were later to become famous in the world of popular song, they were the husband-and-wife team, Miki and Griff. I played their accompaniment for their first demonstation record, and they gave me a pretty brooch. Now they are highly regarded in the world of Country music, and it couldn't have happened to two nicer people.

Summer ice-shows were really pleasant. *Chu Chin Chow on Ice* was very successful; somehow the oriental extravaganza blended with the artificial glitter of a skating-rink in midsummer to make a very effective show, and the music helped too – the audience knew, or half-knew, most of the tunes already. 'The Cobbler's Song', 'The Robbers' Chorus', 'Any Time's Kissing Time' could be heard every day on the radio even if you weren't sure what they were called. Between shows on warm summer afternoons we'd sit on the lawns outside, and a favoured few were even allowed to exercise some of the greyhounds that raced in Wembley Stadium next door. I was never keen on doing this, I'm a cat-person anyway, and greyhounds are huge, sometimes bad-tempered, animals. Even muzzled as these were, they can give you a baleful stare as though they'd like to see you in place of that hare on the end of the pole.

At the end of each show's season Sir Arthur Elvin, the 'Big Boss', would give the whole company a slap-up sit-down knife-and-fork party in Wembley Stadium, and we provided our own cabaret. Those affairs had a family atmosphere in spite of the cavernous spaces of the stadium's dining-hall. It's an eerie experience, at three o'clock in the morning, to look down on to the great football field, a green, silent, dimly-lit Roman amphitheatre. Sometimes our vocal group dressed up in blue blazers and white flannel trousers or skirts and marched out on to that sacred Wembley turf to lead the community singing which was customary at Cup Finals in those days. On all those occasions, F.A. Cup Final, Amateur Cup Final, Rugby League Cup Final, we were conducted by Mr Caiger, a stocky figure in white high on a rostrum in mid-field, and the whole vast arena full of fans joined in 'Roll Out the Barrel', and 'Abide With Me', with that smudgy baritone sound that results from many thousands of men singing together. (A note from Fred G., which I've still got, warns us to 'bring a complete change of clothing in case of bad weather'.)

One day, one of the girls in our company said 'Why don't you audition for George Mitchell, he does a lot of work with choirs? I'll fix a date for you.' I was getting a bit weary of all the travelling that working at Wembley entailed, even though I got a lift home each night from one of the trumpeters in the orchestra – he's immortal as the man who played the muted solo trumpet in the famous Mantovani record of the old tune 'Charmaine'. So I said I'd try, and a date was fixed for me to sing for George Mitchell at the B.B.C. Maida Vale studios when he would be rehearsing his choir for a broadcast. I was too early – I always am, for everything, and I sat in the canteen sipping lukewarm tea. I saw a man I thought was George – I'd only seen grainy newspaper pictures of him – sitting with a tiny Dresden-china blonde. Timidly I went over to their table and told them my name, and we went off to the empty studio for me to sing. I sang a fairly simple song, 'The Old House' – John McCormack fans may remember it – and then a couple of scales, a sight-reading test, and the sort of test where you pick the middle or lower note out of a chord – to see if you could sustain a harmony part in choral music – then a short unaccompanied passage to see how capable you were of keeping in tune unaided. 'Right,' said George. 'Are you free next Sunday? We need an alto voice for the broadcast at the Camberwell Palace.' Could a duck swim? So began an association which lasted for the next fifteen years.

George Mitchell was, and is, an extraordinary person. He had started to form his choir when he was in the army, and at the time I joined they were already very well known on the radio. He is a Scot, but not aggressively so; a fine musician with what is much rarer – impeccable musical taste. His choral arrangements were simple and deceptively easy to listen to, each under-part forming a 'tune' on its own, which is most unusual. His capacity for hard work was enormous, never did anyone deserve his white Rolls-Royce more. But the quality I found most endearing was his wit. Not a mere sense of humour but *real* wit, spontaneous, wry and lugubrious, capable of deflating pomposity and yet kindly enough not to hurt sensitive people. The sort of comical shrewdness that made him say to a row of tenors – notorious for their righteous indignation when caught singing wrong notes – 'One of you fellas is flat . . . and he'll be sittin' next to all of you.' I really loved working for him, and the only quality in him that pained me was the fact that he was a Wagner-fanatic . . . ah well, nobody's perfect! The exquisite little blonde was his secretary Daphne Bell. She looked fragile as a primrose, and was shrewd, hard-working, loyal, and, of all incongruous things, a netball champion and the best Charleston dancer among singers that I've ever seen. She was also capable of making the most hideous faces behind the backs of conceited or boorish people, and the rest of us, half-hysterical with suppressed laughter, waited with delicious dread for the day when one of these oafs would turn round and catch her at it. They never did. She looks exactly the same today, and I'm convinced there's a picture up in her attic that grows old with the rest of us while Daphne Bell like Dorian Gray shines on.

That first Camberwell Palace variety broadcast was a taste of what was to come. We sang 'Anchors Aweigh' (I always thought it was 'Anchors Away', but it isn't!), 'Mardi Gras', 'Sky-liner' and similar numbers. We wore black satin skirts, white satin blouses and black ribbon chokers round our necks. I sang with one of the more experienced girls and enjoyed the nerve-racking precision of the whole show – everything was live in those days, with no going back to correct mistakes. After that, nearly every Sunday meant another broadcast, and during the summer I worked for George in the choir at Empress Hall, Earls Court . . . much nearer to my home than Wembley had been, but yet another ice-show! The set-up was different at Earls Court though. Whereas the Wembley musicians and actors had been hidden away in the 'box', the Empress Hall management liked the audience to actually *see* the dubbers and orchestra sitting in rows and working away like mad for their entertainment. The show was *White Horse Inn*, and the heroine's part was skated by Belita. Belita had been a child-prodigy skater – Belita Jepson-Turner from, of all places, Nether Wallop. She had grown up in America and developed into a skating super-star, with long, elegant legs – very unusual, as most skaters have very thick thighs – and a reputation for being temperamental and of colourful vocabulary, all instantly forgiven when you saw her spin at the end of a solo number, a slender blurred column whirring round like a revolving drill-bit. The great Max Wall was her co-star. Don't ask me how his classic 'Professor Wallofski' piano act got into *White Horse Inn* on ice, but there it was; every night I watched it, and every night I laughed.

That year's ice-panto was *Cinderella* with Tommy Trinder as Buttons, and the musical clowns 'Jo, Jack and Johnnie' as a speciality act. These boys dressed in flapping black tail-coats and bowler hats and pretended to be a lunatic Palm Court trio. They were good, steady lads, and the brother of one of them was an excellent shoe-mender – difficult to find in those days.

The next summer's ice-show was called *Wildfire*, a musical-skating version of the story of Captain John Smith, Pocahontas, and the early settlers in Virginia. The hero's part was taken by that thoroughly nice man, Frankie Vaughan, gamely slithering about the ice on unfamiliar skates. Frank was and is the soul of kindness and would stop his Rolls in the street to pick up any member of the company he noticed on the way to the arena. This may seem a small thing, but you'd be surprised how many show-business types don't think of it. (We had our connections with the classier people in the B.B.C. too – our pretty brunette harpist in the orchestra was sometimes visited between shows by her brother, later to become Sir Huw Wheldon.)

The ice-shows and the Sunday broadcasts meant that I was seldom home in the evenings, and Eddie spent a good deal of time with our friends in our favourite riverside pub – 'All beers drawn from the wood.' An honest, cosy place at that time, with a clientele of sweeps, watermen, commercial travellers and timber-yard workers, it has now been skilfully tarted-up into a haunt for thrusting young executives. Our dear, dreadful little flat was fine for two, but desolate for one.

By now Eddie was teaching full-time at a big school for boys in north London. There were thirty-three different nationalities among the one thousand pupils, ranging from Arabs to Zulus, and never a dull moment. He taught them English, but my husband's English lessons included bits of history, geography, music, drama, poetry, wherever he felt they might light a spark in the minds of boys who might find school difficult. He seems to have succeeded. . . . I've known him to be walking down Regent Street and suddenly be startled by a young man falling into step beside him and declaiming a line of Housman into his ear – a relic of Eddie's half-forgotten English lessons, from a former pupil.

School discipline was strict, but school life never colourless, with many unexpected treats, like diamonds found on paving-stones. A boy who'd appeared only average would begin to concentrate on his work, another who seemed sullen would present Eddie with a wooden bowl or a painting of his own making. Good schoolmasters cannot have favourites, but I know Eddie had a great regard for the Italian boys for their cheerfulness and capacity for work; for the Chinese for their industry and their elegant appearance (I wonder how Chinese mothers keep their children looking so smart?) and for the Cypriots for sheer friendliness and business acumen. One of them took over a hoop-la stall at a school fête because he couldn't bear to watch the well-meaning incompetence of the master who was running it. In half-an-hour he had made a small fortune for the school fund, and a slightly smaller one for himself. I've a feeling he will bestride this narrow world like an Onassis. When Eddie retired from teaching he was glad in many ways; working under modern conditions is becoming unnecessarily difficult, but he missed the boys, and their occasional racing tips for horses or dogs – sometimes good ones! – and their home-made birthday-cards with the signatures of the whole form. The Cockney boy, with his mixture of sophistication and naïveté, can be an endearing or infuriating pupil, often both. His education deserves less windy theory, and more worldly-wise firmness and example.

Since we had left Covent Garden our life had taken a course different, perhaps, from the one we had hoped for – I wonder if it's all 'written down' somewhere . . . ? – but although we were older (I had found my first grey hair on July 23rd 1952. . . . I was sufficiently shaken to have made a note of it in my diary!) we were still together, and our mixture of love and friendship grew stronger day by day. We had made costly mistakes, but even the great strain of acute poverty had not broken our bond of affection. Now *there's* an old-fashioned word, but long experience and observation have taught me that affection, deepening, if you are lucky and work hard at it, into love, will endure when passion cools or even dies. The word 'love' is used very loosely today. I think it is extremely rare in any relationship, and difficult to define. 'Sheer pleasure in watching somebody else living' is one way to describe it. Most people, when they finally grow up, will find that affection will do very well. Love is different, indestructible, eternal, and those of us who feel its presence are truly blessed.

CHAPTER FIVE

Poco a poco animando

SINCE THE END of the war great technical advances had been made in the world of recorded music. Decca had issued their first British long-playing record in 1950, and there was an increasing demand for more music and musicians for radio, television and gramophone records.

George Mitchell had decided that those of us who were good sight-readers would be more use for this work than being walled up in long-running stage shows, so we spent most of our time in the nerve-racking and highly competitive world of the session musician.

'Session' work means that a singer or an orchestral player is hired for a session of three hours to sing or play whatever music is required. The hiring is usually done through a 'fixer' who knows from long experience which musicians are best at what kind of music. This develops into an incestuous process, with the same couple of hundred people being hired in different permutations for different sessions. The men who played in Mantovani's orchestra for one session might be called 'Reg Leopold and his Orchestra' a day or so later. Singers tend to stick more closely to their 'fixer' or choirmaster, for there are more variations between one human voice and another than there are between, say, one trombone and another, and a good choirmaster will know his singers' voices well.

The sound they produce varies with the type of musical arrangement which is needed for each record, but sometimes choirs are used as a backing – mostly ooos-and-ahs – for a popular singer (not 'pop' yet, notice, this was still the mid-fifties), sometimes as extra instruments of the orchestra, and sometimes as themselves, as in the case of Ray Coniff or James Last and their choirs and orchestras.

These musicians, both singers and orchestral players, are extremely expensive, and consequently time is literally money. Sessions must be got through in as short a time as possible, so all the players and singers must be good sight-readers. It's a very masculine world; orchestral players are almost entirely men (and I've only ever seen one woman conductor in the session world) but happily there are few men who can sing soprano or alto, so women are needed for choirs. (Sometimes girls who can sing well below middle C are used to strengthen a tenor line – if an alto voice sings, for instance, G below middle C it can sound like a tenor singing the G two octaves above.) And there was never any question of financial discrimination, both men and girls received the same fee. A session singer who was much in demand could in theory do up to three three-hour sessions in one day, perhaps every day of the week. After working like that for a few weeks you'd be rich but exhausted.

No great voice is required for session singing, although it's as well if you can sing in tune unaccompanied, as some music will be written *a cappella*. This is more difficult than it sounds, as you can prove to yourself. Think of a favourite tune, play the first couple of notes of it on the piano (better still, play the tonic chord, and *listen* to the notes) then sing the tune through to the end without accompaniment. Play the first few notes of the tune again, and almost everybody – particularly men's voices – will be found to be about a quarter of a tone flat, sometimes as much as a semitone. Flatness is not incurable, though. A bit more concentration – 'thinking high' – generally corrects it. Sharpness is more serious, and not much can be done to cure it.

A good sense of rhythm is a help, but it should be the conductor's rhythm, not yours, or in a choir of forty voices there'll be forty different ideas of tempo. Exact rhythm, again, is not easy. Audiences who clap in time to music generally clap faster and faster until it all sounds like applause. Try clapping one whole beat and two halves for a minute or so. It's the two half-beats that begin to get shorter. There are other qualities you'll need if you are to be among the constantly employed chosen few. Concentration is one. You must be able to hold your musical line no matter what the other voices are singing. Obedience is another, obedience to chorus-master and conductor (if he says it's *adagio*, it's *adagio*, no matter if the score says *andante*) and, in the case of classical music, to the style of the composer. Punctuality and good health count, too. You can be late once, although you won't be popular, but not twice, and this can be a problem. Film studios, where much film music is recorded, are often out in 'them thar hills', and it may mean starting from home at about six o'clock in the morning to be at work by eight. And you can't afford to be ill very often, or you'll be classed as unreliable. Appearance is not all-important, unless you do a lot of television work, but what the advertisements used to call 'personal freshness' *is* – you stand very close together in choirs! There is little glory in the job; it's not the career for somebody who feels they must be a solo singer. But there is plenty of respect for anyone who does the job consistently well, and plenty of money, too, although it's not a regular income – several hundred pounds for two weeks, then maybe no work at all for three.

Calmness and self-discipline are essential. You can't panic and stop singing, whatever appears to be going wrong around you, you just keep going and who knows, you may be right. I achieved an entirely unmerited reputation for coolness under fire simply due to the fact that I'm so short-sighted. It was no use a conductor turning the colour of a tomato and glaring in my direction, I'd just smile mildly back at what appeared to me to be a pink blob with two waving arms, and I suppose my expression said 'I've been shouted at by better conductors than *you*.'

Conductors are a very special breed, especially in the session world. Apart from being musically competent they must be able to control anything up to a hundred musicians and singers, some of whom they've never met before, and who will be quick to notice any lapse of either musicianship or authority . . . a case of 'Carry On, Karajan'. Small wonder that some of the more insecure characters develop megalomania ('There but for the grace of God goes God'), and news of a forthcoming session with one of them is received with groans of dismay and a mind fixed firmly on the money, for there'll be little joy in the work. But there are many conductors whose sessions are a pleasure, from 'Monty' Mantovani, through the late Geraldo, Geoff Love, the Canadian Robert Farnon, the Latin-American specialist Stanley Black, witty Harry Rabinowitz, Jack Parnell, Eric Rogers, Alexander (now Sir Alexander) Gibson, composer-conductors Ronald ('Elizabethan Serenade') Binge, Ron (*Robert and Elizabeth*) Grainer, Cyril Ornadel and lots more. All highly competent musicians and reasonable men.

British orchestral players are considered the best sight-readers in the world, so many American film companies, having made their film, move over to Britain to have the music recorded. Some go to Vienna to use the Vienna Philharmonic, but many producers seem to favour London orchestras. The language is the same, for one thing, except that you have to get used to hearing a crotchet called a 'quarter-note' and a bar a 'measure'. It seemed incredible to us that this vast undertaking would be cheaper than using an American orchestra and singers, but they assured us that it was. Sometimes the orchestral track had been recorded in Europe and only the choral music remained to be done. This was carried out by the conductor and singers alone in the sound-stage, all standing in a circle, wearing headphones, and singing to the pre-recorded soundtrack. The conductor's English could occasionally be wayward, as in the case of the great American-Russian composer-conductor Dmitri Tiomkin. He'd never believe this, though, and stomped cheerfully through the language, crushing nouns and kicking verbs aside with zest, for instance in his determination to get real *pianissimo* singing from us for the soundtrack of the film *55 Days at Peking*, all about the Boxer Rising. There was Ava Gardner on the screen, dying beautifully, and Maestro Tiomkin had provided a plaintive Chinese-type tune for us to sing. After making sssh-ing gestures he finally stopped and said: 'No, no, no! Iss too *loud*. Woman in Orient never zo loud zing.' The words of some songs are awkward on the ear too. During the Carl Foreman film *The Victors* we were singing a Christmas song 'Deck the Hall with Boughs of Holly' when the producer charged out of his cubicle. 'What the hell goes on?' he wailed. 'It sounds as though you're singing: "Troll the ancient Yuletide carol" . . . what is it supposed to be?' 'Troll the ancient Yuletide carol', we chorused gleefully. To do him justice, all he said was 'Oh my *Gard*!' and disappeared again.

Recording studios, at least the ones used for large orchestras and choirs, are usually huge, high-ceilinged places, with perhaps a cinema-screen at one end for the conductor to see when sound is being dubbed on to a film. When the session is booked for nine o'clock in the morning most groups of singers have to arrive earlier so that they can run through the vocal parts on their own and thus not waste the conductor's time later. You seldom know what sort of music to expect until you are handed the manuscript. It might be anything from opera to a commercial jingle. You very seldom read from printed music, either, most parts are written out by hand by copyists (who seem able to copy out parts even when a full orchestra is blaring away in the same studio). Nobody in the nineteen-fifties had yet invented (and they still haven't, I believe) a musical 'typewriter', so the copyist generally writes the words in block letters under the stave-lines and you're at the mercy of his handwriting. While you're sight-reading music and words together there's no time to actually comprehend what you're singing about, and I warbled happily through *Gigi* singing 'was I out yonder somewhere bunking at a star'. It should have been 'blinking at a star', but the copyist's 'l' and 'i' looked like a 'u', so 'bunking' it was. And many's the time the word 'legend' has become 'leg-end' when the 'leg' part has been at the end of a line and the 'end' part on the next line. There's sometimes no title or composer's name at the top of the score, just 'Opening' or 'Closing', or in film music: 'Number 5, Section Three', so you never really get to know who wrote the stuff. It's not safe to scowl at it either, because the conductor may have written it himself. The manuscript sheets are stuck together side by side, so that they can open out in a concertina-like strip perhaps four feet long. To add to your woes the words may be in any language from Japanese to Serbo-Croat, so you just read them phonetically and hope that no Japanese or Serbo-Croats will hear the result.

Generally there are two singers on each vocal line, and one of them makes him or herself responsible for any alterations or notes to be added to the manuscript, so in addition to having all your wits about you, you need a pencil and some comfortable shoes – there's a lot of standing to be done. The conductor has a chair so that he can sit down occasionally, the orchestra sit down to play anyway, but choirs generally stand on a rostrum and can only sit on or near it. Even during coffee-breaks it's not easy to find a place to sit, the orchestra's chairs are occupied with several thousand pounds' worth of violins, violas, oboes and clarinets, and it's more than your life is worth to touch them. Coffee-time is fun, though, with the chance to chat with other musicians you may not have seen for some time. In my experience orchestral musicians seldom talk about music. Sometimes it's cars (many of them are dedicated drivers of high-powered vehicles), or holidays, or their families; and coffee breaks are the chance to hear the latest and funniest Jewish jokes, for many top session musicians are Jewish, and consequently love telling barbed and piquant stories, or sharp one-liners like: 'Know how to make a Jewish omelette? Borrow six eggs.'

Sometimes the 'breaks' can be the chance to celebrate something pleasant. One of the happiest occasions was when Leon Goossens, the famous oboist, played a morning session on his seventieth birthday, and was presented with a huge iced cake, enough for a slice for all of us.

During the time I had spent in the ice shows at Earls Court I had taken more singing lessons, this time from a baritone who had been one of England's best lieder singers in the thirties, John Morel. He was a fine teacher, and a cultivated and perceptive man. He had the wife he deserved, a warm and charming Swedish lady whose smile was worth going miles to see. If I had been a few years younger, and stronger, and much, much more dedicated I might have made far more use of his excellent teaching. But the work I was doing then seemed not to require any refinements, and it was unlikely that I'd ever be any kind of soloist. Even so, I'm glad I was lucky enough to have had those lessons, at least I now know really good singing from just good, and I was able to go on singing for perhaps three sessions each day without damaging what small voice I had. Such endurance was necessary, too. George Mitchell's singers were very busy from then onwards, doing radio and television music with most of the star performers of the time. We certainly never had time to get tired of one particular style of artist. Most Sundays we sang in *Variety Playhouse* with Vic Oliver, the Viennese comedian-musician who had starred with Ben Lyon and Bebe Daniels in the war-time radio show *Hi, Gang!* (And if anyone would like to know of a real-life love story they couldn't find a truer or more touching one than Bebe's and Ben's.) Vic loved to conduct an orchestra and chorus, and while he was no Furtwängler his pleasure was infectious. He made us sing operatic choruses, Viennese waltzes, everything, and even though at times there were only twelve singers the B.B.C. engineers made us sound like fifty. The 'drama' spot on the programme was provided by Jack Hulbert and Cicely Courtneidge, with famous actors as guest-stars. Donald Wolfit was one of them, and chilled our blood wonderfully with the 'Death of Bill Sykes' from *Oliver Twist* with that marvellous husky actor-manager's voice – a voice with an astrakhan coat-collar if ever there was one.

Most radio was live then, and television too, which meant that programmes had to be exactly the right length – no cutting or editing, and in the case of television, even when the show could be pre-recorded, if anything went wrong the whole programme had to be done again. Radio producers would go to extraordinary lengths to achieve realism – I can remember one Bank Holiday broadcast from a pleasure-boat moored at Greenwich. It poured with rain all day, and the wind blew our music sideways, but Joe Loss and his band, Dora Bryan, Bob and Alf Pearson ('My brother and I') and the 'Mitchells' played gamely on in the icy downpour. It could all have been done in a studio, with the addition of seagull and river-tug noises, and I doubt if the listeners would have noticed the difference!

There must have been scores of George Mitchell singers in those days. Some were in permanent theatre shows all over the country, but a nucleus of a couple of dozen of us in London were used for all the radio, television and recording work that would require fast sight-reading. George's favourite number of singers was sixteen – four of each voice, soprano, alto, tenor and bass, divided into two top sopranos, two second sopranos and so on. He even had a car number-plate that read GM 16, as the number seemed to have been lucky for him. I don't think luck had much to do with George's success, it was due to a combination of outstanding talent and sheer hard work, allied to a charming and persuasive manner that kept us working for him when we could probably have made more money elsewhere. Working for most other choirmasters after working for George was like drinking Coke after vintage champagne. The one exception to this rule was Mike Sammes, who had been one of the Mitchells and later formed his own group of singers. My own favourite number for radio work was twelve – eight men and four girls, especially for closely-written harmonies, and, apart from the times when the choir was featured on its own, I loved acting as a kind of extra orchestra. We did some of this work with Ronald Binge and his orchestra (the usual collection of top session players). We sang no words, just 'Ah', or 'Oo' or *bouche fermée* – a classy musical way of saying 'humming' – and it must all have been mighty expensive, for it was a large orchestra, with about twenty singers, but the resulting sound was rich, sensuous and dreamy in Muzak-type melodies like 'The Water Mill' and 'Candle-light'. Some of us liked the 'instrumental' vocal work so much that Fred Tomlinson, perhaps our most musically intellectual (and Goon-like!) member, even made purely 'vocal' arrangements for us, just for fun, using the 'Dab-a-dab-a-dah' type of sound. All this was years before the Swingle Singers were heard of.

These different kinds of music were a great change from the Covent Garden days, and it was an intriguing thought that the Mitchells, with, say, sixteen singers, could sound like the seventy-strong Covent Garden chorus, thanks to the excellent sound engineering of B.B.C. technicians. Some of the music we sang was pretty rubbishy (or pretty *and* rubbishy) and the words too, for instance to the 'Galop' from *Orpheus in the Underworld*: 'I can-can and you can-can, so why should not we two can-can?' There's not a lot you can say about lyrics like that, except that it was of the same poetical school as the words to the waltz 'España': 'Sunny Spain *calls* again back *to* those deep *skies* of blue, *days* in the bright *glow* of light are *call*ing to me, *call*ing always'. One of our younger sopranos had a lisp, and it was a treat to hear her beside you, carolling 'Thunny Thpain callth again back to thothe deep thkieth of blue . . .'

Sometimes we would be allowed our own spot in a variety show, perhaps one of George's fine arrangements of negro spirituals or an elegant setting of popular song from a film; 'Secret Love' or 'This is a Lovely Way to Spend an Evening'. One of the most successful show-off pieces for girls' voices was the 'Færy Song' from *The Immortal Hour*, which contains a line very appropriate to describe some of the more ineffectual comedians 'They laugh, and are glad . . . and are *terrible*'.

We began to be in great demand as singers-actors-extras in television variety shows too. These spectaculars were generally built around a star singer or comedian, and we saved the producer a bit of money by 'dressing the set' in street or café scenes. These shows were broadcast from Lime Grove Studios, or the Shepherd's Bush Empire or the Old King's Theatre, Hammersmith – now demolished and replaced by the office-block of an electronics firm, alas. If the show was for one of the Independent Television companies it might be made at the Wood Green Empire or the Hackney Empire. We loved both of those theatres. There was a really fine pub next to the Wood Green Empire and a famous 'marble-hall' fish-and-chip emporium next to the Hackney Empire, and a charming row of ancient almshouses just behind the theatre; I wonder if they have survived the planners' jackboots?

Television was all black-and-white then, so a lot of the care that went into our costumes and sets was wasted, but as we became known to various theatrical costumiers, and trusted by them, they let us wear some genuine garments from their stocks of Edwardian and nineteen-twenties and thirties clothes, with hats and parasols to match. Sometimes we'd find a famous film-star's name-tab sewn into a dress. I got to know that anything with 'Jennifer (*Song of Bernadette*) Jones' on the label would fit me if the hem was let down about three inches. So, all dressed up in 1910 sailor-collared gowns, button-boots and straw boaters, we'd sing 'Moonlight on the Wabash' and perhaps essay a mild soft-shoe dance. I was never much good at this, having what amounts to two left feet, but being taller than most I lolloped happily about in the back row in decent anonymity. The one real snag was that the words and music of the songs we did 'in vision' had to be learned in a very few days, and sometimes refused to stay in our heads. One mind-stopping occasion was half an hour before transmission time when we were due to open a 'nineteen-twenties' musical show. There we were, sitting in our big dressing-room, in cloche hats, low-waisted gowns and pointed toed shoes. . . . 'Right,' said Daphne, our head girl, 'let's go through the opening chorus, shall we . . . er-one, two, three, four. . . .' We all opened our mouths automatically and there was a dreadful silence, not one word or note could we remember. We dived for our music copies with a screech of horror, and 'fa-fa'ed desperately through the maze of notes until we were called down on to the set. Oddly enough, it was one of our best performances.

Singing, dancing and acting in a group like the Mitchells gave us a worm's-eye-view of most of the stars of the day, whether in their own shows or as guest performers in someone else's. Naturally we had our favourites, the endearing Charlie Chester was one, and the late, great Ted Ray was another. Not only could Ted sing a bit, dance a bit, play the violin and do creditable impersonations, he also had one of the finest 'comic memories' I've ever heard. Say any word to him – 'parrot', 'trolley-bus', 'tea-pot' – and Ted would instantly tell you a joke about it. Dave King, that much under-rated comedian (who has a second career now as an actor) had his own television song'n dance series, remembered by us for the weird situations we found ourselves in . . . why on earth was I, at one point in a show, hiding under a shop counter with two huge, malodorous Old English sheep-dogs?

We took part in the Frankie Howerd Show, the Norman Wisdom Show, the Jewell and Warriss Show, Henry Hall's Guest Night, the Billy Cotton Band Show, and shows featuring the occasional female star, one of them a lovely blonde called Yana. We loved her show, it was a chance for us to wear elegant black lace dresses (really black lace leotards with overskirts) and huge 'diamond' collars and earrings – real Hollywood stuff. One of the three men who appeared with Yana was Digby Wolfe, who later went to California to work as a script-writer on Rowan and Martin's 'Laugh-In'.

Another girl we liked to work with was Ruby Murray – top-of-the-pops at the time with a gentle little three-four song called: 'Softly, Softly'. She was the sort of Irish colleen all the songs were about, very pretty and amenable, with a nasally sweet voice and the 'everybody's daughter' air which was – maybe *is* – so appealing. We worked on a series of programmes with her, with the usual company of dancers, singers and guest-stars. The dancers were under the instruction of George Carden, a much-respected choreographer who had taken part in the old 'Sweet and Low' revues at the Ambassadors Theatre. He was much respected, for a very good reason . . . he was the most severe disciplinarian I've ever encountered, and his dancers ('*My* dancers') were superb as a result, with a style and elegance unmatched since. He even insisted that all the girls did their hair the same way, even at rehearsal, with a sophisticated Siamese-type topknot. He was an excellent choreographer where singers were concerned, too. He realised – as very few dance-directors have done – that singers have words and notes to remember, must see the conductor somehow all the time, and must not be out of breath just before they are due to sing sixty-four bars fortissimo. So we approached television shows directed by him with a mixture of terror and delight, knowing that the musical numbers at least would be polished and professional. I think pretty Ruby Murray was a bit of a puzzle for George Carden, she was obedient, and respectful, but there was never a flicker of spirit until one day at a rehearsal of the last programme in her series. George Carden had been placing us for the finale and stepped back to survey the result. Suddenly Ruby Murray broke into a little tap-dance. It only lasted a few seconds, and she did it with a perfectly straight face, but the effect was stunningly comical – as if a kitten had donned boxing-gloves. The whole company collapsed into giggles, and George had to allow a tea-break – the good choreographer's answer to all anarchy.

But the lady we loved and admired most of all, both professionally and personally, was Vera (now Dame Vera – I still think that's an archaic title – why not just 'Lady', I wonder?) Lynn. Vera Lynn had earned a golden reputation as the voice of home to all men and women in the forces during the war, but never was anyone more matter-of-fact about her world-wide fame. Even Field-Marshal Rommel was said to have admired her singing! She seems to me to be the perfect example of a professional entertainer. She has no conceit whatever; she treats everyone, from the grandest producer or conductor to the humblest chorus dancer or singer, precisely the same; she is never late, or discourteous, and she always knows her lines and the words and music of all her songs. (That may sound elementary, but you'd be surprised how many performers are incompetent in that respect – it's a form of bad manners really, I suppose.) She looks neatly and suitably dressed always, and during the occasional bits of dancing she had to do it was apparent during her 'twirling' that the lace on her petticoat was spotless. Superficial observation, you'll think? Well, I can only say that you'd be surprised how many bits of underwear *aren't* spotless, and care taken in one respect generally means care taken in another. Then there is the voice, of course. It could be described as a London sound, rather nasal, which gives it remarkable carrying power. At a rehearsal of a Royal Variety Performance finale the whole cast were on stage, everyone in white tie and tails, singing the Flanagan and Allen number: 'Strolling'. The sound system failed, and all that could be heard was Vera's voice, strong and confident as ever, carrying easily to the back of the theatre. She has had many years of show-business experience, which may account for her complete humility, and she is also a good practical housewife. (It's typical of Vera that she wouldn't mind being called a housewife – she enjoys home-making, and respects other women who enjoy it too.) She is completely responsive to every other human being; whether she's gently teasing one of the boy dancers, or writing out a recipe for ginger beer for one of the girls. She's the sort of woman every man should have as a wife, lively, attractive, practical and kind, and I suppose it was these qualities that rang out somehow in that marvellously strong sweet voice. Dear Vera, you are 'nothing like a Dame', but you *are* a Lady.

Another world-famous star who still shone brightly at that time was Gracie Fields. The famous voice still intact, huskily sharp in her Lancashire songs, and with a referee's-whistle quality in popular ballads. Her favourite style was to be alone on the stage, with just her accompanist at the piano, her only prop seemed to be a big chiffon scarf. Completely professional, and a hard-working entertainer.

But the epitome of the professional approach was made plain to us one evening when we had made a short television film with – I think – Jimmy Young, who was still a singer-pianist then. We were told to stay on the set, and we sat about chatting in our white lace dresses with our 'diamond' collars until we noticed the doors at the back of the stalls opening, and a platoon of men coming down the centre aisle of the theatre. They looked like the board of directors of a merchant bank, which I suppose in a way they were, all wearing dark overcoats and black Homburg hats. The 'chairman' of the board, as he came into the light, was unmistakable, no one else had that hockey-stick nose. 'George,' said the producer to our boss, 'I'd like you to meet Bob Hope. Bob, this is George Mitchell, our musical director.' 'Glad to know you, George. . . . How do you spell your name, one "l" or two? Make a note of it.' (This to a Homburg-hatted aide.) He never forgot names, and was unfailingly polite, but – or do I mean 'and'? – he ran his professional life with ruthless attention to all detail.

Every joke and every 'aside' was carefully rehearsed, and it was no wonder he was famous for his smooth performances – rather as Morecambe and Wise are now. That apparent spontaneity is the result of hours, weeks and years of hard rehearsal.

We were to meet two other eminent American showmen. One was Jack Benny, who proved to be a quiet and apparently modest man. In a 'model village' peopled with show-business personalities (a favourite Mitchell game during long hours of hanging about on the set) he'd probably be cast as the local family lawyer, discreet in manner and impeccably dressed. Nobody could call 'Lee' Liberace impeccably dressed – not on stage, anyway – but he was a delight. Charming, witty and kindly, treating everyone with the utmost consideration. He'd hold doors for all women, stars, cleaners, dressers, chorus-girls, with the same friendly smile, and his piano technique was formidable. The glittering, sugary music which had made him so rich needed as much virtuosity as that shown by any other concert pianist. The sequinned clothes, the satin cloaks, lace cuffs, diamond rings and candelabra were all part of the act. The more po-faced critics expressed their scorn for all this, and one of them ended a disdainful paragraph with a half-wistful quip: 'But I suppose no adverse criticism can affect Liberace, he'd merely cry all the way to the bank.' After that, during one of his performances when he swung sideways on the piano stool to banter with the audience he'd say with perfect timing: 'Y'know that bank I'm s'posed ter cry all the way to? . . . Well . . . I *bought* it!' Unanswerable.

The 1950s equivalent of the B.B.C. television show *Top of the Pops* was called *Tin-Pan Alley*. The idea was similar, showing off the hit-songs of the day, but all the performers were professional, and the staging for each number was generally ingenious and novel. One of the favourite black-comedy songs was from an American revue. It was all about a notorious murder case in Fall River, Massachusetts, when an apparently stainless middle-class girl was accused of murdering her parents, giving rise to the jingle:

> Lizzie Borden with an axe
> Gave her momma forty whacks.
> When she saw what she had done
> She gave her father forty-one.

The song had been written in square-dance form ('Let's have a hoe-down') as a narrative ballad, and between each sardonic verse the

1 *Eddie and me today.*

The band of the King's Royal Rifle
ps at Colchester in 1905. My
er, Edmund Roberts Ready, is
ng immediately behind the right-
d kettledrum.

Standing in the gateway of our
ached' house in Feltham.
With my parents at Ramsgate.

A Sunday afternoon stroll to Staines
ervoir with my grandparents.

6 *My father was a champion bowler. Here he is receiving the Jay Bowls Cup at Worthing in 1948.*

7 *My class at the County School, Ashford. I am sitting on the ground at the extreme right.*

8 *Me at eighteen.*

9 *'The Mayfairs' concert party. I'm on the right.*

10 *(Left) The London Women Officers' Training School, Redington Road, Hampstead, in 1943. I am third from the left in the front row.*

11 *(Left, below) Irene Thomas, mezzo-soprano.*

12 *(Right) With three of my Covent Garden colleagues: Muriel Burnett, Joyce Edmanson and Val Thorne, 1948.*

13 Der Rosenkavalier. *I'm on the left in the group of three maids in the centre of the stage.*

14 The Magic Flute – *Act II, Scene 1. The three spirits (I am on the left) with Tamino (Kenneth Neate), Papageno (Grahame Clifford) and the three ladies (Doris Dorée, Elizabeth Abercrombie and Constance Shacklock).*

15 *Eddie in 1948.*

16 *Some of the 'Mitchells' outside the Camden Theatre. I'm on the right, next to George. Daphne Bell is in the centre.*

17 *Entertaining at the Amateur Cup Final, Wembley, 1954.*

18 *The new 'Brain of Britain' in the B.B.C.'s* What Do You Know? *contest on radio, July 1961.*

19 *What?*

20 *Well....*

21 *Ah....*

22 *Got it!*

HENRY
IRENE

Question-master Kenneth Horne h Ian Gillies and me in World iz '67.

With Bob Dyer, the question-ter, Henry Button and Patrick oles in Australia's B.P. Pick-a- *show, 1967.*

A real live teddy-bear friend.

Bob 'n' Dolly Dyer.

SOS

27 *With Lyell Boyes, Pat Macaskill and Ian Gillies in* Stump the Brains Trust, *played with New Zealand every year.*

28 *With the* Round Britain Quiz *team:* from left to right, *John D. Stewart and the Rev. Dr Michael Dewar of the Northern Ireland team; Sir Jack Longland, then our travelling question-master; Anthony Quinton (now President of Trinity College, Oxford); and Trevor Hill, the producer.*

29 *With Professor John Mays: together as the London team in* Round Britain Quiz.

30 *In the* Mastermind *chair.*

31 *With Thomas Dyer, Walter Dobson and Dr Roger Pritchard in* Supermind.

32 *With Jack Jones on* The 607080 Show.

33 *Roy Hudd and I are entertained by some of our guests on* The 607080 Show.

chorus of 'jurors', 'citizens', and 'neighbours' got up to dance yelling 'You cain't chop y'r Momma up in Massachusetts', for the message of the ballad was that Lizzie Borden would never have escaped unpunished if she had not been one of a wealthy and respectable family. There was a lot of hearty dancing and singing to do, and we had a royal guest as an observer, for Princess Margaret was visiting Lime Grove Studios. We stood in two tidy lines while the small blue-eyed figure passed by with attendant satellites, on her way up to the control-room to watch the show. We really knocked ourselves out – we loved the number anyway – and when it was over we leaned against the scenery, panting and sweating, waiting for a 'clearance'. Instead of a dismissal, the floor manager told us that the princess had enjoyed it so much that she would like to see the whole thing again. Flattering, but exhausting, especially in our ill-fitting button-boots.

Television shows when the singers and dancers were not on the set every minute of the time were much more peaceful. 'Better than working' was an in-phrase professionals used then when, as priests were supposed to in ancient Greece, they could hardly meet each other without exchanging covert smiles at the thought of their luck at being able to deceive the public in such a pleasureable way. It was fun in breaks during rehearsals to sit playing cards with Dave King, or to do tough crosswords with Tony Hancock's brother Roger, or listen to Jack Parnell and a few of his band busking quietly for their own – and our – amusement. Twenty years later, Jack Parnell still reassures me that I'm not losing my sense of pitch when he takes part in the television 'discoveries' programme *New Faces*. Some aspiring groups make my ears shrivel, but none of the other appraisers appears to have heard what's wrong until Jack Parnell says in his mild voice: 'I think perhaps this group need to pay a bit more attention to their intonation'. And I know I'm still sane, the poor lads' guitar strings were not even in tune with each other, let alone with those of the next chap.

Work can be a kind of gentle anæsthetic against private troubles and sorrows, and in the autumn of 1956 I was glad not to have much time to sit and sigh. My father had retired from his job with the gas company, and he and my mother had gone to live in a small bungalow in Sussex. Their life there was quiet and pleasant, my mother made friends easily and enjoyed living by the sea, and my father was a leading player in the local bowling-club. He had always been an excellent player – the marksman's eye again, maybe – and he often played for Sussex against other counties. One evening, after he and my mother had been having supper with friends, he said he had a headache and would lie down for a while. This was unusual, he was generally very healthy, and a stoic about pain. He went into the bedroom and my mother heard him fall. When she reached his side he was dead. The neighbours had called the doctor, but nothing could have been done to save him. My mother was very shocked – they had been married for almost forty years, and she had relied on him utterly, for everything. Eddie and I went down to Sussex the next day, as there was a lot to be done, and we stayed until a few days after the funeral. On the way to the burial service I reflected that this was probably the only time my father had ever travelled in a Rolls-Royce, and with so many honours. It was a green and gold September day, and all the friends and acquaintances he had made during the few years he and my mother had lived in Sussex were grouped at stations along the road. Labourers in the fields took off their caps and watched him pass, and the members of the bowling-club stood by the roadside in their blazers and white flannels with their panama hats held chest-high. One very old gentleman raised his silver-topped cane in salute.

I thought of my father's early life and realised that by present-day standards he would have had every excuse for becoming a thorough nuisance to society – no name, no parents, no family, no money, not much education except for what the army had given him. He had survived loneliness, disease, and danger, conquered his natural shyness and reserve, and built a modest and decent life for us. He was the soul of honour, with a chivalrous and courteous manner which never altered, and he had the kind of natural refinement that cannot be learned or forgotten, and which can be observed in some people of all classes. His word, once given, was never broken; for him to cheat or lie would have been unthinkable. He had almost no money, and yet gave what he could and never mentioned it. There was a stoic composure about him, which later softened to graceful resignation, but not a shred of self-pity. Perhaps he had never heard of Marcus Aurelius, but he would have read: 'Nothing happens to any man that he is not formed by nature to bear' with complete comprehension.

There is a word which describes him, and all men like him, of whatever class or race or station; men who put a sense of duty above all other considerations, and show a sweet generosity of spirit in the smallest actions of everyday living. 'Progressive' people may hear the word with an embarrassed smirk, but the rest of us know exactly what it means; the word is gentleman.

CHAPTER SIX

L'istesso tempo

WITH MY FATHER gone, my mother's life lost its positive quality, leaving her in a state of growing bewilderment. Even though she was a cheerful and determined woman she had been totally dependent on him for even the smallest practical details of everyday life like writing a cheque or filling in a form. Money was not the worst problem. My father once said that he would like to leave 'perhaps as much as five hundred pounds' when he died, and he had left almost exactly that amount. With a bit of help from me, my mother could live fairly comfortably in her own home, but loneliness defeated her, and it became obvious that she could not go on living by herself. So a few months later we began to look for a house where she could come to live with Eddie and me. We had to find one quickly, so we had no time to ponder. The only suitable one was an ordinary 1927 semi, not very attractive, but sound, and in a very pleasant district near our dear dreadful flat. We are still living in that same semi, although we have improved it, and we are happy with the district and our neighbours. Our road is a surrealist mixture of architectural styles, from huge 1880 houses with twenty rooms and vast gardens, through semis and 1950s neo-Georgian to small blocks of modern flats replacing some of the great 1880s houses. Viscount Montgomery lived in one of the old houses as a child, and when it was demolished (with great difficulty, as it was built like a cliff) we bought half of one of the great sash windows for ten shillings, to use as the top of a garden frame. So our early lettuces now gaze up under the same piece of glass as the little Bernard Montgomery looked through at the towering horse-chestnut trees which are our road's chief attraction.

With families of a certain temperament, warm, close and gregarious, the generations may mix happily, but even in those cases, particularly when the younger generation has made its own life-style for perhaps a good many years, the addition of another person can never be easy. Perhaps the only solution is for the older person to have his or her own rooms, particularly a kitchen and bathroom, right from the start. In our case all our combined money had to be spent in buying the house, and there was none left for converting it into two separate apartments even if we had considered such a course. As a result, life for all of us could sometimes be difficult. It was nobody's fault, merely an occasional lack of harmony, but I have since met people who have lived in similar circumstances to ours, and people who have kept separate establishments for each generation in the same house, and I think a certain amount of 'generation-apartheid' can be more pleasant for everybody concerned. This is especially noticeable where there is a parent living at close quarters with an only child, there can never be any relief for either generation. I have great sympathy for single women who have given up a career to take care of one or both of their elderly parents. For the most part they perform their loving duties with grace and gratitude, sometimes in trying conditions, and up to now daughters in particular have been bred to expect this situation. ('A son's a son till he takes a wife; a daughter's a daughter all her life.') The present younger generation may be a different case, I think.

My work, in those days of live television and radio, meant that I was not often at home in the evenings, and although my mother occasionally visited her friends most of her evenings were spent watching 'the telly', which she loved – particularly when she could catch a glimpse of me in some light-entertainment show; no matter what strange costume I might be wearing, my mother could always pick me out of the crowd.

It has become tiresomely fashionable in some quarters to take a patronising attitude towards the people who depend on their television set for most of their entertainment, as though the inveterate 'telly-watchers' were somehow intellectually inadequate. Not so. I don't feel intellectually inadequate, and I can and do watch one channel or another for hours every evening, from the *Magic Roundabout* to the little white dot when you switch off, and some of the most brilliant and distinguished men I know will happily do the same whenever they can. To the lonely and the old – many people are both – television has come as a godsend.

To disabled or housebound people of all ages the set in the corner of their room is welcomed as a trusted friend, whose company brings new interests and information. Most programme-makers know this, and make an honourable attempt to justify the trust of their viewers. A few seem too zealous – or too obtuse – to consider that trust, and kick a figurative hobnail boot through the screen. There must always be a welcome for new ideas and fresh angles in comedy, documentary, drama and educational programmes, but not at the expense of bruising the feelings of the audience, no matter how backward and complacent that audience may seem to an eager producer. Contempt for the susceptibilities of the viewer seems to have created a new puritanical tyranny. I sometimes feel like some raddled old hag left over from the rip-roaring Regency days being lectured for her frivolous backsliding by a pious young Victorian reformer. Audiences are not as daft as they may seem, and there is generally only one result of such a reformer yelling at the apparently insensitive viewers contemptuously referred to as 'Joe Public'. Joe Public goes deaf.

But in the late nineteen-fifties there was a growing thirst for light entertainment of all kinds, which meant that the Mitchells were always in work, and in addition to our work in B.B.C. and I.T.V. variety shows there was a new field of employment for us . . . jingles. Jingles are the lyrics used in the short advertising films you see between programmes on commercial television or, now, hear on commercial radio. They are expensive to make, and quite unbelievable care is taken in their making. For the performers it is very well-paid work, not so much because of the initial fee, but for the residual or 'repeat' fee which comes every time the jingle is used. A small group of Mitchells took part in a lot of the sound recordings for jingles, and it proved finicky work. Every single person had to sing his or her part in *exactly* the same manner as the next person. In fact it was the kind of polished perfection I wished we had time for in our usual light entertainment work, where we always seemed to be in a terrible rush, with no time to rehearse long enough to give a perfect performance. But in jingles precision is vital. Everyone must breathe at exactly the same moment, and if a word ends in a consonant, like 'that', the final 't' must be pronounced at the same time by everybody, otherwise there'll be a 't-t-t-t-t' noise which will irritate the listener even though he may not realise how he's being irritated. And in a word like 'fresh', which is always cropping up in advertising, the final 'sh' must not turn into 'ssshhh'. This is an extremely difficult technique to perfect. By the time you've sung a jingle ten or fifteen times it begins to sound strange and silly, like writing or saying one word over and over again. Then when you've got your six or eight people singing all this right, the tempo may have speeded up a bit and the jingle is now taking twenty-seven seconds instead of the required thirty, so it all has to be done again. ('Take sixteen'!) We did commercials for prams, sweets, biscuits, beer, petrol, cakes, airlines, wine – everything whose consumption could be increased by repetition of slogans – and we turned many an honest penny that way.

Commercial television (Independent Television is the more genteel description) had proved very valuable to us. For some reason it paid better than the B.B.C., but even down at our level we could feel that it was a more brash and philistine world than 'Auntie's'. *Sunday Night at the London Palladium* always seemed the prime example of I.T.V. variety. Very slick, noisy and polished, with a game stuck in the middle of the show in which contestants chosen from the public could win prizes by throwing tennis-balls into wastepaper baskets or similar garden-fête jousting. No harm in that, but it seemed to bring out the worst in some people, and even more embarrassing were the giggling interviews before the games. At rehearsals some of the Mitchells and dancers who might be unwary enough to be sitting in the stalls were made to act the part of the contestants, and if the comedian-host was in a petulant mood it could be a real penance. I never liked the Palladium as a theatre anyway, its atmosphere seems coarse and meretricious, and I for one was always thankful when the finale came and we were all driven on to the great revolve on the stage to stand and wave to the audience. This revolve sometimes started turning with a sudden jerk, so it was prudent to position yourself so that you could hold on to one of the big glittering letters that said S–U–N–D–A–Y—N–I–G–H–T—A–T. The 'S' was my favourite – nice and solid.

In other I.T.V. shows we worked with some of the most popular entertainers in television; people like Arthur Haynes, with his 'straight man' Nicholas Parsons, whom I was to meet years later in a very different role; and Adam Faith – an amiable lad always willing to sit and have a smoke and a chat. David Jacobs used to appear in some variety shows too, and we even worked with those two comic monuments, Flanagan and Allen. Some years later, when Bud Flanagan was to retire, we took part in his radio life-story, and I asked him if he'd be sorry to leave the theatre after all those years. 'In a way, love,' he said, 'But it'll mean I'll be able to stay for the last race at Kempton Park – up to now I've always had to leave before then to get to the theatre on time.' Tommy Cooper was another of our favourites – he's even more amusing off-stage than on, with his cameo description of the type of fan who comes round backstage to see a well-known star – diffidently at first, then with increasing impudence until he is finally telling the star how to run his act.

There are some comedians who have a very special gift – and it *is* a gift, it can't be acquired – of making people smile before telling a single joke or performing any piece of comic 'business', in fact you laugh before he does anything at all. Tommy Cooper is one, Benny Hill, Harry Secombe and Roy Hudd are three others. We almost fought to be allowed to take part in a Harry Secombe show, our affection overcame the knowledge that he is almost impossible to work with because his fellow-artists are in a state of near-hysteria all the time, such is his inexhaustible fund of goonery. From the time when he sings a fine B-flat at the end of a song and immediately falls flat on his back, to the time when he whips off his glasses and puts them round a pewter tankard and cries: 'Look, folks . . . my little brother!' when you're all trying to rehearse a *Student-Prince*-type tavern scene, it's laughter all the way, and kindly laughter, too, never hurting or embarrassing anyone else.

Benny Hill can convulse an audience with the kind of sly, blinking leer that implies that he has just thought of a good idea for a seaside post-card. He's a one-man *Carry-On* film, and his ribaldry is so patent that to the connoisseur that fact becomes comic in itself. I'm happy to say that I've taken part in many of his 'medieval ballads' as a member of the 'hey-nonny fa-la-la' chorus of steeple-hatted ladies.

The fourth and youngest member of the quartet of favourite comedians is the one I've worked with most often, the endearing Roy Hudd – much more about him later.

In February 1957 George, our boss, would reach the age life is supposed to begin at, and we thought we ought to make it a special birthday. Fred Tomlinson (the brother of Ernest Tomlinson the composer) made a beautiful arrangement of 'Ye Banks and Braes o' Bonnie Doon', and as many of us as could be got together went to Levy's in Bond Street to make a recording of the song. On the other side of the record was a collection of 'endings', the sort of harmonic arrangements that we sang so often as the last few bars of popular songs, and Fred had written them in George's own style as an in-joke only he and we would understand. It must be one of the rarest records in the world of popular song.

That world is, according to its own publicity, always on the lookout for new songs, although at that time all popular tunes seemed to be written by the same few composers. Maybe that was because they were the best, or just that they formed a tight little circle, like a mediæval guild, I don't know. But the B.B.C. decided that there should be a more or less open competition to find new British songs, and that viewers should decide which songs they liked best. Each song was to be sung twice, presumably so that the jury would not vote for or against it just because they liked or disliked a particular singer. This taxed the producer's imagination a bit, and resulted in one song about 'waiting for you to come home' or some such wistful sentiment being sung, for its second appearance, by Petula Clark, apparently waiting for a huge shaggy dog. I can't remember any of the songs except one, which never came within a thousand miles of winning, called 'Under the Sycamore Tree'. It was a weird little three-four ditty with odd repeated phrases: 'Grandfather died and he buried his buried his money, his money under the sycamore tree, tree, tree, tree', and would perhaps have been better as a number in an intimate revue, but we enjoyed singing it, and we were allowed to wear some genuine Edwardian costumes. The whole farrago has now evolved into the Eurovision Song Contest, and between then and now strange things have happened to my ears, because most of the Eurovision songs sound to me as though they were written by some computer for singing to other computers.

In July of that year George told us that we were to be given our own television series, and we would at last be featured as ourselves instead of as players in other people's shows. The series would be live, of course, and it would be seen at 6.45 to 7.15 p.m. every Friday. We would start each show in the same way, with a song that sounded like 'Maryland, My Maryland' but wasn't. George wrote the tune and I wrote the words. The show was meant to look rather like an American college glee club. The changes of costume for each number had to be done in seconds; we started off wearing blouses and skirts, with the men in blazers and flannels, everybody wearing academic caps and gowns, and our costumes all laid out in order at the side of the studio. Bizarre combinations of clothing could result from frantic quick-changes in the half-light away from the set, and I have a piquant recollection of a line of girls in frothy tulle dresses gazing upwards and singing a romantic song . . . very elegant, except that one of them was still wearing the cowboy boots she hadn't had time to change from the last number. The whole costume business can be very confusing, especially during quick tea-breaks in the canteen where you can see a monster from *Dr Who* next to Henry the Eighth, next to a French hussar. I once chatted affably to a man behind me in the queue who was dressed as an Air Vice-Marshal of the R.A.F. 'Rehearsing for *Moonstrike* are you?' I said – there was an adventure serial called that at the time – 'Er, well, no,' he said mildly. 'This uniform is real – I'm here for *Panorama*.' So *that* was why I'd thought his make-up was a bit pale. . . . One great novelty in our *Glee Club* series was a medley of Stephen Foster songs in which, just before the final number, we bent our heads, put on curly wigs and came upright again with the traditional 'black-face' make-up. This startling effect was achieved with a special make-up and a sudden change of lighting. The make-up consisted of a red face with the wide nigger-minstrel mouth left white. The red colour, in those days of black-and-white television, did not show until a green filter was used on the lights, then the red faces became 'black' and the white mouths visible.

Later that year, at the Radio Show at Earls Court, the Mitchell Men were seen in what was to be the first *Black and White Minstrel Show*, singing a mixture of popular songs and sentimental ballads. There were no girls in the show at first, but later the Television Toppers – six blondes and six brunettes – provided extra glamour with their dancing and their glittering costumes, and then girls' voices were needed for the singing, so a few of us were used as female voices for the Toppers to mime to. I don't think anyone realised that the Minstrels would become one of the most popular light entertainment shows of all time, but viewers seemed to love it right from the start. Even in black and white it looked lavish – all satin and sequins and feathers and smiles; and the sound of men's voices singing together – and singing well – is irresistible. Every tune we sang was short – seldom more than sixteen bars of anything, with one song sailing smoothly into the next, thanks to George's superb talents as an arranger, so the result was a fast, tuneful, good-humoured show. The sterner critics hated it, and tried to condemn the whole thing on racialist grounds, but without much success as the race-relations industry was but a toddler in those days. They seemed to think that the men were meant to be *real* blacks, dressed up for the entertainment of unfeeling whites, and appeared totally ignorant about the history of black-face musical shows, whose make-up is as traditional as that of a clown or an auguste in a circus. The more the critics carped the more the viewers loved the show – it was just golliwogs and china-dolls to them, and very pretty too. Incidentally I've never yet met anyone in the entertainment business who gives a damn what colour you are as long as you are a good colleague – a 'trouper' – and have talent. In fact it has since become a positive advantage to be black or brown in some cases; it can add an extra interest to any success story. Many of the people we most enjoyed working with were black or brown anyway, from the dear, kindly baritone Edric Connor, to the glamorous and amusing Elizabeth Welch, and one of our greatest treats had been the radio variety show when Leslie Hutchinson ('Hutch') was one of the stars. Hutch had been world-famous as a pianist-singer ever since the 1930s, and had lost none of his superb showmanship and sophisticated skill. He was a fine pianist, and sang songs like 'When they Begin the Beguine' in a voice that was the essence of white-tie-and-tails and pre-war nightclubs full of duchesses, debs, and Guards officers. We applauded him so loudly that even he was startled and he sent us a bottle of champagne by way of thanks – what style he had.

Island in the Sun and *Carmen Jones* had made the black American singer and actor Harry Belafonte very popular with British audiences, and we worked on two television 'specials' with him. The first show was a collection of songs from all round the world, and the songs in the second show were American work-songs, both 'black' and 'white'. Harry Belafonte was a very handsome, serious young man, with a small, husky tenor voice which he could use to spell-binding effect in quiet songs, and as he grew to know us better he showed a mischievous sense of humour. I'm indebted to him for two cartoon-like Christmas jokes; a nice one-liner which goes: 'I don't care *whose* star you're following, get those camels off my lawn!' and the other about the Wise Men approaching the stable where the baby Jesus lies. In the darkness one of them treads on a rake which cracks him cruelly on the shin. Hopping about in agony, he clutches his leg and shouts: 'Jesus Christ!' One of his dimmer, Runyonesque companions says: 'Oo . . . er . . . dat's a good name for der kid!'

His musical director was a delightful man called Robert de Cormier, whose name was sometimes de-glamourised into Bob Corman. A few years later the Mitchells worked with him on a series called *Round the World in Song*, which used music from almost every country – and in almost every language too. Much care was taken to get the pronunciation right, and many a startled announcer from the World Service in Bush House was shanghaied into our rehearsal hall to drill us in his native language – Polish, Czech, Serbo-Croat, Spanish. Our favourite was the smart young Japanese who not only told us how to pronounce the words of the cherry-tree song 'Sakura' but actually *sang* it to us, in an excellent light-baritone voice. Our baritone section fetched an extra chair and tried to make him join us permanently.

The songs we featured in that series were of all kinds, love-songs, work-songs, folk-songs. Some we had already done with Harry Belafonte, like the charming lullaby from Indonesia 'Suliram', but some were new to us, and there were fascinating American examples of how old English songs crossed the Atlantic with settlers throughout the centuries and came back again with words and tune slightly changed. One of these was 'Coffee Grows on Whiteoak Trees'. Bob said it might once have been: 'Coffee grows on white folks' trees'. The next line was 'The river flows with brandy-o'. The words were sung to a tune that is almost exactly the same as 'The Eriskay Love-lilt', and even some of the words had the same basic sound as the Gaelic ones. I wondered if the black workers had made up their own words in imitation of what they thought were English words sung by their masters. Altogether the programmes were a delight to us, and Bob was the most considerate and kindly of conductors. We were genuinely sorry when he went home to America, he was the kind of man to whom only the good things should happen, and I hope they have.

Every Christmas in those days was marked by a kind of end-of-term romp on B.B.C. Television, a Christmas pantomime in which all the stars of the day would take part in *Cinderella* or *Aladdin*. They were just beginning to be called 'television personalities', which is a phrase used when it's quite difficult to say what anyone's particular talent is. These pantos were jolly affairs for the principal players, but for the singers and dancers they were much more tedious than any normal variety show, for rehearsals often went on far into the night. The one I remember best was *Dick Whittington*, in which Mary Malcolm and Sylvia Peters played the parts of Dick and Alice, and that Wodehousian character Fred Emney was the King of Morocco. The Mitchell girls were his 'wives', dressed in gold turbans, little gold jackets, and pale blue and gold trousers. The wife with the two black knees showing through her trousers was me, having tripped over my little gold turned-up-toed slippers in the rush to get up the canteen steps at the tea-break and bruised both knees. One of the worthies welcomed to the King's court with Dick and his cat was an intrepid explorer in khaki shirt and shorts, David Attenborough, later controller of B.B.C. 2.

After marathons like that, ordinary television light entertainment shows were a 'doddle', some of them ludicrously so, thanks to a union regulation that only live singers were to be used. I can remember one series called *Hi, Summer!* in which our only contribution in one particular week was to sing 'Hi, Summer, Hi Summer!' in the opening bars. Then we went home. 'Better than working', indeed. There wasn't much to do, either, in shows like *Six-Five Special* when we were occasionally used as backing for the new breed, the 'pop' singer. *Six-Five Special* used its studio audience as part of the show, as *Top of the Pops* does today, and I can recall one girl among all the youngsters quite clearly. She was small and curvy, with a magnesium-blonde plait of hair down her back – it was the era of the pony-tail hairstyle and the circular tight-waisted skirt. Since then she has become almost notorious as the hypermammiferous blonde in what is one of Britain's most profitable exports, the *Carry On* film series. Her name is Barbara Windsor, a serious and conscientious young woman, quite unlike her screen image.

We were given another series of our own television *Glee Club*, but most of our work was our customary back-up job for other performers of all kinds, giving plenty of opportunity for observation and sometimes amusement. Some stars twinkled wanly and then went out. Some are still glowing even more brightly, like lovely Percy Edwards, with his uncanny knack of becoming a bird or animal in, literally, one second and his kindly humour which makes you fonder of him than ever, even when he has just frightened the daylights out of you with his 'angry lion' voice – all done with a lamp-glass. Two comedians whose technique was especially fascinating were Al Read – a pie-manufacturer turned character comedian – and the late, great Jimmy James. Al Read was one of those comics, like Max Wall and Albert Burden, whose act is almost a ritual which everybody knows, but you still laugh at it. His most enchanting creation is the happily drunk Northern chap staggering homeward and shouting through his neighbours' letter-boxes: 'We've soopped soom stooff tonight . . .' Jimmy James was a comedian who was in the Rob Wilton class, really a superb character actor, not so much a 'comic'. When he did his masterly 'drunk' act he seemed the very epitome of all the good-natured inebriates you'd ever seen, you could almost hear the alcoholic ringing in his ears as he swayed backwards and forwards, his eyes marvellously out of focus, and every unco-ordinated gesture ever-so-slightly missing its mark, while he tried to sing whatever scraps of tunes drifted into his poor head, managing only the famous crooked phrase: 'Er-fa-a-fa-a'. In real life he was a teetotaller. On some radio variety shows we used to meet a plump dark-haired young man who showed the same fine acting ability, and has since become one of the greatest British character actors, Ronnie Barker. I call this type of entertainer an actor rather than a comedian. He – or she in some cases – is seen mostly in 'situation comedy' – short, amusing plays using the same set of characters in each episode of a series. Audiences tend to think that these favourite performers will be as funny off the screen, but I think most character actors would admit that without a script that suits them they cannot be expected to make people laugh in panel games or interviews without their humour sounding forced, no matter how skilful they may be. In that respect they differ from the stand-up comedian, who can work on his own, sometimes with his own material, at what must be one of the loneliest jobs in the world.

By this time the Mitchells were like a family unit, all types and ages and temperaments making up an organisation which had its own way of working, its own catch-phrases (anything slightly inaccurate or out of tune would be 'Near enough for jazz' or 'Very adjacent.') and its own jokes. If George himself was not able to take a rehearsal Fred Tomlinson would be in charge. Fred was our wild boy, our own brilliant eccentric, one of whose tricks for calling everyone to order at the start of a rehearsal was to pound out the opening bars of *Belshazzar's Feast*, *fortissimo* on the piano, bawling 'In *Ba*bylon . . .' in a deafening baritone. The accomplishment of his that I most envied was his ability to blow his nose on a perfect B flat.

Very often we had to rehearse – when there was time to rehearse at all – in small rooms full of upturned tables and piles of chairs, with no piano. On those occasions we relied on Phyllis Whitaker. Phyl had 'perfect pitch', and could hum any note asked for with complete accuracy. Useful, for other people, but the gift can be a curse when a piece of music is for some reason performed in a different key. Then the luckless possessor of 'absolute' pitch has to transpose the music in his or her head. If Phyllis wasn't there we had to make a guess at the right pitch. A typical Mitchell exchange in an upstairs rehearsal room would be:

GEORGE: 'Oh hell, no piano . . . give us an A, somebody.'
DAI FRANCIS: 'Fa. . . . There y'are, George. I know it's right, I brought it all the way up from the piano downstairs.'

GEORGE (*not to be outdone*): 'Somebody must have trodden on it on the way up, then.'

Phyllis was an excellent pianist, and sometimes spent a whole day playing accompaniments for the auditions which George occasionally held when we needed more singers. There were some good, fresh young voices among the hopefuls, but it was sad to realise how few of them could read music at sight, even though some of them had studied at one or other of the music colleges. So they were not suitable for session work, although they were very useful in stage shows. Some of the Welsh candidates could sing tonic sol-fa, which can be a help when you're sight-reading. I sometimes used it myself when we came across a difficult interval between two notes, but I don't use it properly, nor did my colleague Moira, who often sang on the same 'line'. When we wanted, for instance, to find a B flat in the key of G minor we both thought of the B flat as 'mi minor', whereas every good sol-fa expert knows that the B flat is still 'doh' and the G is 'la'. Even our garbled version was very useful though – a half-remembered system that we had learned at school. We always knew when George had spent the morning at auditions; he'd sit over a cup of tea and shake his head glumly threatening to grow long ears with flaps like a spaniel's to let down whenever he heard the opening bars of Adele's 'Laughing Song' from *Die Fledermaus*. Once is nice; three or four times in a morning is tedious, and there were days when he was glad to leave the auditioning to Daphne and Phyl. Phyllis had once been a concert-party pianist, faced with the usual weird musical conundrums during children's talent contests. Her Waterloo had come one day when a small boy was lifted on to the stage by the comedian-compère. 'What're you going to sing, love?' said the comic. 'Er slicky eye ger slucky ee', piped the tot. 'What?' 'ER SLICKY EYE GER SLUCKY EE!' 'Look, dear,' said Phyllis, 'you face the people and sing your song, and I'll play it for you.' He toddled off to the front of the stage and began a curious quavering wail: 'Ger slicky eye . . . ger . . . slucky ee'. Phyl played bits of tunes that she thought might fit: 'I Love Little Pussy', and 'Little Boy Blue', until suddenly the mite turned round to look sternly at her, and in a voice of piercing scorn said: 'You don't *know* it, do you?' After that, Adele's 'Laughing Song' is a picnic.

Towards the end of the 1950s we could reflect that some of the people who had sung with us at one time or another were beginning to be better known in their own right. In addition to the three *Black-and-*

White Minstrels principals, Tony Mercer, Dai Francis and John Boulter, we had as old boys and old girls people like Dorita, who became part of the distinguished Latin-American duo 'Dorita y Pepe', the actors Glyn Owen and Peter (*Onedin Line*) Gilmore, and Mike Sammes, who had formed his own vocal group with its own elegant and sophisticated style. Mike was, like George, a highly talented musician with a wonderful Goon-like sense of the ridiculous. (His fiancée Enid and I were always cast as tarts in street scenes in television musical shows; it became so inevitable that we automatically went to lean against any lamp-post which might appear on any set, and braced ourselves to wear red satin dresses and five-inch heels – the Wardrobe's standard uniform for tarts in those days.)

One of our youngest sopranos was Maryetta Midgley, daughter of the same Walter Midgley who had sung the Prince in *Turandot* opposite the formidable Eva Turner. Another second generation soprano was Margaret Eaves, the daughter of the first Margaret Eaves who sang so sweetly in the wartime *Garrison Theatre* radio show, which had starred the incorrigible 'Private' Jack (*Dixon of Dock Green*) Warner. It seems incredible to me now, but one of the girls who occasionally sang second alto with me was Heather Harper, now an internationally famous soprano. But to many instrumentalists the most noteworthy member of our group was Tommy Sampson. Tommy once had his own band, much admired among musicians, and he was a great asset to us on the musical side, but what enthralled us most about Tommy was his vast and varied fund of scatological tales about some of the cabaret artistes he had worked with. He was an educated Scot, and knew the value of money in spite of his zany, happy-go-lucky ways. Once when we were helping him copy out vocal parts we said: 'This is worth seven-and-six a page, y'know, Tom.' We were only teasing, but he paid us! One of my happiest moments in our *Glee Club* television series was when Tommy and I were partners in a reel during our 'Scottish Medley' number. Tom was slight, and pale and bespectacled, but he was a grand dancer.

Sometimes the irregular work and sheer nervous tension of our job was enough to make some singers need a change – rather like going into a 'retreat', and they joined one of the various theatre companies in one or other of the musical shows of those days. But compared with the hectic session world a long stage show must be like becoming one of the crew of a luxury liner on a long cruise after being on a fast, battle-scarred destroyer. One of our brightest girls took ship, as it were, in

The Sound of Music, and spent some calm and uplifting months as one of the nuns. At length, however, the religious life proved too much for her, and after a tiff with the stage manager she gave in her notice. On the afternoon of the day she was to leave, in the time between the matinee and the evening performance, she glided out of the stage door, still wearing her nun's costume, and went into every pub in the Charing Cross Road, ordering half a pint of bitter in each one. To this day publicans and elderly topers of the district remember the sobering sight of that nun standing at the counter, one foot on the brass rail, knocking back halves of bitter. In these days of trendy religion it probably wouldn't increase a bishop's heartbeat under his 'Jesus Rules O.K.?' teeshirt, but it was enough at that time to ensure her a place in the folk-lore of Soho.

CHAPTER SEVEN

Con sordino

ONE DECEMBER evening in 1959, I was watching a television programme about the diagnosis and treatment of cancer. It was late at night, and everyone else had gone to bed except me and my cat Twm. During the course of the programme one of the doctors taking part said that he wished all women would look for signs of breast cancer in themselves, so that it could be treated early.

Two days later I went to the doctor and told him what I had found. Our doctor is a quiet, serious man, with, thank goodness, no jolly jokes or heartiness in his manner. He said he thought I should go along to a clinic at our local hospital, the West Middlesex at Isleworth, a sprawling Victorian building with, at that time, a fine reputation as a teaching hospital. The consultant whom I saw said he thought I ought to be admitted as an in-patient, 'just so that we can have a look'.

So a week later there I was in an old-fashioned ward with about ten beds in it, all polish and sunlight and chintz bed-curtains. It hadn't been a very jolly Christmas. I knew by some instinct that what I had found was not just an ordinary lump, and the thought of what might happen if I had discovered the thing too late had made everything in normal everyday life seem like a film with no soundtrack – a mass of meaningless images.

In my job it is essential to look cheerful and alert even when you don't feel like smiling – the 'On with the Motley' attitude. When I sat up in the iron-framed bed and looked round at the other women in the ward I stretched my lips in the grin we all use when we don't want to be accused of looking doleful. To my surprise it worked. Everybody smiled back, and one or two dressing-gowned ladies plopped over the polished floor in their pink furry slippers to have a chat to the new girl.

The West Middlesex at that time was a hospital which drew its staff and its patients from the surrounding district – any patient of about twenty-four or twenty-five might find themselves being nursed by a girl who had sat next to them at school. But the registrar who was to be my surgeon couldn't have come from anywhere on earth that was farther away from our district. He was a Tasmanian, a large, thoughtful young man who did me the favour of laughing when I said I thought Tasmania was a neurosis, not a place.

Two days after my admission I was taken to the operating theatre for a biopsy. That same evening the staff nurse drew the curtains round my bed and said 'Mr Muir would like to talk to you,' and he came through the curtains, a file under his arm and sat down on my bed. The conversation couldn't have been briefer. 'Mrs Thomas, we've reason to believe that the growth is malignant, and I strongly advise you to have that breast removed.'

'Oh . . . when can you do it?'

'Nine o'clock tomorrow morning.'

'Thank you.'

Even though I had half expected the news it was still unpleasant. It would mean permanent disfigurement, for a start. I'd never be able to wear the low-necked leotards and other costumes we used for our stage and television appearances. I could well understand why some women dreaded the operation when they had husbands or lovers who would be repelled by the result; but I believed that Eddie and I had been through too much together for any physical disaster to affect our love for one another. And it wasn't like losing an arm or leg, so I'd just have to make the best of it.

It was the sister in charge of our ward who gave me courage and whatever hope she could. She was a tiny thin woman with a sardonic sense of humour and a sweet, husky Geordie accent. She put on her dark blue cape and walked beside my 'trolley' when I was wheeled down to the operating theatre. The West Middlesex was not designed for comfort, and on the journey to the theatre all trolleys had to be wheeled over a bridge between two buildings, and along a concrete path, both open to the sky. It was all right for the patient, half-drugged, dressed in a comical white hat and gown and woollen stockings, and wrapped in warm blankets, but the nurses and porters must have cursed the whole arrangement. Snowflakes floated down and fell delicately on my face. Once inside the theatre building Sister Wilson said 'This is Sid. He'll put you to sleep.' I wasn't going to sleep without trying to raise a laugh, though. Through the warm narcotic haze I mumbled 'My newspaper horoscope today says I shouldn't make any social arrangements for this evening.' Sid grinned, and it crossed my mind that he must be an expert at interpreting patients' semi-conscious murmurs. 'Better not, then,' he said. 'What's your zodiac sign, anyway?' 'Cancer,' I said, and fell into a black lake.

Late that evening I awoke. The ward was dark except for a dim lamp over the staff-nurse's desk, and my bed-curtains were closed. I lay still, getting used to being conscious. Minutes later the staff nurse came through the curtains, and we smiled at each other. 'I expect you're thirsty,' she whispered. 'I'll move this trolley so that you can reach the soda-syphon when you want it.' Next morning the syphon was empty, I must have drunk the lot during the night. The twenty-four hours that followed were among the nastiest of my life. I couldn't move very easily, for there were so many tubes attached to me – drainage-tubes, I was told. And the bandage round my chest was almost unbearably tight, but would have to be endured if the draining process was to be successful, Eddie came to see me – my mother later told me he had stayed up all night before the operation – and I think I must have looked a bit wan, because he had tears in his eyes when he left. I put it down to Celtic emotion.

When the nasty twenty-four hours was over I reached for a mirror. Something would have to be done. After a very painful and awkward ten minutes I had a wisp of mascara on, and a touch of lipstick, and managed to comb my hair, which was agonising, and drew a round of applause from the other patients – very gratifying to any performer! 'Move about as much as you can,' said Sister Wilson, 'It'll help the circulation.' So I did, and a couple of days later I was allowed out of bed, with the wretched tubes now disconnected. Standing up straight was painful, as I couldn't lift my left arm without pulling on the stitches down my side, but it was good to be out of that bed for a few minutes. It transpired that I was Mr Muir's first mastectomy, and every morning he would come bounding up the stairs before he started the day's work, and stand at the foot of my bed chewing the ends of his muffler thoughtfully. A Goon-like conversation ensued: 'G'morning Mr Muir, how are you?'

'I'm supposed to ask *you* that!'

'O.K. Let's start again. G'morning Mr Muir.'

'G'morning. How are you?'

For the next few days I tottered about the ward when I was allowed out of bed, and thought how glad I was to be getting about at all. I had said I didn't want any visitors, but flowers and cards kept arriving, and I had plenty of books to read, and the other patients to listen to after each visiting time was over and eyes had been wiped and noses blown. Those of us who could walk would sometimes gaze out of the windows at the traffic bowling along the London road outside, and marvel at the people getting on to buses. Such strenuous exercise seemed impossible to us.

One day, the staff-nurse, wearing a white mask, came to take 'alternate' stitches out. My face was covered with a cloth while this was being done, so that the sight of the wound wouldn't be too much of a shock, I suppose. 'Staff' left me for a minute to tell Mr Muir and the students that I was ready for inspection, and while she was gone I had a look at the damage. It was indeed a nasty, unnatural-looking thing, but neatly done, and obviously healing well.

A week later I was home, very weak, but somewhat reassured by what I'd been told – that the cancer had been in its early stages, and that it might not recur. I had to go to the Middlesex Hospital in Mortimer Street every day at half-past four for radio therapy. This is an eerie process, like a science-fiction movie. First they measure up the area to be irradiated, and draw squares on your skin with a wax pencil ('Try not to wash it off'). The treatment takes place in a white-painted room with a long padded table in the centre and a huge grey-painted machine balanced above it. They take one of what look like glass flower-vases of different shapes from a shelf on the wall and fit this 'vase' on to the business end of the X-ray machine. Then they lower the machine until the glass vase is clamped hard against your chest (on half-healed flesh this is very eye-watering), give you a buzzer to call for help 'if necessary' (. . . what did they mean 'if necessary' . . . blue flames coming out of the machine? Little green gnomes? . . . What?), and then they swing the heavy sliding doors shut, and run! They wave to you through their glass panel, and it struck me that the whole set-up was rather like being in a radio studio, when you are alone with a microphone. The silence was disturbed only by the traffic outside, and a short crackling sound from the machine. A tap dripped over a sink in the corner, and I read the maker's name-plate – PYE, CAMBRIDGE., it said – on the machine. I knew how butterflies would feel if they knew they were pinned down in display cabinets. The machine above me obviously weighed several hundred-weight, and I hoped it was securely balanced, otherwise I'd be crushed like an ant. After one minute I was released, and sent home until the next day. Meantime I would have to follow the rather bleak instructions on a printed leaflet . . . 'Don't wash the irradiated area with soap. Use only unscented talcum powder. Drink at least six pints of liquid every day.' After three weeks it was over, my skin had become a bit inflamed, I had felt slightly sick towards the end of that time, but I was back at work by the end of the second week. Monthly check-ups followed, then six-monthly, then yearly.

It was obvious that my days as a 'showgirl' singer were over. Apart from the obvious disfigurement, my left arm was puffy and swollen, and likely to remain so for some time. There was plenty of other work though, and I was glad to be back with the Mitchells. I reflected with some amusement as we rehearsed the music for the Jack Payne television show that not only had the B.B.C. helped to educate me when I was a child, and provided me with work now; it had even seemed to warn me, by means of that medical television programme weeks before, to watch out for any signs of ill-health!

We had a good many radio and television shows to take part in, *The Charlie Drake Show*, a Royal Variety Performance, *The David Nixon Show*, and the official opening of the Television Centre at Shepherd's Bush. We had been rehearsing there for some years, in what was called the 'Canteen Block', although there was no canteen in it yet, it was just a vast bare room, with literally nothing in it except a piano, a trestle table and some clattering metal chairs. Outside all was mud, duckboards, concrete-mixers and scaffolding. But at last the twelve-million-pound complex was ready and we opened it with a gala variety show. I can't remember a thing about that show, except that we and the dancers began the opening routine crouched down on our knees waiting for the orchestra to play the introductory chords, and it seemed hours before the floor manager started the countdown, with consequent yelps and moans of simulated agony from all of us as our muscles became cramped. It's a custom – amounting almost to a fine art – that whenever dancers and singers see the opportunity to make a bit of a fuss about some minor discomfort they relish doing so . . . who knows? it may result in being given a ten-minute tea-break, or just a chance to sit down and have a cigarette and a chat.

Two things happened in 1960 which were nothing to do with the song-and-dance world I had known up until then. I saw an advertisement in a newspaper asking for applications for membership of the MENSA Society. I had seen some members of the society on the television programme *Tonight* and they looked and sounded very amiable people. So I applied for membership, took a Cattell intelligence test, and passed into their 'top two per cent' category. I haven't all that much trust in intelligence tests, in some cases several different answers seem possible to the same question, but it was very gratifying to know that if I *had* been given the chance to go to a university I would probably have been able to take a degree of some kind without too much trouble. There was another sense of relief, too, more difficult to explain. Everyone in the session world, singer or musician, is extremely bright, they have to be or they would not survive in that highly competitive world. But for some time I had felt that perhaps music was not the only area in which I might flourish. This may have accounted for the occasions when I would be chattering and laughing with my colleagues and suddenly would feel like an observer; one of the group and yet somehow outside it. But here's yet another puzzle. Even though I knew I was a MENSA member I never told more than two or three people about it, and I never wore the badge or went to the meetings of the society. It was, I suppose, like gaining an academic honour of some kind, you know you've got it, but you don't go around the streets wearing your cap and gown. And anyway, though MENSA seemed a fine idea for anyone who found it difficult to find friends of their own standard of intelligence, I had scores of such friends around me nearly every day – in fact it's warding people *off* that has been my trouble!

The second diversion came when I saw a paragraph in the *Radio Times* (which in those days carried civilised items like a crossword, and gardening and cooking columns instead of jokey pages full of comic-strip illustrations and articles about football), a paragraph asking for more women candidates from Wales to enter the general-knowledge contest called, in those days, *What Do You Know?* – it's now called *Brain of Britain*. I wrote to the producer and said would I do, as I was Welsh by marriage? Alas, no, you had to be born Welsh. A few weeks later I had another letter asking if I would like to try as a London contestant. I went to an audition – I think one had to get about thirty-three per cent of answers right to pass – and in December I began the climb up through the first round, played before an audience at the B.B.C. Playhouse theatre, in Northumberland Avenue, where the Mitchells worked on so many radio variety shows.

The question-master at that time was the late Franklin Engelmann, an urbane and civilised man who would probably have done extremely well as a contestant himself. A quiz like *Brain of Britain* is almost entirely a question of luck. Questions can be about any subject, and you either know the answer or you don't, no clues are allowed. If you get five consecutive answers right you are given an extra mark as a bonus. The other candidates may answer if you are wrong or can't answer at all. The worst part of the whole affair is to hear the next fellow being asked all the questions to which you know the answers yourself, but that only confirms what John P. Wynn, who set the questions in those days, used to say: 'An easy question is one you can answer. A difficult question is one you can't.' By the beginning of 1961 my luck still held, and I was still in the running for the semi-final. The questions would not be more difficult, but the other contestants would be the wilier survivors from previous rounds. You can't do any 'revision' for this kind of quiz, it's luck, luck, luck all the way.

The Mitchells had a lot of work to do during this time. One of our most fascinating jobs was to 'back' the black American singer, Josh White. Josh was a man who had come up the hard way, and his face and voice showed it. He accompanied himself on an ordinary guitar (no 'electrics' then!) and sang in a husky, whisky-tinged voice songs like 'Black Girl', 'St James Infirmary', 'Boll Weevil', 'House of the Rising Sun', and spirituals too. He was an amiable man, with only one fault as far as we were concerned . . . he would only start recording in the evenings, and so the end of each session was very late. We also worked on a series with David Hughes, one of the few popular singers who has ever graduated to Glyndebourne, and Edmund ('Ted') Hockridge. Ted was a Canadian, a fine singer whose success in *The Pajama Game* made him well known in Britain, but who was capable of much more subtle work like the charming old Canadian 'Chanson des Voyageurs'.

1961, one of my star-gazing friends said, would be a lucky one – the date could be turned upside-down and still look the same. The last time this had happened would have been 1881. However daft this sounded it *was* a lucky year for me, and for the Black-and-White Minstrels. They won the Golden Rose trophy at the Montreux television festival, and on 6 July, Eddie's birthday, I became the 1961 'Brain of Britain'. The two other finalists were women, and very bright they were. (One of them, Mrs Joan Taylor, was television 'Brain' a few years later.) For some reason a record of that final is preserved in the B.B.C. Sound Archives, and there I am, fighting a lingering Cockney accent – not at all fashionable in 1961 – and stumbling my way towards the title. The Final was held in the concert hall in Broadcasting House, and the prize was the two-volume *Shorter Oxford Dictionary*. I was naturally delighted, and grateful to see so many of my former opponents in the audience. There's remarkably little animosity in that contest, it's still fun, which can't be said of some other quizzes. Eddie met me outside (I can never bear to have anyone who is close to me as a member of the audience in the theatre or hall) and I rang my mother to tell her the news. As I put the telephone down, I thought of my father, and of how proud he would have been.

While my luck seemed to be in, I thought I'd try another venture. For many years past I had been listening to a radio programme called *Round Britain Quiz*. It seemed to be the most erudite and devious quiz of all, and the players – they were 'players' rather than contestants, as most of the entertainment came in the incidental chat, not in the exact answers to the questions – the players were mostly academics . . . professors, critics, authors, and so on. I found that I could answer most of the questions, so I wrote to the producer, Patrick Harvey, to ask why there were no women in the London team playing against teams from the regions, the North, Wales, the Midlands and so on. Back came the reply I had expected, the time-honoured B.B.C. answer to all such questions: 'We've never found a woman who would be suitable.' (I'm still getting this same reply, nearly twenty years later, from a few producers!) The answer to that is: 'Then try *me*.' Sometimes it works, sometimes not. Mr Harvey gave me an audition, but, with a commendable show of regret, turned me down. Among the other distinguished hopefuls that day was Rupert Hart-Davis, the publisher, and he was never used either, so I had been in good company. I was determined to accept defeat, as it were, like a gentleman, so I wrote a note of thanks, and that was the start of *seven years* of intermittent letter-writing. Every six months or so I would jog the producer's memory with short notes (sometimes these took two or three days to compose!) and rhymes for use as 'mixed stanzas' – a favourite type of question for the teams in those days, using a line of poetry from four different poets and making a coherent verse out of them. Very difficult to do! Connoisseurs may like to try their luck on this one: (the answer will be found on page 144).

A voice cried through the startled air:-
'She was a phantom of delight.'
Sir Ralph the Rover tore his hair,
And cut her throat, and serve her right.

I could see the producer's point of view. Here was this woman, bright enough in some ways, but with no 'distinguishing marks', no degree, no background, and only this 'Brain of Britain' title to her name – and even that might well have been some kind of fluke – trying to be accepted as a player in one of the most prestigious quiz-games in the world. But he was a courteous soul, and answered each painfully-hewn note of mine with a friendly line or two.

In August that year I made my very first solo television appearance, on the children's programme *Summerhouse*, a modest magazine programme produced by Rosamund Davies. It was, I suppose, a forerunner of the marvellous *Blue Peter*, but of course more limited, for enormous technical advances have been made in television since then. Luck got me *that* spot, too. One of my Mitchell colleagues was married to a cameraman who told the producer about me, and she asked me to do a short piece about cats. In the end, there I sat, almost numb with fear, clutching a rather cross kitten, and telling viewers about well-known historical characters and their cats. The beloved Kenneth Horne was the show's anchor-man, and he read a poem for me – the famous verses found scribbled on a manuscript in a monastery in Carinthia, by an Irish monk:

I and Pangur Bân, my cat,
'Tis a like task we are at . . .

The other people who took part were the gentle and charming Anthony Oliver, an actor whose passion for cats equalled mine, and a pretty girl called Pat Pleasance who reviewed children's books. Apart from my jellied knees it was a milestone for me. Even though I had faced a television camera scores of times before I had always been singing and dancing with my colleagues, and mostly dressed in costume as somebody else; I had never appeared as myself.

The rest of 1961 was fun. The Gilbert and Sullivan operas were at last out of copyright and we took part in a series of programmes about them. I had never been a Gilbert and Sullivan fan up to that time, but when we came to learn the choruses the ingenuity and wit of the words and the sheer quality of the music captured me for life. (W. S. Gilbert would not be needed, except for rhyming, if the operas were to be adapted for today's audiences, present-day politics and social mores are dafter than anything he thought of.)

William Cox-Ife was our 'instructor' in the style required, and he read to us from the D'Oyley Carte Opera Company's regulations, one of which ran: 'No lady in the company shall at any time be forced to appear in a costume which she could not with propriety wear at her own dinner-table.'

We provided the backing, too, for a television 'special' starring the American singer Jo Stafford. She proved to be a tall, rather morose lady, but with a voice that haunts me yet, tinged with a sunset melancholy that enhances the strange words of old American 'mountain' songs.

I was invited to appear from time to time in the B.B.C. television quiz called *Ask Me Another* – a kind of visual *Brain of Britain* but played with two teams, one composed of radio quiz people and one of 'regulars'; Ted Moult, Dr Reginald Webster and Olive Stephens. And I was asked to compile the quiz-questions in an excellent television programme for children called *Playbox*. The producer was John Furness, an ex-Gurkha officer with a sharp and educated wit. (It was he who first told me that there is a Gurkhali folk-song which runs: 'Across the river there lives a boy with a bottom like a peach, but alas, I have no boat.' We all howled with laughter at this gem, and said the equivalent of get-along-with-you. But there really *is* such a song. Moral, never laugh at what seems incredible, ten-to-one it will be true.)

Thinking of questions for a children's quiz is far more difficult than compiling one for adults. After all, adults should know something about everything, but each question for children is restricted by their limited knowledge . . . 'can't ask them that, they won't have learned it yet.' And the answer should be expressed in one word . . . 'How many gold rings did the man in the "The Twelve Days of Christmas" send his true love?' 'Five.' The question-master for this part of the programme was Eamonn Andrews, one of the most pleasant people in the business of entertainment. If the world was full of Eamonn Andrewses it wouldn't be a bad place. He treated our twelve-year-old quiz contestants with a mixture of courtesy and humour that was a treat to see, and he is the kind of man who, once having heard that your mother, say, is not well, asks how she is next time he sees you – without any reminder. Tony Hart, that imaginative genius whose *Take Hart* and *Vision On* programmes can be watched with delight by grown-ups as well as children, was our resident artist, with fresh ideas every week. A most happy programme. Later I compiled questions for the *Tich and Quackers Show* quiz. I never saw the producer, but sent the questions by post each week, which seemed to work well. I adored Quackers – a kind of infantile duckling – a natural anarchist with a genius for getting his own way.

After that I compiled the quiz for *Crackerjack*. I stood by the camera each week to give a nod or shake of the head if a child gave any doubtful answer, so during the rest of the show I had time to observe the children in the audience. It was the beginning of the 'pop' era, and each week a spot in the show was devoted to a group or a singer. One of our regular solo singers was Tom Jones. His nose in those days was his own, and I think it suited him better. He was a very affable fellow, absolutely happy to sit in the canteen scoffing tea and buns with the rest of us, and one of the few pop-singers who was audible without a microphone. At the end of each show the children were asked which groups they would like to hear in future programmes – anyone who asks any audience question like this gets a cacophony of shrieks in reply, and I saw one child near me with her eyes shut rocking backwards and forwards in her seat and shouting 'The STONES, the STONES, the STONES', like an incantation, and it was then I realised that even twelve-year-olds were going to be the next target for the hard-headed businessmen who invented and ran the pop industry.

The summer of 1962 brought me a small success and one of the greatest blessings of my life. The success came on 28 June – my birthday – when I won the title 'Brain of Brains' in the contest that is held every three years when 'Brains of Britain' play each other. Sheer luck again – it could have been either of the other two contestants.

The blessing was something much more important. Along with his father's charm and intelligence my husband had inherited his drinking problem. Anyone who has watched someone they love dearly destroying themselves in that way will know how I felt during the ten years or so while it had been getting worse. And quite apart from the dreadful injury to his health the injury to our finances was disastrous. For a while I had tried to, as it were, keep him company during those long and expensive evenings in pubs and bars, but I often had to work at that time of day and I was always worried about what was happening to him. Whether the alcoholic's condition is physiological or psychological I don't know, but one thing is certain, the victim must realise *of his own accord* that his condition will eventually lead to degeneration and death, and only he can decide to get help for it.

One morning Eddie went to see our doctor, and the result was an appointment at St George's Hospital. I went with him on the day, and sat in the waiting-room while he was with the consultant. The room was painted in bright colours, with handmade posters on the walls telling about the various social functions that patients could attend, and meetings where they could talk to each other. My Danish ancestors in the Dark Ages used to build great fires in their halls, and feast and sing to forget the darkness and danger outside. This determinedly cheerful waiting-room had the same effect, that of a heroic effort to keep despair and horror at bay.

The receptionist asked me to see the consultant too, and the first question he asked me was 'Mrs Thomas, when your husband goes to bed at night does he hang up his clothes or leave them in a heap?' 'He hangs them up' I said, and he seemed satisfied with that answer, as if it gave him some clue to Ed's condition.

Two days later Eddie was admitted to the Atkinson Morley Hospital at Wimbledon. He was there for four weeks, and it must have been an experience no one would want to repeat. His courage and determination were incredible, and he never uttered a word of self-pity. The cure is drastic, and must be a once-and-for-all treatment. If you are a real alcoholic, and want to be cured, then it is not a question of 'cutting-down' or 'moderate social drinking', you must never take another drink in your life. If you do then the misery will be twice as terrible and difficult to cure. Eddie's wardmates were from several different professions, and they were all highly intelligent men, with stories to tell that would have been comic if they were not so appalling. Some had whole weeks missing from their lives, with no recollection of the past seven days until they woke up on some remote beach clutching an empty bottle. (I think Alcoholics Anonymous helps a great many sufferers, but not everyone can fit in with their methods, and some people would rather fight on their own if they can. Eddie is one of these.) What impressed me even more than the bravery of the patients undergoing the 'cure' was the obvious affection and devotion of their relatives and friends I saw on visiting days. The hospital's system was truly ingenious; towards the end of the 'course' a doctor would say 'Why don't you go out for a walk on the common?' This would be while all pubs and off-licences were shut. A few days later the walk would be allowed while the pubs were open. If you passed that test you were allowed home for a week-end – 'paroled' – and soon after that you could be discharged. Follow-up visits to the out-patients' clinic acted as a guide to a patient's progress, and after a few years the doctors say goodbye. The people I talked to while waiting for Eddie to come out of the clinic's consulting-room were among the nicest I've ever met.

There is no more delightful person in the world than a truly 'recovered' alcholic, I suppose because he or she has been through so many horrors, and now knows the true value of everything.

After some heroic deed – and being treated for alcoholism *is* an heroic deed – there is inevitably a kind of anti-climax, when life has to be re-built, new habits explained to friends and acquaintances, and debts paid off. In our case it wasn't too bad. I'm a good, almost dedicated saver, and in a year or so our finances were beginning to be our own at last. One of the greatest problems recovered alcoholics have at such a time is in finding other interests to fill the lacuna left by not drinking. In Eddie's case it was easy, poetry and music had always been vital to him, and now he seemed somehow relieved at not *having* to drink, and not having to spend time doing it.

My own work was getting more varied too – I did some interviewing for *Woman's Hour*, one with Selwyn Lloyd, the Chancellor of the Exchequer (he got sacked ten days later, poor man – I do hope it was not the result of that interview!) and one with the forthright and monumentally hard-working opera-star, Joan Sutherland. One of my Mitchell colleagues, Mike Sammes, had formed his own group of singers and I worked with them on some commercial recordings – the ones I remember best were an L.P. of Stephen Foster songs, and a collection of favourite 'Sunday'-type tunes like 'The Lost Chord' and 'Onward Christian Soldiers'. Marvellous stuff, recorded in Walthamstow Town Hall with an orchestra so huge that in *fortissimo* passages we literally could not hear ourselves singing – and there were about fifty of us.

One of the most moving radio programmes the Mitchells took part in was called *The Long, Long Trail*. It was about the songs of the First World War, and was produced by the B.B.C.'s greatest expert on the history of popular song, Charles Chilton. That radio programme was later made into the successful stage show *Oh What a Lovely War!* To work for Charles was always fascinating. The songs were usually familiar – the ones that weren't were well worth discovering – and the narration – the words linking the musical numbers – always taught me something I didn't know. It was hard work though, anything up to fifteen numbers for a half-hour programme, and never was good sight-reading more essential. Two more of his programmes which I remember vividly were one about the Salvation Army (I got to bang a tambourine in that one – very satisfying!) and one about the Mormons and their great trek to what was to become Salt Lake City.

But my favourite was *The Blue and the Gray*, which started me off on my long love-affair with the songs of the American Civil War. I can't think of a better way of teaching history than by means of a Charles Chilton radio programme.

Ever since 1960 I had been going to the radiotherapy clinic at the West Middlesex Hospital for a check-up from time to time. When I kept my appointment in the summer of 1963 the doctor at the clinic found two small lumps – so shallow as to be hardly noticeable – on my ribs near the great scar of the original mastectomy. 'We'd like you to come in as soon as you can', he said, 'Just so that we can have a look'. A week later there I was again, in the same ward as three years before, with, luckily, the same sister in charge. 'What's this, what's this?' she demanded. 'Back again?' 'Can't keep away,' I said. We grinned at each other, but after that we didn't talk much. There wasn't anything to say, after all, nobody can look you in the eye and say 'You're cured,' I knew that, and I had known that something like this might happen. This time the operation was small, the two lumps were removed, and in two days I was back at work, calling at the hospital a few days later to have the stitches removed from the two tiny scars. Sister Wilson said goodbye to me in the corridor outside her office. 'Try not to worry', she said . . . 'And eat nice things like grapes and milk chocolate.' As I waited for the lift I stared in a daze of anxiety at the cream-painted wall. An appointment had been made for me to attend the radiotherapy clinic at the Middlesex Hospital again (nice and handy for Broadcasting House, I thought). On the day of the consultation I had a demonstration of what all National Health Service treament should be like. 'We shall be a few minutes yet, Sir Brian Windeyer has been detained with a private patient upstairs, so sorry to keep you waiting.' (According to egalitarian thinking N.H.S. patients are supposed to be thrown into an apoplectic rage when they hear this sort of thing. In reality, of course, they are delighted to be attended by the same top-class consultant as someone who can afford to pay for him, and thankful that he is just a few floors up in the same building, and could be reached within minutes during any treatment considered necessary.) And a few minutes after that: 'Do you mind if Sir Brian brings some students with him?' He could have brought the entire medical school for all I cared, but there were only about five of them. He prescribed four weeks of X-ray and said, 'Then we'll see how you get on.'

So there I was again every day, on that long table under that huge machine in that white-walled room with the great sliding doors and the glass observation panel. Same instructions as before . . . at least six pints of liquid every day, no soap-and-water on the marked area, no scented talcum powder. This time, I learned later, the radiologist had told my husband that the treatment would prove to be 'rather harsh'. He was dead right. When the specified four weeks were over the verdict was 'We think that, to make sure, you should continue for another week.' This time, in spite of all the water-drinking and other precautions like dabbing the treated area with surgical spirit and applying clean dressings each day, the skin over my ribs, from collar bone to waist, had begun to crack and blister, and as the weeks stretched farther to five, six . . . then seven, the burns had to be dressed with gentian violet. Very pale skins react like this to sunburn, and I suppose the effect of X-ray is much the same. But you can have enough sense to come out of the sun, and I couldn't give up the X-ray course. In the fifth week I began to feel slightly sick all the time and most dreadfully tired – not with the kind of pleasant, natural fatigue one feels after work. This was a draining-away of all energy, and a fading of all colour from everyday living. There were days when I'd get up at seven, try to do housework, and have to lie down again for about ten minutes every hour of the day. I had to restrict my session-singing to mornings only, so that I could go to the hospital for the X-ray and then go straight home afterwards. At the end of the seventh week I seemed to have had enough, so they let me finish. I suppose now that I was experiencing a form of radiation-sickness. The burns took weeks to begin to heal – usually I'm a good healer – and the great red scars are there to this day. But the awful tiredness persisted for a year or more, then gradually lessened. I plodded on, taking each twenty-four hours at a time, and thankful for not being dead. Each day now is like a gift, and I've cured myself of worrying overmuch about the future. That may be just a sign of maturity, but an experience like those seven weeks certainly gives you a sense of proportion about what matters and what doesn't!

I've wondered since then if it wouldn't be possible for some kind of survey to be taken of the kind of people who develop cancer. Surely there's some great computer clicking and humming away somewhere that would be happy to do it. I used to notice while I was waiting at the radiotherapy clinic that many of the other out-patients seemed to be the same type of person, not physically, but in demeanour. Rather over-alert, given to quick smiles, and lightning reactions, as though they were always at a high tension like a piano-wire. Then there were those other strange symptoms, unusual 'cold-sores' on my forehead and cheeks – I'd never had them in my life until then. Maybe it's a certain type of person who develops cancer – or perhaps inherits a predisposition to develop it (the 'temperament' theory again!) Maybe we just poison ourselves with hidden stresses.

One pleasant outcome of all the wretchedness was that I wrote a short item for a radio magazine-programme about the odd scraps of thought, like coloured feathers, that floated across my mind while I waited in the out-patients' department and that piece was the start of many more. I still visit the hospital every year, and apart from one scare a couple of years ago there seems to be an air of sober optimism. The thing may get me in the end, I know that, but until then I am grateful for every new day.

A voice cried through the startled air
(Longfellow, 'Excelsior'.)
She was a phantom of delight
(Wordsworth, 'She was a phantom of delight'.)
Sir Ralph the Rover tore his hair
(Southey, 'The Inchcape Rock'.)
And cut her throat, and serve her right
(Stephens, 'Nora Criona'.)

CHAPTER EIGHT

'. . . *and tell 'em Bob sent you!*'

IN THE AUTUMN of 1962 a letter arrived from the London office of B.P. Australia, asking if I would be willing to take part in a test to find a British opponent for the Australian quiz-champion, Barry Jones, in their television quiz *Pick-a-Box*. The letter had been addressed to 'Miss Thompson', and sent to one of the *Brain of Britain* contestants called Christine Campbell-Thomson. Out of sheer kindness and courtesy she re-addressed it, as the message was obviously for me. She need not have done so, and I would then probably have missed the journey of a lifetime.

Barry Jones was Australian television's Man-you-Love-to-Hate; a younger version of Gilbert Harding, making a career of being apparently gauche and boorish, arguing with question-masters and protesting gruffly at any decision not in his favour. His quiz-game winnings were enormous – some said as much as £30,000 – and finding somebody to defeat him was becoming an Australian national sport. Barry's real-life character was utterly different, most of his adversaries found him pleasant and easy to get on with, but those are not qualities likely to make you into a notorious television personality, so he must have developed the fangs and claws and hairy pointed ears that seemed necessary.

The selection of the quiz-gladiator took place at B.P.'s headquarters in the City. I found many former Brains of Britain there, and MENSA members, too. We were given a general knowledge examination, separate interviews, and a fine lunch at the Great Eastern Hotel – with a handsome B.P. cigarette-lighter for each of us as a memento. Then we saw a film of the Australian television show.

Some weeks later we were told that the challenger to meet Barry Jones would be Dr Reginald Webster, a formidable player in the

B.B.C.'s television quiz *Ask Me Another*. 'Doc' Webster made the trip to Sydney, but was beaten by Barry Jones, and we all thought that was the end of the matter.

One evening four years after that, the telephone rang, and a voice said 'This is Bob Dyer here . . . you won't have heard of me, but . . .'. 'Yes I have,' I said – I remembered the B.P. film – 'You're the host of *Pick-a-Box*.' Bob and his wife Dolly were staying at the Dorchester, still searching for a British opponent for Barry Jones – would I like to meet them there, with Patrick Bowles and Henry Button, two other Brains, to take yet another test for the game. Henry, Patrick and I had of course already taken part together in the three-yearly *Brain of Brains* game. I was the winner that time, but by a mere two or three points. Bob didn't even have to drop a hat.

We were shown up to the Dyer suite, and for the first time we met 'Bob'n'Doll' as they were called all over Australia. They both seemed seven feet tall to me, but had the warm and kindly manner of homegrown Australians – generally much more pleasant than some London-based types. They gave us another general knowledge test and told us we three were so close in competition that it was hard to choose, and they'd let us know.

A few weeks later we did know . . . Bob had the idea of bringing all three of us to Australia for two weeks, where we would play each other in twelve programmes, and the winner would take on Barry Jones six months later.

When my Mitchell colleagues heard about the proposed trip they had varied advice for me: 'Wear your woollies – it'll be winter there – August.' 'Australia! The only way you can tell 'em from the sheep is that the sheep don't wear hats with corks dangling round the brim.' 'You won't be able to answer any questions – the blood'll run straight to your head. Do you realise you'll be walking about upside-down?' And various other witticisms.

But at last it was all done, the date fixed, the cases packed, the passport in order, with visas for America – and Mexico too, as we might stop there on our return flight. At the United States Embassy in Grosvenor Square they needed a written assurance that I'd only be passing through America, and not lingering to be a one-woman threat to peace and order. At the Mexican Embassy they didn't seem to care a fig for that sort of fandango, but offered me sweets, and chatted amiably while their plump, pretty clerks filled in their forms – on which my occupation was given as *Artista*.

Patrick and I had never flown anywhere before, Henry was the worldly one of the trio, so he had to reassure us that yes, the pilot *would* know the way, and no, aeroplanes did not have propellers any more, or people in goggles leaning out of cockpits shouting: 'Chocks away!' Even with such reassurances the take-off from Heathrow one cloudy August evening in 1967 was a bit frightening, with that eerie rushing roar and the fumes filling the air in the 'plane.

We were travelling as guests of Qantas, first class, an experience not likely to happen to us again – total luxury all the time. Too much of it at once, really. I often wished the next fourteen days could have been spread over a few years – having them all at once was like living on crystallized fruits, and what with the delicious meals and the immobility of air travel we felt like geese being force-fed for pâté de foie gras.

If ever you have to fly twelve thousand miles you cannot have better travelling companions than two distinguished British civil servants. This maligned breed is generally well-educated, amiable and sensible, and in the case of Patrick and Henry blessed with a fine sense of the ridiculous and an ability to preserve a friendly silence for hours at a time.

The two were totally different, Patrick from National Savings the traditional rosy-cheeked country squire type, and Henry, from the Ministry of Agriculture, 'Ag'n'Fish', more studious-looking, with a faint Lancashire accent underlying the Cambridge tones.

Few passengers seemed able to afford first-class travel that night, so we had the pale-blue and beige cabin almost to ourselves. Our first delay came at Frankfurt. Two hours, during which time we had a marvellous dinner at the airport restaurant. Patrick said the Germans were probably sending for 'your traditional genial Black Forest toy-maker mit der lederhosen and der jazzy braces' to repair the plane. Henry said better a few hours delay here than inflating our life-jackets over the Persian Gulf.

Before the days of Universal Airport architecture every city airport had its own style. When the doors of the 'plane opened at Cairo we stepped out into a velvet-black jasmine-scented night, and drank thick coffee in the silent lounge, with pamphlets in French on each table giving the Arab account of the Six-Day war.

After hundreds of miles of desert like the waves of an orange sea, Bahrain, even with a dawn temperature of 98°F, was fascinating. The heat was like a hammer-blow to the head, but the restaurant had the atmosphere of a seaside cafe – red and white checked tablecloths and plain wooden chairs. More trees than I had expected – one with scarlet flowers, obviously cherished, with its own hosepipe lying near. . . . Small, dignified Arabs, with their ladies like little cones of black silk – only their blank brown eyes and tiny feet visible. The crew who serviced the plane here couldn't start their own truck when it was time for them to drive away and had to be towed. Henry said he hoped they'd had better luck with the 'City of Townsville', as our aircraft was called.

A different kind of heat met us at Palam Airport, Delhi. This was like a great wet claw dragging the energy from our limbs. . . Photography not allowed (whatever was there to photograph?), very smart policemen, a gallant attempt to grow flowers in oil-drums full of earth, wheeling birds (kites?), pi-dogs, and the lounge full of red velvet seats and a faintly mouldy smell – in spite of the revolving fan in the ceiling. A superb cup of tea was served to us . . . Indian, naturally.

Bangkok's night was black and clear, and warm. Announcements in French, and jewellery and leather shops in a big Lyons-Corner-House-type lounge. Henry bought a bottle of beer with an unusual label for his collection. That label later defied all attempts to soak, peel, rub or steam it off all over the world. Thai glue must have special properties.

The Thai people were the most elegant I'd ever seen – all of them, men and women, tiny and exquisite, as though God had made them to put on his mantelpiece. When we got back into the plane, and settled down after the customary fruit juice and ice-cold face-towels I found that the exquisite Thais had lifted my Qantas travel-socks . . . ah well, 'Handsome is . . .'

Singapore Airport lounge was like the old Long Bar at Waterloo Station, but incomparably cleaner. Shop-fronts covered in sequins, with tinsel trees on the tops. Everything open and business going on full blast – at midnight.

The plane filled up with Australian business-men going home to God's Own Country from a conference. Only another four thousand miles to go. The dawn woke me over north-west Australia, an eerie sight, a land quite empty, the air glass-clear over thousands of miles of nothing but yellow desert and red-plasticine mountains. A vast, silent country, but not in the least sinister, just waiting, either for people to come to it, or for the people who are there to go away.

White scratches appear on the tawny ground; roads connecting groups of huts with silver roofs flashing in the sun . . . geological surveyors? . . . miners? The roads seem to lead off into nothing. A few farms appear . . . why in that spot? Who says: 'This is the place'?

Hours later the long scratches are black, and the ground is white . . . snow! Forests, mountains and clusters of houses. Forms to fill in declaring that we haven't brought any forbidden plants or seeds, or 'visited any farm or abattoir where there were diseased animals'.

Then a great city below, and farewell to our blue and beige cocoon, with its cheerful, pretty Australian stewardesses, and all the terrifying literature about 'What To Do In An Emergency'. We were met by B.P. advertising men, and whisked off through the streets to our American-style hotel. It's fashionable to jeer at these places but I love them, they are extremely comfortable, highly efficient, and the same all over the world – you know exactly what to expect. (Local touches can be endearing. My husband tells me that in the Singapore hotel of this type your clean socks are pegged neatly in a row on a coat-hanger.)

From my room, eleven floors up, I had a superb view of Sydney harbour and its great bridge. I couldn't wait to go out into the streets. It was mid-winter, but the temperature rose to 70°F, and the air was clear and golden, like a September afternoon. So many things were strange – the sun in the *north* all day, the unfamiliar sweet-toned birds in the city trees, the pavements covered with awnings and shop-signs facing you as you walk along underneath.

I was enchanted by the rows of Victorian terraced houses, with wrought-iron verandahs and balconies. In some streets these were being restored and obviously cherished, in others the balconies had been filled in with glass, often broken, and the houses looked like the ones in Ruth Park's novels about Sydney. Argyle Place – 'once the haunt of sailors' a white notice-board said – was an example of how delightful these old houses can look, but we found that most prosperous Aussies like to live in the handsome bungalows and houses with big gardens in the city suburbs.

The stranger can easily see why that part of Australia is called New South Wales. Sydney is like a warm Pembrokeshire coast – with skyscrapers. All round the Harbour there are tiny bays and creeks, with woods running down to the water, and it was on one of these bays that Bob and Dolly Dyer had their house.

At that time, Bob and Dolly were probably the most famous couple in Australian television. The *Pick-a-Box* quiz show had been running for many years, and the Aussie television audience was fiercely partisan, as each winner emerged. The contestants were all viewers from all over Australia, and the game involved a certain amount of chance – gambling being the national Aussie vice. At certain points in the programme a right answer would give the contestant the chance to open a box from a row set up behind the question-master's desk. The box might contain just a can of motor-oil – or a voucher for a whole house-full of furniture. 'TAKE THE BOX!' the studio audience would yell. I've always been amazed at the attitude of studio audiences in television quiz-games where money or goods are the prizes. Far from being envious of the winner's luck, they seem to love to see other people winning things. *Sale of the Century*, and *The Generation Game* are two more examples of this.

At set times during the programme Bob would do the commercials – for B.P., the Bank of New South Wales ('You can bank on the "Wales"' – which he was horribly afraid he would Spoonerise one day . . .) and Qantas, the superb Australian air-line. The advertising for B.P. exhorting motorists to buy their products at the local garage always ended with '. . . and tell 'em Bob sent you!' which became our catch-phrase.

Losers on the programme were sent away with a handsome wrist-watch. ('Wear a Bulova watch, folks, and see that Bulova difference!')

'Bob'n'Doll' (car number-plates BOB and DOL, of course) lived in some style in a lovely house with the usual upper-middle-class swimming-pool in the back garden (arum lilies blooming there, too!) And *one* ornate 'Tudor' chimney-pot on the roof. One of Bob's most endearing qualities was his realisation of the difference between this affluence and his childhood poverty. He was an American, from the wilder part of Tennessee, and by sheer hard work, energy and luck had made his name in Australian radio, and later, television. He looked like a retired colonel – tall and lean, and was a complete professional where television was concerned. If the show was under-running, and one-and-half minutes extra 'chat' was needed, then Bob would supply it – ninety seconds, no more, no less. This is much harder to do than it appears – and of course the art lies in making it look easy.

Bob's greatest asset was his wife Dolly. Like him, she was tall and elegant – and beautiful, too. They had been married twenty-seven years, and obviously loved each other dearly. Dolly's warmth and sweetness added an even more homely touch to the programme; she always reminded me of the archetypal heroine in a Western – the angelic wife who gets killed by Indians in the first reel.

Doll's sweetness was not just for television shows – it went right through her personality. Australian women must surely make the best wives in the world – often beautiful, practical and kindly. Sometimes Australian men do not deserve them – but more of that later!

Their home was different from others of its type for one main reason – Bob's lifelong devotion to big-game fishing. Moored at his private landing-stage, down 200 steps, was a superb ocean-going launch, *Tennessee II*, with a big 'chair' on the prow from which he – and Dolly too – played the huge sharks and marlin, sometimes for hours.

To dine at the Dyers' was an odd experience. You'd look up from your half-pound steak to see the huge jaw-bone of a great shark mounted on the wall. In their sitting-room there were *two* of these huge creatures – whole – covering two walls, with engraved steel plates under each; one reading 'His' and the other 'Hers'. One of our greatest treats was the day Bob'n'Doll took us on a trip round the Harbour on *Tennessee II*. It was a golden, sunny day, full of laughter and good comradeship – with a stop whenever the green-and-gold B.P. shield on tankers and oil installations could be included in a photograph.

Home-made films were another of Bob's enthusiasms. He showed the best ones on the *Pick-a-Box* programme, including one of his friend Harold Holt, the Prime Minister of that day, on a fishing trip. Mr Holt had been given a spear-gun by the then American President Lyndon B. Johnson. The thing proved difficult to handle, and the prime-ministerial blood was soon seen flowing from a cut on the finger. The film broke down once, after a sequence showing the P.M. swimming, and one of the soldiers (on leave from the war in Vietnam) in the studio audience observed sardonically 'P'raps a shark got 'im!' This proved tragically possible a few years later when Harold Holt was lost while swimming among the rocks near his beach house at Portsea, Victoria.

The *Pick-a-Box* shows were recorded at A.T.N.-7's studios in Epping, outside Sydney. One television studio is much like another, but the people who worked there – production staff, technicians, make-up girls, canteen staff – were the friendliest I had ever met. Australians must be the easiest people in the world to talk to, and only aggressively defensive when insensitive outsiders imply that Australia is a cultural desert, or that other countries are better. Different they may be, better they are not.

The shows themselves were great fun. As there were three of us 'Poms' the rules had been altered so that we all sat at one table instead of in separate glass boxes. Perhaps that was a mistake, because audiences hate change of any kind in a quiz-show formula.

Among the studio audience were groups of people like wounded soldiers from Vietnam, Rotary clubs, and on one occasion a ladies' Bowling Club. God help any invader of Australian soil who confronts these cheerful, forthright women, Brünnhildes in panama hats.

The questions were formidable . . . well, what *is* the name of the book by Mary Mapes Dodge with 'Peter and the Dyke' in it? (*Hans Brinker and the Silver Skates*, that's what, but I didn't know at the time.)

After twelve games Patrick emerged as the winner, but we were all richer by a few hundred dollars ('You can bank on the "Wales"!') Dollars and cents ('Dolls'n'Sense' in 'Strine' language) had just been introduced, and were treated with some contempt by most Aussies. 'Cup of coffee? One-and-six please, dear' . . . and items marked in dolls'n'sense lay next to those marked in pounds – in the same shop window. But how sensible was the 'ten-bob dollar' – after all, one cent was then about equal to the old penny, instead of being two-and-a-half times as expensive, as in our own lunatic decimal currency.

One day Rod Taylor, B.P.'s advertising manager, drove us on a sixty-mile trip to Katoomba, a holiday resort 3,000 feet up in the Blue Mountains. We stood on Echo Point and looked out over red mountains covered with blue-gum forests – totally silent except for the sound of the bell-bird (exactly like the ringing of a tiny silver bell). The spicy 'herby' aroma of the gum-trees is the scent of Australia to me – they should bottle it to sell to nostalgic exiles.

The road there and back followed what had been the old pioneer track cut out of solid rock. Strange names appeared like: 'Knapsack Gully' which I thought might have been the place where some depressed pioneer sat on his bundle to rest. Rod said it was more likely the place where the pioneer had his knapsack pinched by another pioneer. All along the road were signs illustrating the perky 'Strine' methods of selling. On the back of a lorry 'Hit me nice'n'easy, mate, I'm full of Frank's Ice Cream'. And 'FREDDO chocolate frogs' – apparently all small boys in Australia had been nourished on those for years. One battered roadside eating-house said 'Captain Bligh's Panorama Look-Out Café'. The next sign said simply 'OBEY GOD'. Among the roadside stalls selling oranges and grapefruit there were puzzling notices which said: 'CHOOX HERE'. We Poms had to have it translated – a 'chook' is a chicken, and so naturally 'choox' is the plural, like 'sox'.

The catch-phrase 'Tell 'em Bob sent you' was vividly illustrated one morning when Bob asked the curator of the Aquarium at Marineland to show us the big fish being fed. This was done by a frog-man (Freddo?) swimming coolly round the vast tank feeding the huge, flat sting-rays . . . with a man-eating shark flicking its way round him. . . . I was assured that sharks eat only once every few weeks. Pom sang-froid was further tested when they handed me a tiny sea-horse to hold – not at all slimy; like a very light papier-mâché toy.

There's an awful lot of wildlife in Australia. Kuringai Chase, about fifteen miles out of Sydney, is a National Park with zoo where you can walk among the tame kangaroos, and even stroke their beautifully soft fur. Real-live koalas clung sleepily to the trees – a koala spends most of its time literally up a gum-tree. Koala means: 'never-drink', and all this endearing creature does is reach out a paw for the next bunch of gum-leaves. The oil in these, I'm told, makes the koala slightly drunk all the time, which accounts for his dazed expression.

I was allowed to hold one of these charming animals on a publicity trip to Taronga Park Zoo. Valda Marshall, *Woman's Day* journalist – and now a playwright – needed some pictures for an interview she did with me, so we asked Mr Thomas, the curator, if we could include the animals. Mr Thomas, with his own black and white cat, Matthias, in attendance, let me hold a 'joey' – a baby kangaroo – whose mother had been killed by hunters – and then he introduced me to 'Pooh', the most amenable koala. Pooh was surprisingly heavy, but as cuddly as a favourite teddy-bear, except that his claws could be painful if they landed on your face or neck. Koalas don't see too well, and they think everyone they cling to is a tree. (It was a chance remark from Valda that convinced me of my unfitness ever to be an immigrant. She had, she said, opened the front door of her house one morning to find a snake on the doorstep.)

I think it must be far more difficult to be an immigrant than most people realise. The right attitude must be the one expressed by a Frenchwoman we met, the owner of an elegant restaurant. When I asked her if she ever longed for Paris she said: 'I sometimes go there for a holiday, but I never consider it as my home. I am an Australian now.' And yet there were people in the audience for our quiz-show who came up to us afterwards, and almost wistfully enquired after Walthamstow, or Ealing . . . had those places changed very much? . . .'We've been here forty-five years and we still think about home'.

I only really longed for home on one occasion, that was the afternoon I took the steamer from Circular Quay (which is *not* circular!) to see Ruby Zlotkowski, an old show-business colleague of mine who is now teaching singing in her native Sydney. We talked, and ate iced sponge-cake, and listened to records of her pupils, and it was only when we heard a tape of one of her friends playing the piano version of Schumann's 'Widmung' that I thought how wonderful it would be to get home again. No explanation . . . the song isn't even English, for heaven's sake! But that was on the posh 'Norshore' (Strine for North Shore). The city itself was a daily delight, so like and yet unlike home. Suburbs with names like Chiswick, Putney, Croydon, Paddington, and then names straight out of Billy Bunter's mouth: 'Yaroobah Road' for instance, and 'Wahroonga'. ('Turramurra' had a pleasantly Tennysonian ring to it – 'Turra-murra by the river, sang Sir Lancelot'?) Handsome streets full of big stores, but where in Regent Street would you see people carrying swimsuits and towels under their arms – the beaches in 'Sinny' are only a bus-ride away.

Huge policemen – not necessarily tall, but huge – like old-fashioned 'bobbies', friendly and helpful as at home . . . but everybody had to fetch their own tax-return from a post office, *and* pay the postage too!

Every other shop seemed to be either a bank, a chemists, or a lottery-ticket office. Daffodils on the market flower-stalls . . . but with marigolds as well. Commercial radio stations chattering on about a 'Saucepan Event in Parramatta', and the stolidly worthy wavelength that broadcasts the proceedings in the Australian Parliament. The day I listened it consisted of a somnolent drone about sheep, but as well as the speaker's supporters saying 'Hear, hear!' as at home, there were some murmurs of 'My word, my word!' – much more encouraging.

The King's Cross district, where we were staying, was the night-life quarter of Sydney, with girlie-shows ('STRIPERAMA' . . . I'm convinced it should have been spelt with two p's!) and exotic restaurants. From the window of my room I could watch the lights flash on over the city – no long slow winter twilight as at home, the Sydney sky was dark in ten minutes with a great orange moon and the bridge looking like a coathanger made of gold beads. The liners and tankers in the harbour wailed and boomed, and an icy wind blew . . . from the *south*, straight from Antarctica.

The shops by day were a show in themselves – full of strange fruit and meat . . . with kangaroo-meat sold as pet-food, alas. One of my wanderings took me past the Alamein memorial. This looks like a huge dandelion-head on a stalk, and water flows over the metal 'puff-ball' at the top. At night the head lights up, and the effect is beautiful. I never found out why it was made in that form, as it seemed unconnected with the El Alemein battle of 1942, but it was most impressive.

It was fashionable in Britain in those days to decry the nineteenth-century concepts of honour and patriotism. Those were the days of the Cult of Youth, which was really a creed fostered by shrewd business-men who saw ways of making money out of the newly-affluent young. The infection no doubt reached Australia later, but most Australians still kept the old values, and expected other people to acknowledge them too. Nowhere was this more evident than in the Anzac Memorial in Hyde Park, a tall, cenotaph-like building at the end of a long avenue. Stone Anzacs with reversed arms outside; and inside, a circular, domed hall. Gold stars glint on the ceiling, and the old names are carved on the walls in cold, plain capitals: 'Gallipoli, Ypres, Fressines, Hill 60.' A notice says simply: 'Quiet. This is a sacred place.' From a marble gallery you look down into a dimly-lit well, and at the figure of a young man carved in bronze, staring upward, dead on a shield, with arms hanging limp over a long sword. No sound at all, just the hum of traffic outside. The memorial is simple, but a heart-rending reminder of the men from the dusty outback sheep-stations, the city banks and the factories who went to fight in remote countries for a cause perhaps only partly understood, out of loyalty to a country most of them had never even seen. Outside on the marble steps there were old men sitting in the sun, and the gardens were full of violas and marigolds. I wondered if the scorn shown by young people for supposedly outmoded beliefs is not sometimes a kind of resentment for not having shared in that mixture of dreariness and danger that their elders knew in wartime. For some older men, war is possibly the most important experience they will ever have had, as childbirth is for some women, and the rest of their life is a diminuendo.

The curious relationship between Australian men and Australian women may have changed by now, but I think the so-called Women's

Liberation movement may have had a hard time trying to alter the traditional Australian male's attitude towards women.

The Australian man has a long tradition of hard living, hard fighting, and hard drinking. It seems to me that this is a relic of the old pioneer days, when women, no matter how loving, tough and devoted, were, because of their inferior physical strength, a liability in times of adversity. When faced by drought, floods, storms or bushrangers, only your 'mates', your male comrades, would be of much use, so males must always stick together. This tradition persists even among the men in sophisticated cities in the twentieth century. Heavy drinking seems to be taken as a sign of masculinity – a great pity. In some areas pubs are still for male drinkers only (I would have liked to have seen the famous *art-nouveau* decor in one particular Sydney pub, but I had to be content with a description!)

Anyone who really wants to understand how Australian attitudes have formed could not do better than to read the stories of Henry Lawson (or Larsen), the great Australian writer of the late-nineteenth and early twentieth centuries. A strange, manic-depressive man, deaf, drunken and, in the end, disillusioned, but his writing – a mixture of Dickens, W. W. Jacobs, Mark Twain and Maxim Gorky – gives what must have been the very sight, sound and smell of Australian life, particularly vividly in stories like 'A Child in the Dark', 'Telling Mrs Baker', 'Water Them Geraniums', and 'The Union Buries its Dead'.

Australia seems to me a place full of vitality and energy, and unaffected enjoyment of its prosperity. But there is – or was – a certain wistfulness there, too, rather like the demeanour of a rich uncle who has never quite been accepted by the rest of the family. Nowadays the 'family' is poor, and 'uncle' has been asked to take in the relations – sometimes churlish and ungrateful ones. No wonder he occasionally makes a bitter and defensive comment about the old family.

On the night before our stay was over we all had a farewell drink in the hotel bar. The bartender had just won a prize for inventing a new cocktail. It looked exactly like copper sulphate solution – bright blue, and probably lethal – but it tasted delicious. We were all to go our separate ways home, Patrick via New Zealand to see his son and daughter-in-law, Henry to a conference in Canberra. As Kingsford-Smith airport ('Mascot' to Sydneysiders) fell away below my 'plane I found myself crying. I clutched a copy of *The Australian* and a tiny orange that the wife of one of B.P.'s executives had given me from the tree in her garden.

I still remember my Australian friends most vividly, from the hotel doorman whose passion was rose-growing, to the kindly, genuine (in the Cockney sense) people who showed us such warmth and hospitality. 'Bob'n'Doll' were awarded the O.B.E. and M.B.E. a few years later, and no two people deserve the honours more, for sheer hard work and enthusiasm.

Our first stop was in Fiji, at Nadi (pronounced 'Nandi'!) and we spent an hour or so in the pretty, homely airport with its bamboo decorations, soft voices, smiles and, outside, the blue skies, distant mountains with black rain-clouds over them and always the warm wind tugging at your hair.

When we got to Honolulu, the night was black and rainy, so apart from the airport itself I saw nothing. We had some hours to wait, and I thought what an exotic mixture the passengers at our table in the deserted restaurant were. There was an Australian scientist; the wife of a racing motorist on her way to join her husband in the States, an Irish diplomat and his wife, and a small, plump, middle-aged woman who seemed to have known everyone in every consulate and embassy all round the world. She must have retired by now, and perhaps she's living in a comfortable small hotel in Bournemouth, in a room full of photographs in silver frames. I think she was the most practised traveller I've ever met. She could have been set down anywhere in the world, and in an hour she would have got herself a room, a job and some acquaintances. She made us forget the continuous Hawaiian-type Muzak, and the sight of all the empty coffee-cups.

San Francisco airport was a relief from being pinned down in that pastel-coloured prison of an aircraft, but I don't think I've ever felt so alone as I did then. It was full of rushing crowds, and the sun burned through the glass walls of the main hall. My case felt unbearably heavy, I couldn't find a bank to change my money into dollars, and had to ask a kindly black porter to mind my luggage while I trudged to the cash-desk. When I finally got back – expecting him to have gone away long before – there he was, serious and patient in his smart uniform and spotless white gloves. A reassuring introduction to America, but alas the cab-driver who took me to the hotel overcharged me after a few adroit questions to find out just how much of a stranger I was!

I had three days to spend in the city, so I used the introductions I had been given by the B.P. men in Sydney. Australians are great travellers themselves, so they know how valuable and time-saving it can be to have a 'name' to ask for in the air-line office or bank. The Qantas men in Post Street took me out for a drink (funny how all Australian men seem to have one-syllable names . . . Bruce, Fred, Vince . . .) and told me that the best way to see as much of the city as possible would be to take coach trips . . . and would I like to go on the local television chat-show? I wish I had, now, it might have been fun, but I was far more eager to explore the city. My hotel was late-nineteenth century and my room had a huge walk-in clothes closet which must have once been used to accommodate the vast satin-and-taffeta dresses of railroad kings' wives. But no food on the premises, so I had to eat next door in a Korean restaurant where the proprietor cooked the food in what the Chinese call a wok over a gas stove. It was delicious, and so plentiful that I only needed one meal a day, apart from what a nearby early-morning café called a 'Slimmer's Breakfast' – egg, three slices of toast, preserves and coffee . . . whatever did *non*-slimmers eat, for goodness sake?

San Francisco coach-drivers are guides as well, and have all the enthusiasm for their job which I find one of the most attractive American characteristics. The man who drove us to see Muir Woods, the forest of giant redwood trees about seventeen miles north of San Francisco, was driver, guide, historian, naturalist, linguist, philosopher and comedian.

'My name's Bob' he said – he pronounced it 'Barb'. 'Now, where are all you folks from?' From various parts of the coach came timid voices: 'Noo York', 'Saynt Loois', 'Wisconsin', 'Noo Joizey' . . . and I realised that though all my fellow-passengers were American, they too were tourists, and California was new to them as it was to me. After a few jokes about football, Bob told us that it is easy to tell native San Franciscans from tourists . . . the tourists are the ones with the goose pimples, the natives are the ones with the overcoats. We laughed but it is true that the cold Humboldt current off America's west coast makes the sea chilly and the shore foggy even in summer. The giant scarlet 'ladders' that hold up the Golden Gate Bridge disappear into the mist, an eerie sight.

The woods were awesome. Five hundred acres of huge red trees, some of them 300 feet tall. Insects do not thrive on the bark, so there are few birds, and the silence is total. The great trees grow in families of five or six together and give the effect of groups of silent giants, some 2000 years old, waiting politely for the pygmy tourists to leave them in peace again.

On our way back to the city Bob sighed philosophically at bad drivers, chatted in Japanese to a small boy newly home from Kobe with his Air Corps father, and drove along a winding precipice telling us that the army had rejected him for having bad eyesight. We stopped in a pretty, sunny little town called Sausalito – 'Little Willow,' Bob said. It was an artists' colony, with a marina, and a tiny 'village green', where middle-class 'flower children' – it was their hey-day at that time – sat on the grass and sang to the music of flutes and bongoes, and played with their pet cats and racoons, and would obviously put their bangles and headbands away neatly when they went home to supper. Self-consciously chic, but charming. Bob found the father of a lost child, told us the best and cheapest cafés to visit, and gave a short talk about the various trees in the woods at the roadside. Then we drove on into the city down Powell Street, which seems almost vertical – even the two ladies from Maine who sat behind me held their breath while Bob made his frightening jokes about the brakes.

That same evening most of us booked the Chinatown trip too – with a Chinese guide – a young student called Steve (*Steve?*). The mist had come down again, and the top floors of the Empress of China hotel faded into the night sky as though into the darkened flies above a stage. Everything was almost aggressively Chinese – the street-lamps, the telephone-kiosks like little pagodas, and the shops with misty neon signs. Steve told us about the Chinese telephone operators – the jobs are passed down from mother to daughter because there are, for example, over a thousand people called Lee in the district, and a directory is not much use. So the girls have to learn about all the Lee families by word of mouth . . . rather like knowing Jones the Fish and Jones Top-Shop in Wales.

Steve had blood-curdling tales, too, about the days of the Tong wars, when rival tongs would line up on both sides of a street and at a given signal would go at their rivals with hatchets. Lovely tourist stuff, but there were the tong 'family' names in discreet black letters over office doors – 'Friendly Societies' where any member can go for help or advice; like the Oddfellows in Bolton or Wigan . . . well, almost.

Of course we had our fortunes told with joss-sticks and cards chosen by small birds. I was born in the year of the Monkey, so I'm 'highly observant, curious, clean (thanks!) and agile . . . excellent in work requiring curiosity *but* not likely to mind own business.' True, true.

We munched fortune cookies, those sweet crisp biscuits with paper mottoes inside, and drove home along a street full of jazz clubs and topless shows. Outside one of these was a big neon-lit birdcage with a girl go-go dancer inside it – our driver tooted our coach-horn at her and she waved merrily back, and went on go-going to music inaudible above the clanging of cable-car bells.

Next morning, the survivors among us – that included the two ladies from Maine, of course – staggered back to Union Square for yet another trip. This time it was to be the 'San Francisco de Luxe' tour. The first part was de luxe all right. We drove past palatial homes where the really rich people live – the ones you never hear about, the ones who never need gossip-column publicity. I suppose San Francisco must be the most elegant city in America – a mixture of Bournemouth, Torquay, Cardiff and alas, some touches of Slough. The hills are so steep that cars park at right angles to the pavement, and your front door may be level with your neighbour's roof-top. The site is just above the San Andreas Fault – two plates of rock which may some day grind together with disastrous results, but few people seem to worry about that. It must be the ideal city to be rich in – better even than Paris or London. It has that elusive quality, style, and there can't be much wrong with a place that insists on calling its dockside area the Embarcadero. That name is a relic of the days of the Spanish settlement, like the rugged little church of the Mission Dolores, founded in 1776, with its tubby white columns and chalet-type overhanging roof. We stopped for coffee at the 'world-renowned Cliff House' (dated 1858) on the rocks overlooking the melancholy and misty Pacific, and heard gruesome tales of unwary swimmers being eaten by sharks. Real hippies stood on the pavement outside, selling an outlandish-looking magazine full of rather good *art-nouveau* drawings and totally incomprehensible reading-matter. Back through Golden Gate Park ('The glasshouses here are modelled on the famous one in Kew, England') and its enchanting Japanese garden.

The plane I was to travel on left the airport at one minute past midnight – Bruce said it was known as the Red-Eye Special from its arrival time at crack of dawn in New York. I can't say as the song does: 'I left my heart in San Francisco' . . . but perhaps the left ventricle may still be there somewhere. When I had my last coffee at the airport café (with the inevitable glass of iced water as soon as you sit down, of course) and thanked the waitress, she smiled and said 'Y'r welcome, come back soon.' I'd love to, some day.

Breakfast in New York's Kennedy airport – Idlewild had surely been a much more intriguing name – with a zoology professor from

Hawaii, a sales director of Rothmans and a pretty girl who never said a single word to anybody even though we all tried hard.

The yellow lights of the M4 motorway as we approached London were like so many hundreds of little harvest moons to my eyes. Even the grudging service and martyred air of porters and waitresses had the grubby familiarity of an old pair of gardening-gloves.

There really *is* no place like it.

CHAPTER NINE

Scherzando

EVER SINCE I was a small child I can remember being curious about almost everything. I learned to read in greedy haste because I wanted to know what it was that grown-ups saw when they looked at books and newspapers, and how they could tell me stories just by looking at all those black marks in rows on white paper. I loved listening to them talking to each other, too, especially about their own childhood days. When I could read for myself it was like giving roast beef to a starving man, I read *everything*. From the Rawlplug instruction leaflet to the side of the OK Sauce bottle ('OK' may be derived from the Choctaw 'Oke', or 'Hoke', but has also been said to come from the expression 'Orl K'rect'). You could learn French that way, too: 'Cette sauce de premier choix . . . ' and so on.

My avid thirst for not so much *knowledge* as simply *reading* would give a sharp attack of the jim-jams to any of the compilers of carefully-structured reading courses for modern children. I got through such literary fare as *Tiger Tim's Weekly*, *The Butterfly*, *Schoolgirls Own*, *The Diseases of the Horse* (my grandfather's bible), *Yarns on Heroes of India*, *A History of British Battles*, *Jane Eyre*, and a huge book of bound volumes of *The Girls' Own Paper* of 1885. And the *Lady's Companion*, *Tit-Bits*, *Everybody's Weekly*, *The Young Soldier* (the Salvation Army paper for children), *Little Women*, *Grimms' Fairy Tales*, the parish magazine, *White Fang* and *A Peep Behind the Scenes* – all before I was ten. Traditional children's books were not my real favourites – *Peter Pan* seemed rather silly, not a patch on Marie Corelli, and the only page of *Alice's Adventures in Wonderland* that I really liked was the one where the print curved down the page as the letters got smaller and smaller, forming a tail. I didn't read about Winnie the Pooh until I was past forty – it was worth waiting for.

When examination-time came at school I found the occasion exhilarating. I loved the excitement of the whole thing, and it was thrilling to turn over the question-paper to see what questions were to be answered. There was much less fuss about examinations in those days, for we were always having small tests of one kind or another, and an examination was just a longer, quieter test. Even if you didn't know much about the answers to some of the questions on the English paper for instance, you could always use your imagination to write something that would be interesting for the examiner to read, rather like writing a radio piece based on a flimsy idea.

I'm convinced that the fine teaching in my schooldays provoked my curiosity about almost everything, and as I get older the scraps of information fit together like the apparently random pieces in a patchwork quilt going to make up the larger pattern. For instance, a date in history will not only remind me of the events, battles, statesmen, kings and queens of that time, but a whole set of connected features like the music of the age, the painting, architecture, costume, literature, food, transport and language. A dictionary or a map open before me means an hour or more spent in idle exploration, and a reference book, from the *Daily Mail Year Book* to *Brewer's Dictionary of Phrase and Fable* is like picking gold nuggets out of gravel. The fascinating items mined in this way range from gems of daftness like the description of the death of the holy St Sigbert: 'Such was his faith that he went to battle against Penda, King of Mercia, armed only with a wand. . . . He was instantly killed' (it's the thought of the look of sheer incredulity on the faces of Penda's army that's so intriguing) to vulgar music-hall gags like the fact that Baron Woolley and Baron Winterbottom both appear in the list of peers, and should surely to introduced to each other before the cold weather sets in.

Being a devout pedestrian has meant that I have plenty of time to read oddities like the old London Transport bus-timetable notes ('The Board does not undertake, nor shall it be deemed to undertake, that vehicles will arrive at the times specified, or at all . . .' I love the sonorous majesty of: 'Nor shall it be deemed to undertake') and the railway regulations about what may be carried on trains – no 'noxious substances' or unattended violoncellos. The excellent modern London Transport posters might have been devised specially for me, but I seldom buy magazines or books to read on train journeys – there's always so much to see out of the window, especially if the train goes through mysterious regions like East Anglia. I can remember one eerily fascinating journey like that, over the flat, black Fen country – so flat that on a clear day you can see the train coming *over the horizon*. This was a winter afternoon of icy mists, silent swans on the fens, and Ely Cathedral materialising out of the fog like the Flying Dutchman's ship. People left the train at tiny halts and faded away down wispy pearly-grey funnels. A girl with a basket got off at Manea – pronounced 'Maynee' – and drifted away . . . where to? There wasn't a sound, or the sight of a building anywhere. With all that going on, who needs a magazine? Local papers are captivating, too . . . *anybody's* local paper, from Cleckheaton to Carmarthen – especially Carmarthen, where half the news is printed in Welsh, and some of the forthcoming funeral announcements are followed by the phrase: 'Gwron yn unig' – 'gentlemen only' – in some quarters it's still not customary for ladies to attend funerals. Some local papers have part of the small-ads page devoted to a lost-and-found column which can generate Byzantine flights of conjecture . . . for instance, under what circumstances did someone lose: 'one black glove, two swimming costumes and a teddy-bear'?

These jewels lie about everywhere, bits of coloured glass waiting to be picked up and stuck into the cement of one's mind like the scraps of broken china and stones in old-fashioned garden walls. Even on the draughty and gritty bus-ride to the Television Centre place-names flicker past my eyes like bunting . . . 'Weltje Road' . . . Weltje was George the Fourth's cook, it is said. 'Starch Green' . . . a relic of the days when that part of West London, from Shepherd's Bush to Brentford, was the capital's laundry centre, where the merry, brawny washerwomen slammed and pounded the clothes with wooden dollies. This Aladdin's Cave of baubles that lies about us everywhere can be a time-waster, though, like stopping to exchange compliments with the local cats. There is an elegant theatrical wig-maker's in Marylebone where the waiting-room table was laden with Edwardian ladies' magazines. I used to arrive at least half an hour early for a fitting, just to read about how to drive a pony-and-trap ('Motor-cars will always stop to let a horse-drawn vehicle pass, especially if it is seen that the driver is a lady.') and how to inform the waiter that you will not be taking any wine . . . (roll up one of your white kid gloves and put it into the wineglass). Lovely, useless, enriching stuff.

'But you have such a marvellous memory' people tell me. I don't think my memory is much different from anyone else's, perhaps it's just that I use it more. Most women who run a home have excellent memories – after all, you don't reach for a cookery book every time you want to make a Yorkshire pudding, do you? And you carry thousands of other pieces of information in your head, like your children's shoe-sizes, and your friends' birthdays. But memory neglected becomes like a fountain-pen unused. Unless you thump the thing smartly the ink won't start to flow. My memory is certainly not infallible – I've been known to leave washing on the line for two days . . . that was before I made myself a little card that says: 'Fetch washing in', which goes with the card saying: 'Switch off immersion heater'. Names I remember well, no matter how long ago it was that I heard them, and especially if I've seen them written down. Faces are much more difficult, particularly if I see the person out of the environment in which I first met them. This is probably due to the fact that I'm dreadfully short-sighted and never saw them clearly in the first place. I lose my way continually in large buildings, no matter how many times I've been there. (One day a pile of my whitening bones will be discovered in some remote corridor of Broadcasting House.) Outside, though, it's easier. If I can only see a street plan of a city I've never been to before, I'll be a proper little Marco Polo. Perhaps there are several different kinds of memory. Mine seems to be the semi-photographic type. When I was session-singing for television shows I could usually 'see' the page of music in my mind's eye, about eighteen inches in front of my head, with the stave-lines, the words, any alterations, blots or smudges, and, at the foot of the page, where to turn over. I say 'semi-photographic' because this memory is sometimes wrong, and the edges of the 'pages' get misty. But I can usually remember whereabouts a quotation came in a book – right-hand or left-hand page, top or bottom of the page . . . but not the page number! This gift has its disadvantages though. If I'm to learn a script it is fatal for me to write out my lines on another piece of paper, which helps many actors remember their part. If I do this I get confused between remembering the original page and the re-written one, so I must always try to 'photograph' the original.

Silent concentration helps memory, if you are seriously trying to learn something. I know you're probably saying scornfully 'Our Jonathan got ten O-Levels and had Radio One blaring away all the time he was studying'. I humbly suggest that your Jonathan, if he'd switched the radio off, might have got fifteen O-Levels. Saying that background noise helps concentration is a form of self-deception, like that of the musicians who take drugs, or drivers who drink, deluding themselves that they become more skilful. They *think* they do, that's all. No matter how sick with nerves you may feel when faced with a theatrical performance, or an examination, or an interview, it's best not to rely on drugs of any kind – even the ubiquitous tranquilliser – to help you through the crisis, for two reasons. One is that some day you may not have your dream-drops with you, and you'll have to face whatever it is without them. The other reason is that any form of sedation or mental anæsthetic must slow down the lightning reaction that all performers (performers on a stage or performers in everyday life) must have, and must numb the delicate antennæ which are so essential for instinctive knowledge of what will be the right thing to say or do. (The remedies for nervousness among entertainers are as numerous as the stars in the sky, from: 'Take six deep breaths before you go on,' 'Concentrate on your *eyes*, think of nothing else,' to the coarse: 'Check that your flies are done up, and avoid stumbling over the furniture, then just say the lines.') Nothing helps much, except to remember that nerves are ninety per cent bad conscience. If you *know* your part, or subject, or speech, thoroughly, you'll be a lot less nervous. But he who has no nerves at all is no artiste; even I, the singer of whom Toscanini once said: 'Who . . . ?' knew that.

My almost unconscious accumulation of knowledge had won me my 'Brain of Britain' and 'Brain of Brains' titles, and given me a mind filled with sequins – nothing very valuable, but showy. I thought how pleasant it would be if I could use some of the sequins to decorate a radio programme. I was still writing brief, light-hearted notes to the producer of *Round Britain Quiz*, but there seemed no real hope of my being allowed to take part, and to be quite fair I realised that to disturb the monastic calm of the game with the presence of an ex-chorus-girl, even if she had won a couple of quiz-contest titles, would be like encountering Annie Oakley in the chaste corridors of the Athenaeum. But every six months or so I wrote another note, just to keep my memory green.

I had compiled what I thought would make a pleasant musical half-hour for radio. It was a collection of songs which had been best-sellers at the turn of the century – all of them written by women; songs like 'I Passed By Your Window', and 'The End of a Perfect Day'. I knew several producers of musical programmes, but this sort of project would, they said, be undertaken by the Gramophone department. So I sent the script there. Six months later I had heard nothing, but a few weeks after that I had a letter from a totally different producer from the one I had originally approached saying that the script might make two fifteen-minute items in an afternoon 'magazine' programme. Eventually it was broadcast in 1965, and from the time I first submitted the script to the date of the actual transmission was eighteen months. Somehow I had a copy of my script misdirected back to me during that long wait. Attached to it were inter-departmental notes which I still cherish to this day. I should have sent them back, I know, but that might have embarrassed the people who wrote them. My favourite one said: 'Do we *know* anything about Irene Thomas? Has she done anything for us?' Those two sentences encapsulate the difficulty a would-be broadcaster had in finding a producer who'd take a chance on an unknown writer. Even though I had been working in Light Entertainment programmes for over ten years and had won two of the B.B.C.'s own 'titles', it all cut no ice with other departments, which seemed totally unconnected with each other. It's probably easier now, but in those days each department seemed to need some outside recommendation before you were accepted as a solo broadcaster, even though the actual script you had written remained unaltered on the day of your broadcast. You needed corroboration of your worth, a kind of abstract 'Accused's Friend'; like having a first-class honours degree, or running a home for delinquent donkeys, or having sailed across the Channel in a plastic bucket. Without such credentials the going was rough and very, very slow, like climbing a steel wall in bedroom slippers. Everyone was extremely pleasant, and very polite, but expert at writing the kind of letter that takes up exactly one-third of a page, full of wispy evasion and promising nothing. (Everyone, that is, except one man, who was supercilious and unpleasant.) I'm not really pushy enough to embark on a campaign of that kind. If people say no to me I generally go away, remembering to shut the door quietly as I leave. If I decide to persevere I can be tenacious, but it takes a long, long time to see results.

My colleague Phyllis, she of the absolute pitch, was also trying to achieve her aim of becoming a staff accompanist. One day we were sitting on a table in a rehearsal room, idly munching crisps. 'Any success from any of your letter-writing, Phyl?' I asked. 'No,' she said. 'Not a thing so far. But I get some lovely replies.' We laughed till we cried at that phrase, and to this day I have a file marked 'L.R.', which stands for Lovely Replies, for there are even now a few examples of second-generation B.B.C. 'lovely-repliers'.

I had taken part in the television programme called *Ask Me Another*, like most winners of the radio 'Brain of Britain' title, but that was an infrequent job, and consisted of a game against the regular team, Dr Reginald Webster, Olive Stephens and Ted Moult. It was a very pleasant affair, but not an opportunity for developing one's own style of answering questions – not really my type of quiz.

There are three types of quiz-game. The first is the straightforward question-and-answer, either-you-know-it-or-you-don't kind, like *Brain of Britain* or *Mastermind*. The second is the kind of quiz you can see mainly on commercial television channels, where the questions are not all that difficult for any of the contestants who have been chosen to play the game (they must be very bright or they wouldn't have got that far) but speed is vital. You must be that tenth-of-a-second faster than your competitors at pressing the buzzer or switch that says you know the answer. The third kind is the one I like best, and *Round Britain Quiz* is the perfect example of it. The questions sound perfectly incomprehensible at first, and must be unravelled before you can get a clue to the answer. It's not so much the answer that's intriguing, but the *finding* of the answer, and the people who set the questions, whether the questions come from listeners or whether they are devised by the question-master, have to be even more ingenious than the players, for clues must be given – as grudgingly as possible! In the first two types of game an audience can contribute to the excitement, but in *Round Britain Quiz* the fascination lies in its unique atmosphere of after-dinner conversation in dark-panelled, candle-lit rooms, with dons enjoying their port and walnuts, so an audience is not needed. Apart from possible quiz-work in the mid-1960s there were great preparations being made for the B.B.C.'s second television channel, with a certain amount of nursery-style jollity over their kangaroo symbols, Hullabaloo and Custard. (Nobody seemed to know what this meant, except, presumably, the chaps who thought of it in the first place, but we smiled knowingly at it just the same, with the same smile as we used during rehearsals for the staff pantomime.) It was rumoured in the bazaars that research assistants would be needed for the new channel, so I applied. I didn't really know what a research assistant was, but as it happened I didn't need to, for I was turned down without ever having been interviewed. The story which prevailed at the time implied that to be considered for the job you needed a degree – preferably a Cambridge degree too, but that may have been a *canard* put about by disappointed Oxford graduates. I wasn't very surprised at the rebuff, for I'd already had some experience of being interviewed by television executives. One man, to whom I'd submitted some modest programme ideas, seemed far more interested in the Winter Olympic Games which flickered on his television screen in the corner of his office, although it was instructive to see how many of those ideas were made into programmes in later years, long after my interview had been forgotten. Encouraging, really, for it showed that my notions had not been too fanciful after all.

The one programme which often invited me to take part in short quizzes and brain-games was *Woman's Hour*. They didn't seem to care a fig about anyone's qualifications, just about whether you'd be suitable for what they had in mind. Luckily I was able to offer the extra gimmick of being the only woman who had ever won the 'Brain of Brains' title. On one literary quiz I partnered the novelist Pamela Frankau against Maurice Richardson and Peter Forster. I'd never met anyone like Pamela Frankau. She seemed totally opposite to what I had imagined a 'literary lady' would be. She was as thin as a stair-rod, with enormous dark eyes and a husky voice like the *chalumeau* register of a clarinet. Her manner was warm, charming and truly humorous – I wish she were alive now; she'd make an admirable *Round Britain Quiz* player. Miss Frankau and I won the game handsomely, which added to our delight.

Another *Woman's Hour* game entailed answering questions about Shakespeare's plays. Alan Dent was the question-master, and my two fellow-players were Jonathan Cecil and the delightful Diana Graves, a lady straight out of Congreve. Then I was one of the 'victims' in an intelligence-test game chaired by a professor of psychology. Just before the recording I began to draw parallel lines on a corner of my notepad, then similar lines crossing them, and then filling in alternate squares to give a chessboard effect. 'I'm always doing this,' I said to the professor. 'I wonder what it means in psychological terms?' 'I dunno,' he said, 'but if you ever find out, tell me. *I* do it too!'

In the spring of 1965 I had a go at the long-running ITV game *Criss-Cross Quiz*. It was a combination of noughts-and-crosses and general knowledge questions. I won £250. It would have been £350, but for my reckless conceit in trying just one more round and losing some of my winnings. I should have remembered the old theatrical adage: 'Take the money and run!' The people who took part in that game were among the nicest I've ever met in the quiz-world. We waited in a dimly-lit dressing room before the show, for there had to be a few players in reserve in case one of the contestants got knocked out of the game early. I remember with particular pleasure a young man called Harry Davies, who that very morning had received his degree at London University from the Queen Mother. I hope the Premium Bonds he won turned lucky for him.

All this time the Mitchells were still working in radio and television shows and commercial records, but there were signs that the new pop cult would have a serious effect on the use of so many session-singers. Pop groups needed a good many orchestral musicians, but few singers, as they made their own vocal noises. The whole pop industry had begun in the 1950s – or, some would say, as early as 1941, when Les Paul made a recording with his electric guitar in a bathroom, and started a new type of sound. Since then a whole new world has been manufactured by the men who make most money out of young people. It is an almost totally artificial culture which has now gained a momentum of its own, carrying it to the heights where it has its own statesmen – the managers, producers, and promoters of records; its own saints and heroes – the stars; and its own proletariat – the youngsters who buy the records and imitate the clothes and lifestyle of their idols. Even more than in most other branches of the entertainment industry, sheer luck plays an enormous part in the success of a group or a solo singer, and money an even greater part. The now-canonised Beatles had been a flop in America at first until their near-genius manager, Brian Epstein, organised a vastly expensive promotion campaign.

At first, professional musicians treated the new cult with amusement, and in-jokes were retailed about the more moronic groups' lack of skill. (One group leader to another: 'We play our numbers in F, what do you play yours in?') But orchestral musicians soon learned to hide their sardonic disdain when lush orchestral backings were needed for pop records. Serious musicologists were heard and seen on radio and television solemnly analysing examples of pop-tunes: 'This 4–4 bar is followed by a 2–4 and then, intriguingly, a 3–4.' No-one seemed to realise that the tune had been left that way to fit the often illiterate and pretentious words, but by then nobody dared to say that the emperors had no clothes. The real skill in the making of records lies in the great technical ability of recording engineers, who use their multi-track facilities to produce sounds which could never be imitated by live performers on a stage. Some producers and engineers could take almost any four or five youngsters off the street and make a pop-group out of them in a few weeks, whether they could sing or not. In fact this was done in America with a group called The Monkees, four actors needed for a television comedy series about a pop-group.

The brilliant and sometimes unscrupulous men who run the industry are capable of making some lad, whose natural musical abilities should be confined to a cheerful whistling while he rides an errand-boy's bicycle, into a millionaire living uneasily in a Queen Anne mansion full of hi-fi equipment and lifts lined with white leather. Once on a misty winter afternoon in Belle Vue Zoo, Manchester, I saw a doleful chimpanzee sitting in a corner of his cage and consoling himself by rocking to and fro while pushing an empty biscuit-tin backwards and forwards. The similarity between that chimp and the average howling, twitching pop-singer is very sobering, but at least most pop-songs have lyrics with no message except the obvious joys of barnyard copulation, and the men who pull their puppets' strings are motivated by nothing more than honest avarice. The worst that most frenetic pop can do is to make children more hysterical than they are already. But the 'Protest' singers who strummed and wailed their woolly way through the 1960s purveyed a quack sociology and pretentious sentimentality which was enough to curdle the blood in a road-manager's alcohol-stream. That breed seems rarer now; drowned, maybe, under the waves of pallid imitators, who keened their homemade ditties recounting nebulous grievances to baffled audiences. One was tempted to quote Al Capp's description of pop-art, and apply it to 'pop-folk': 'A product of the untalented, sold by the unprincipled to the utterly bewildered.'

But even though some of us considered the pop industry to be the greatest 'con' since the South Sea Bubble, there was no doubt of its power and potential influence. When John Lennon described the Beatles as being more popular than Jesus he spoke no more than the truth. He did not say they *deserved* to be more popular, he simply said they *were*. Politicians were not slow to discover pop culture, either, and saw its possibilities as a means of 'keeping the proles happy', like the music in *1984*. Names of pop-groups could be used in speeches when you needed to show what a man-of-the-people you were. More ludicrous still, the latest styles of dancing and dressing were tried by people old enough to know better, a chilling and unseemly sight.

The principal contribution pop has made to society seems to be the provision of work for so many people. Managers, producers, agents (who can take as much as 25 per cent of a group's earnings), record companies, owners of recording studios (scores of them in London alone), costumiers, makers of electrical equipment, session musicians, and of course the marvellous recording engineers. And whatever the ethics of the whole business, one can only stand awestruck when contemplating a five-thousand-million-pound industry built almost entirely on rubbish. For a pleasantly dry-eyed and fair-minded survey of the pop world one cannot do better than read Michael Cable's excellent book: *The Pop Industry Inside Out* (W. H. Allen, 1977).

There was still enough work to keep the Mitchells well occupied in the mid-1960s, and one of the most enjoyable television shows we did was in a series called *Songs of the Times*, a programme of popular satirical songs of the early Victorian age. Charles Chilton and John Furness were the producers, and the only factor against us was the weather. The programme entailed a lot of dancing and running about, and on the July day when the recording was made the air being blown into the studio was even hotter than the air already there. At every point in the show where we could rest we flopped down on the floor behind the set, limp and dripping like victims of a typhoon.

We worked with Josh White again, and it was fascinating to compare Josh's brandy-roughened croak with Belafonte's silky tenor, two sides of the same sampler; one showing the elegant pattern, and the other showing all the knots and roughnesses of the work, but each man totally sincere in his own way.

Irving Berlin visited Britain, and some of us worked with him. George was intrigued by the fact that the great man played all tunes in the key of F sharp. Most composers who are not instrumentalists have a favourite key to illustrate their ideas to arrangers and orchestrators, but *F sharp*! Six sharps, with all those dangerously narrow black notes!

In 1965 Fame tossed me a bit of laurel that she'd found lying on the floor, in the shape of a recording of extracts from *The Gondoliers*, thanks to Mike Sammes, whose singers formed the cast. Mike and I sang the parts of the Duke and Duchess of Plaza Toro; no great voice was required, just fair diction and a modicum of humour. The orchestra had been pre-recorded, so we made our contribution wearing headphones, fitting our voices to the unseen conductor's beat. It was a most happy occasion, we were sustained with cups of good, strong Cockney-Italian tea made by the wife of the studio's owner, and I even got my name on the record sleeve next to that of Mary Thomas – no relation, alas – who sang the soprano part. Mary not only has a fresh and sweet voice, but she is a fine musician as well, much in demand for singing 'difficult' modern music. Some of the weirder works require her to dress the part too, and she once travelled to Boston, Massachusetts, to sing in Schoenberg's *Pierrot Lunaire*. When she arrived at the building housing the concert hall she was shown into her dressing-room, and began to dress for the concert. When she was ready she left her room, and once out in the corridor realised that she had no idea which direction to take to get to the hall. Somewhat alarmed, she hurried along dim blank passages, and finally getting really panicky she began opening any doors which seemed to have music coming out from behind them. None led to the *Pierrot Lunaire* stage, and the various ensembles – small choirs, string quartets, chamber orchestras – in each studio stared astonished at this wild-eyed, desperate figure dressed in the traditional floppy satin pierrot costume, with its red-white-and-black clown's make-up. Finally she found the hall and sank down into a chair to recover, while the waiting musicians mouthed 'Where've you *been*?' at her. That story is a great comfort to me, for it reassures me that I'm not the only one who gets totally lost and dismayed in large buildings.

'Lovely Replies' to my would-be non-musical efforts came regularly, but there were some small rewards. I took part in the radio version of *Call My Bluff*, and was auditioned for the television discussion programme *Three After Six*. It was good fun, and when the audition was over I caught sight of the producer's clip-board where she kept a list of the candidates for that day. Denis Norden once said that two of the essentials for success in the world of entertainment are the ability to yawn without actually opening your mouth, and the ability to read upside-down words on executives' note-pads. I haven't needed the first of those two skills, thank goodness, but, short-sighted as I am, I could see that against my name on the list was a long row of marks – crosses or stars, I couldn't decipher which. Whether this meant that I was better or worse than most of the other auditionees I don't know, and anyway it was purely academic, for the television company's 'lease' ran out just after that, and the programme never returned to the screen.

B.B.C. 2 had the reputation of being the more 'intellectual' of the channels, and a new game called *Crossword on Two* was devised, with two teams of three people trying to solve a giant lit-up puzzle. My two colleagues on the London team were Neil Stein and Chris Anderson, both MENSA members, and both celebrated crossword-solvers. My crossword solving is confined to occasionally finishing off other people's puzzles – which is sometimes merely a case of thinking of some new angle after the original solver has done all the really hard work, so I was there to supply the low cunning. The question-master-referee was the intelligent and urbane Derek Hart, and the puzzle-compiler was *The Times* crossword man, Mr Akenhead – which is as appropriate a name for a crossword-setter as I can think of. Mr Akenhead was a delightful man who wore a splendid tweed hat decorated with fishing-flies, and we loved his ingenious puzzles. Luck favoured the London team, and we were unbeaten for about eight games. Then another puzzle-compiler took over, and the clues Derek Hart had to read out got longer and longer, and more convoluted. In the end a three-letter word like 'Sue' was taking thirty seconds to define, and the game nearly halted completely. The viewers were as mystified as we were, and the game never returned. One heirloom from it was my lorgnette – I'm so near-sighted that I couldn't see the puzzle, and ordinary glasses were frowned upon in those days because of the shadows they cast on faces and their tendency to reflect the lights. So I got a 'dirty look on the end of a stick', which was useful, but my hand shook so much when the puzzle got unsolvable that it must have looked worse than glasses. I've kept the thing, though – it may become a useful prop when I'm old, for the sight of it certainly startles everyone, and I must look like a dowager in some remote colony, quelling rioting coolies with a glance.

As Eddie's health improved, so, a little, did our finances, and at last we felt we deserved a holiday. We could not afford a continental holiday, and I was secretly glad. Like the late Lord Redesdale I hate 'abroad'. No matter how beautiful the scenery, how delicious the food, how charming the people, I am suspicious of their drains, fearful of their tap-water and anxious about their plumbing. Another drawback is the Thomases' lack of what the Vikings used to call 'weather-luck'. I can remember an Italian holiday when rain fell like metal stair-rods for nine of our ten days. It began the instant we stepped off the aeroplane. The motorway round Naples was flooded, so our coach had to crawl through the city centre in a hooting, howling traffic-jam of cars, lorries, buses, carts and motorbikes, all driving on the pavements, apparently aiming straight at any pedestrians inquisitive enough to step outside their houses to see what all the extra noise was about. I wouldn't have missed that journey for the world, for during the interminable stops we could see into all those one-room shops in the back streets of Naples, each containing the family in earnest commercial conference round the table, with a naked fifteen-watt electric light bulb lending the scene – huge sideboard, knitting grandma and all – a green-tinged gothic gloom. It'll be a brave man whoever tries to organise the Italian people. Each of them is a potential one-man business. But what style they have. . . . I bought a modestly-priced scarf, and was prepared to take it as it was, but the ten-year-old tycoon who seemed to be in charge of the shop with his sister (at least a year older) dragged it back and insisted upon wrapping it in pretty paper. On our one fine day we decided to go into Naples to see the Botanical Gardens. Once out of the sleek new station the noise battered at our ear-drums. I added to it with my shrieks every time we tried to cross the street, feeling like the Egyptian army galloping through the two parted halves of a Red Sea of snarling Fiats waiting to mow us down. We realised how to survive when we noticed two ancient-faced children strolling unconcerned through the traffic. The secret is to pretend that you, too, are a vehicle, and show no alarm. While drivers think that you are made of metal they will not hit you for fear of scratching your paint, but nervous flesh and blood is fair game.

We got happily lost, in spite of profuse instructions from a heavily-armed policeman, and wandered through streets and alleys hung with washing and redolent of fish, a district like a set for a Vittorio De Sica film of the late 1940s. The one-man businesses appeared again; rows of card-tables displaying one nylon shirt, two cigarette-lighters, a pile of gramophone records and some mauve plastic washing-up bowls, each table with its pale-faced eleven-year-old entrepreneur in charge. Who buys it all, I wondered? And why weren't those children at school? Why are Neapolitans always having – or about to be having – local elections, judging by all those posters? When are they going to re-wire the place and do away with the festoons of electric cables draped along the outside of every house? No wonder all the light-bulbs are of such low wattage, maybe the wiring won't stand any more. Why don't they let the splendid Italian *women* run the country and keep the men as pets?

As a well-deserved punishment for all this stern Scandinavian musing the Botanical Gardens were closed.

But even up to that time whenever I heard that any of our friends were going abroad for a holiday I'd say with as much envy as I could feign: 'How lovely!' and think to myself 'Thank God we can't afford it!' for I am an obdurate, woad-dyed, raincoat-and-sunglasses-wearing Little Britainer. I find these islands enthralling, from Welsh valleys where the rows of terraced houses – obviously built by the mayor's brother-in-law – cling to the mountainside like a row of bad teeth in a beautiful face; to the chaste elegance of Edinburgh's New Town or the medieval glories of York or Salisbury. I love the sights the tourists flock to – Windsor, Stratford-upon-Avon – but the real enchantment of Britain for me lies in the faintly sinister atmosphere of places that you feel are best left alone, the bare hilltop darkening as clouds move across and turn the grey dolmens black, the smell of ancient graves and honeysuckle in the bat-haunted dusk of a Suffolk churchyard, even a curving tree-lined road in some mysterious, unfamiliar suburb.

For this holiday we went to Barmouth, the tiny resort jammed up against a mountain on the coast of Merionethshire. I'd buy Barmouth if I could, to keep it just as it was in the mid-1960s. No end-of-the-pier shows full of television stars working their catch-phrases to death, in fact not much organised commercial entertainment at all. The chief attraction seemed to be the local sheep-dog trials, but the high-spot for us was an amateur concert in the next parish. I hesitate to use the word 'amateur' for the Welsh are natural entertainers, and there wasn't an amateurish performance in the whole of that concert, from the blind clergyman who sang 'O Ruddier Than the Cherry', the violin-and-piano duet, the lady who recited a dramatic poem in Welsh (no need for a translation – you *knew* it was all about a storm at sea) to the tenor and baritone duet 'The Moon Hath Raised Her Lamp Above', and the 'siffleur', a rosy-faced lad who had to be a bit late because he had been helping his father with the harvest. He whistled to a record of the 'Tritsch-Tratsch Polka'. And of course a male-voice party who led us all in singing a closing hymn and '*Hen Wlad fy Nhadau*', 'Land of My Fathers'.

Replete with culture we reeled out into the fern-scented evening and ambled back to our hotel, past the tiny ancient church half buried in a sand-dune (there's an altar inside made of a single slab of dark stone with an inscription said to be fifth-century) and past the Olde Welsh Gift Shop with woolly dragons dangling in its darkened windows among the bowls of home-made fudge – a confection of such sinful richness that I'm convinced the old boatmen with brown faces and bright black eyes who chatter and chirrup to each other in Welsh down at the quay are not talking about taking tourists on fishing-trips, but arranging fudge-smuggling expeditions to alien lands like England and the Isle of Man, to spread moral and dental decay among the heathen '*Saes*', the Saxons.

We walked a lot in those days, so we enjoyed places, like Barmouth, where there's not much else to do. The Isles of Scilly, full of flowers and Arthurian sunsets, were perfect for pedestrians, or, if you were feeling really rakish, cyclists. We found a tiny guest-house where exquisite meals were served on china so fine that it deserved to be displayed in a glass-fronted cabinet, but Mr Fleet and his partner seemed to have confidence in their guests – a fine compliment. For cat-lovers the Scillies are a paradise. The local colours are mostly shades of ginger or tortoiseshell, and half-wild cats can live out of doors in the mild winters. You can be sitting among the warm heather eating your lunch under a Corsican-blue sky, and suddenly there'll be the thump of paws padding down the hillside and a great furry tortiseshell head will bury itself in your lunch-box. If you're very good the owner of the head will go to sleep on your lap as a mark of special favour.

One happy Easter we trudged all over the Gower peninsula, in those days full of violets, lambs, gorse and wild ponies, but I suppose by now covered with a bungaloid growth of scampi-pink brick with a caravan-park in every valley. Gower seemed to be full of mad Celtic signposts. 'To Cadiz Farm ¼ mile' . . . and farther along in that same direction: 'Cadiz Farm ½ mile'.

But, alas, Wales is becoming as unfit for pedestrians as everywhere else. There are few places where I've felt absolutely unmenaced by cars. One is the almost vertical flight of stone steps leading down a head-spinning Pembrokeshire cliff to St Govan's (Sir Gawain's?) Cell . . . you certainly had to be a fit man to be a saint in those times. And the other is on the clifftop Turf Walk from Freshwater to Alum Bay on the lovely Isle of Wight. That island seems a microcosm of Britain, with little mountains, little moors, little ports, little towns and a little palace, the charming and homely Osborne House. If I were the Queen I'd live there.

As Eddie improved it was as if the sun was coming out through grey winter clouds, and on one memorable day he was told that he need not visit the hospital again for progress reports. We were delighted at this proof of his victory over what had been such a formidable adversary, and we went for a celebratory trip to one of our favourite places, Richmond on Thames. As we walked along the towpath we saw a neatly-painted placard advertising trips to Teddington lock; and on an impulse we went aboard one of the smaller boats. Some days, for no very clear reason, stay in the mind for ever, and this is one of them. It was a quiet and totally unremarkable journey, we chugged softly along past Marble Hill Park and Eel Pie Island, with the sun warming the varnished wooden benches and sparkling on the brass fittings. The smell of engine oil mingled with the scent of the boatman's pipe-tobacco and his plump black Labrador dog lolled on the deck, panting sleepily. Ice-white swans floated disdainfully by, frowning at their reflection in dark green water, and rotting houseboats and tiny ram-shackle bungalows with fretwork verandahs peeped through the drifting green willows, abandoned stage-sets for some 1920s comedy. We turned for home as the light faded, with a transparent half-moon in the sky. 'Sweet Thames' indeed. I hope the Styx will be like that.

CHAPTER TEN

Allegro con brio

A FEW WEEKS after I came back from Australia I had been asked to take part in a radio quiz-series played between teams from London, Melbourne, and Wellington, New Zealand, called *World Quiz '67*. My partner on the London team was Ian Gillies, who had been a 'Brain of Britain', a 'Brain of Brains', *and* a 'Top Brain' which is the title won when 'Brains of Brains' play each other every nine years! The Australian and New Zealand teams had to get to their studios at nine a.m., while we lucky Poms could have our supper and then go to our studio at eight p.m. It always seemed to me to be a fearsome technical feat to link us all up at the right time, and we got to know the voices of the Australian and New Zealand producers and engineers almost as well as our own studio managers. The producer in London was Joan Clark, who had been in charge of *What Do You Know?* (before it became *Brain of Britain*) for years. Joan is a small, elegant, French-looking lady, absolutely unflappable, an essential quality in a round-the-world producer. The question-master was the late, beloved Kenneth Horne, just as popular with Australian and New Zealand audiences as he was at home in programmes like *Round the Horne*. Ken was that rare type, a natural personality, with a 'board-of-directors' voice, and, in *Round the Horne*, a kind of rock-like sanity impervious to the lunatic antics of the rest of the cast of that greatest of all the 'how do they get away with it?' radio comedies. He was a thoroughly nice man, too, always on the look-out for comic schoolboy wheezes like tricksy arithmetical riddles and word-puzzles. The series was very popular with the overseas audience, especially in New Zealand, for their team always won. We in Britain said that it was due to a kind of intellectual fluoride that the New Zealand government were putting in the water, but the truth was we knew when we were licked. Barry Jones, still the Australian television quiz-champion, was on the Australian team, partnered by Stephen Murray-Smith. It was very much a quiz of the strict 'question-and-answer' type, with not much chance for digression, but there was a good deal of teasing between the Australian and New Zealand teams, with Barry making quips like 'I went to Auckland once, but it was closed.' It was a most happy series, and I was delighted when I was asked to write a short paragraph about it for the New Zealand *Television Times*. I took the view that the New Zealand team was not two people, Jim Winchester and Ralph Dearnley, but one single creature, the 'Jimmanralph', that the New Zealanders were secretly rearing somewhere in the mountains of South Island, all ready for a world take-over. That's what it felt like as we ended each game well crushed.

One day in November 1967 I got the telephone call I had dreamed of for the past seven years. It was from Patrick Harvey, the producer of *Round Britain Quiz*. Cedric Cliffe, one of the London team, an eminent music critic, had fallen ill. Would I like to stand in for him? I felt as though I were living in some fairy-tale – the one where you are given gold coins which may turn out to be leaves when you wake up. But the coins were gold. It was true; and on 9 November I arrived – much too early – at Broadcasting House, sick with apprehension, and worried that I would not measure up to the intellectual standard of my partner, Sir Denis Brogan. Our first meeting was a shock to us both. He hadn't been told that his new partner was to be female, but he took the sight of me like a trouper. On my part the shock was the splendid hat he was wearing. Not only had I never seen a real live human being wearing a deerstalker, but this deerstalker was being worn with the earflaps *untied* and hanging down like the ears of a green tweed spaniel.

We settled into the studio, where there was a tray of sandwiches, coffee and claret. I was the only one who drank the coffee. After a few anxious minutes of difficult conversation I discovered that Denis Brogan knew extraordinary things like the *verse* of 'Mountain Greenery' – that was quite apart from being one of the world's great experts in French and American history and literature. From that moment on we were a team. I dreaded the first question, but when it came it was about fifteen gentlemen in black and a Russian Prince – a reference to Prince Obolensky's famous try against the All Blacks. I thanked the gods for all the times I'd heard Eddie talk about Rugby, even though I'd only understood half of his remarks. The rest of the two games we played that day was great fun, and I was booked for four more in the series. In those days the question-masters were the gentle and charming Lionel Hale, and Roy Plomley – *Desert-Island-Discs* Plomley. He is one of those broadcasters who are a godsend to nervous newcomers; efficient, kindly and a mine of information himself – absolutely vital for a *Round Britain Quiz* question-master. He wore a striking thick-woven woollen tie, bought in Leeds, he said. The whole company was full of such sartorial quirks, from Denis's imposing hat to the waistcoat of one of the visiting professors, who had perfected the dangerous art of smoking a cigarette until the ash was inches long, and even those who had seen it all before waited agog for the grey cylinder to droop and fall.

When the game was over the professors had arranged to lunch at their club, where I could not be admitted – no women allowed – but the next day when we played two more games we all had lunch together in an ordinary restaurant. This made me very happy; at least I had been accepted not only as a player but as a person. After two more games in March the next year, this time partnering Barry Carman when Denis Brogan was in America, the series came to an end. The programme had been running for many years, and apparently it had been decided to give it a rest. I had taken part in some of the last games. Naturally I was downcast, but at least I could say that I had achieved my ambition.

Later in 1968 *Woman's Hour* asked me to do several three-minute pieces, on various themes. I loved doing those, and I had the chance to use a light-hearted style which the listeners seemed to like. There was a weekly 'View of the Week' spot, too, commenting on the crazier aspects of the past week's news. I contributed to the series they called 'My Favourite Novelist'. Choosing is difficult in these circumstances – it's a matter of picking an author nobody else had yet thought of. I chose J. B. Priestley, who is one of them – a kind of twentieth-century Dickens (or was Dickens a nineteenth-century Priestley?). After that item I was actually noticed by a radio critic, one Gavin Millar, in *The Listener*. 'Cosy' was the word he used to describe my attitude to Priestley – and maybe he included Priestley in that description too. A bed-of-nails' approach would have pleased him better, and 'cosy' was as dirty a word as he could think of. I wrote a sharp note in reply, and to my surprise and delight *The Listener* printed it. If only I could have neard the first cuckoo, I thought, groggy with success, then I could try writing to *The Times*.

In November I wrote something for *Woman's Hour* that I had been wanting to do for years, a Remembrance Day collection of glimpses of my schooldays, with sketches of the small boys who had grown into young men killed in the war, and some of the poems that seemed to fit; some Housman; 'Into my heart an air that kills . . .' and 'Here dead we lie . . .'; and some of those haunting First World War poems like Robert Nichols' 'For the last time maybe upon the knoll I stand' and Wilfrid Gibson's 'We who are left . . .' My usual style was light and fanciful, and this item was very different, even though I tried to make it as unsentimental as possible. I got some letters afterwards which made me feel that I had succeeded, and that particular piece remains in my mind as one I'm most proud of. Radio is ephemeral – once the word is spoken it has gone for ever. A magazine or newspaper article can be kept and re-read, but the air is transparent and reflects nothing but present sights and sounds. So I've nothing left of that item except the script and the appreciative letters.

B.B.C. producers' attitudes towards letters from listeners vary wildly. Some show you everything that comes, good or bad. Some keep the bad – and mad! – ones from you, and show you only the favourable comments. Some show you nothing, and let the rather bleak-sounding Programme Correspondence Unit deal with everything. I dislike that procedure very much. If a listener writes to me, or even simply to the programme, I want to read what he or she has written, and send a suitable reply myself, no matter how long it takes to get through the mail. It is kind and thoughtful of listeners and viewers to take the trouble to write when they've heard or seen a programme that they want to comment on, and they deserve courteous and considered replies. Not only does it make them feel that there is really some contact between the broadcasters and themselves, but their comments are valuable – and sometimes chastening! – to people whose sole aim should be to interest and entertain the public. Sometimes the writer merely needs information – or perhaps a correction . . . there can be a considerable difference between what listeners heard and what they *thought* they'd heard!

In the spring of 1969 our cat Twm fell ill, so ill that the vet said it would be more merciful to end his suffering. Twm had been with us for fifteen years, through good days and bad, and many's the time I had cried into his soft fur in moments of despair, or told him of small triumphs until his green eyes blinked slowly in the way cats' eyes do when they smile. Many years later I still miss his benign furry face and wilful ways, for like Mark Twain I wish people were more like cats, elegant, clean and polite – even if they cannot be as beautiful. I find that one's friends can be divided into cat-people and dog-people, utterly different from each other. Not better, or worse, just different.

Later that year there was another of the yearly series of *World Quiz*, but Kenneth Horne had died a few months before and even though the question-master's chair was taken over by the excellent John Tidmarsh, Ken had been such an essential part of the programme for so long that John had a really thankless task. In any case, the series ended that year, as it seemed to be a highly expensive half-hour and the B.B.C. was, like every other organisation professed to be doing, making economies.

There were still plenty of pleasant jobs coming my way, though. I met and interviewed one of my favourite authors, Laurie *Cider with Rosie* Lee, and took part in a programme called *Conversations Off the Record* in Birmingham. It was a civilised idea; you tried to identify various recorded voices – politicians, actors, people in the news – and then talked about what their voices or views called to mind. One of the other contributors was René Cutforth, journalist, war correspondent and broadcaster, who combines a vast and kaleidoscopic experience with laconic good sense. After the broadcast we sat together in the hotel lounge and talked. I listened enthralled to his grim and hilarious tales of the time he had spent in a prisoner-of-war camp; and learned about his great mistake in trying to wash a sturdy pair of woollen combinations in the interests of hygiene. They washed well, but nothing would get them to dry, so the Cutforth limbs had to be protected from the intense cold with several thicknesses of newspaper. He had tried many different journals, but the most effective was the *Corriere della Sera* – nothing like it for keeping out the draughts.

Armed with knowledge like that, even a trip up to Manchester to take part in *A Word in Edgeways* seemed less frightening. Cockneys are always scared to go north. It's a well-known fact that Picts begin at Watford. The journey was the result of one of my many letter-writing efforts, but even though the programme was rather less full of social significance than it is now I was still too much of a lightweight for it. One consolation was a meeting with that engaging character Brian Redhead, surely one of the brightest minds in radio. His round, cheerful face was without the 'Newgate fringe' it wears to-day, so he looked about eleven. With it he looks at least twelve. Brian is one of those people you can meet once every seven years and it'll feel like last week, but his affable manner hides an iron professionalism. A 'cat-man' too, what more do we need? He was also question-master on a jaunty television panel-game called *Not a Word* where each player supplied a letter to a word but tried to avoid completing one. The other players on my team were the actor-writer John Junkin and Sir John Betjeman, and we fought gamely on to words like 'Garblowy' which Sir John said sounded like some Welsh hamlet – or did he mean Hamlet? The series never returned, I think because word-games were rather unfashionable at that time – it was the end of the so-called swinging sixties. Maybe it should be tried again some day, now that literacy threatens to break out all over the place.

At the beginning of August 1970 my mother's health began to fail quite quickly. She was eighty-four by then, and up to that summer she had been very bright and interested in everything although physically rather frail. Now she began to tire very easily, and she stayed in bed until afternoon, which was not normal for her. One day our doctor came to see her, and she recognised him, but soon forgot that he had been, and became drowsy during the next few hours. As I made her comfortable for the night she said, 'Did someone call today?' 'Yes,' I said, 'the doctor came just to see that you were all right.' 'Oh yes,' she said, 'I think I shall be all right now.' I left a dim light beside her bed, and as I bade her goodnight she smiled at me and said: 'God bless you.' It was somehow saddening to hear her say the words so seriously, and yet smiling. She closed her eyes and I went downstairs. As I went to bed about half-past one in the morning I looked into her room. She was sleeping quietly, and she seemed warm and comfortable. At about six o'clock I went to look at her again. It was light by then, so I drew back the curtains and switched off the bedside lamp. She was lying in precisely the same position as she had been in when I saw her last, but she was dead. I knew it seconds before I took her hand, icy cold on the bright August morning.

After her funeral I had time to think of how conscientious and practical a mother she had been. When I was a young girl I felt she had understood me better than my father did at the same time, and she was always ready to laugh and sing and chatter. As time goes on I remember her even more clearly, particularly her slim, elegant good looks, her fastidiousness and her great talent as a needlewoman. I sometimes come across articles she made, or mended, and marvel at the tiny, neat stitches and the care and skill she always used for the most mundane repairs, to pillowcases, for instance, or to the neatly-darned finger-tip of a cotton glove. She had a habit – which she taught me – of keeping soap amongst handkerchiefs and linen and underwear, and whenever I was doubtful about a present for her I knew that a deliciously-scented soap would delight her. I got a cheque-book cover for her once, just an ordinary plastic thing from the bank, and she kept it in her handkerchief-drawer. I use it now for my own cheque book, and there is something about it that puzzles me. Even though it was not near any scented soap when I found it, and many years have gone by since her death, it still carried a faint scent of carnations, one of her favourite flowers.

By this time Eddie was looking forward to taking advantage of the early retirement scheme available to teachers. He'd once said that he envied the lollipop-men who guided children across roads . . . 'they don't *start* working until they are sixty-five.' We wondered whether to stay in London or move to Wales. We'd often dreamed of owning a small stone cottage in the country – hasn't everybody? So we put an advertisement in several Welsh papers to see if there'd be any response. Half Wales, it seemed, had cottages to sell, so we made a list and I went down to look at them. I chose one, a tiny grey-stone one-storey shack about six miles outside Carmarthen, set in lovely rolling hills. No transport nearby, so we'd have to buy a car – we hadn't owned one since Eddie came out of hospital nearly ten years before. But living would surely be cheaper in Wales, even after we had paid for the repairs and alterations to the cottage. We even began to negotiate another quarter-acre of land from an amiable neighbouring farmer. But months went by, and nobody in Wales seemed keen to start our re-building, and as time went on we wondered if it was such a good idea after all. We were not used to the country, we were not young, and the farmer had warned us that the hillside was bleak and cold in winter. But the oriental-style Welsh procrastination seemed to have been designed by fate, as it happened. I was still hoping that *Round Britain Quiz*, or something like it, would return, although the outlook seemed bleak. Patrick Harvey had retired by then, so I wrote to Anthony Whitby, Controller of Radio 4, to ask if there was any likelihood of another series. He wrote to say that he thought it wasn't the right time to bring the programme back, which is a polite B.B.C. way of saying that there's practically no chance at all.

'Lovely replies' of all kinds were fairly frequent, and I began to think that nothing exciting would ever come my way again. Never believe this. One of my friends said to herself on her fiftieth birthday 'Is this all there is, then?' and three months later she was on a world tour with a musical show. In the world of entertainment you are never sure that there'll be no more work for you. You're never sure there *will* be any more either, but it's hope that keeps actors living, never fully committing themselves to any other work they may do for a basic income, like running a boarding-house, or keeping a shop. This may explain why there seem to be so many half-hearted shopkeepers.

1970 was the eight-hundredth anniversary of the murder of Thomas à Becket, and the city of Canterbury had arranged for a special production of T. S. Eliot's *Murder in the Cathedral* in the cathedral itself – but without a real murder. *Woman's Hour* asked me to help with a radio portrait of the city at this time so Anne Howells, the producer, and I went down to make some recordings in the city and the cathedral. Years before, Anne had been the production assistant who auditioned me for *What Do You Know?*, and I had often worked for her on *Woman's Hour* since. We got very good interviews with schoolchildren and citizens of Canterbury, and some of the organisers of the centenary celebrations. We were taken on a fascinating tour of the cathedral itself, and we looked forward to the performance of the play in the evening.

The cathedral lies down among Canterbury's narrow streets like some great golden lion, a building as much French as English, designed by a French architect – William of Sens (who fell off some scaffolding, poor chap, and had to pass the work on to William the Englishman) – built of Norman stone; with a weekly service in French, a place once equal to Rome and Jerusalem as a magnet for pilgrims. In 1170 the interior would have been unlike the pale, elegant, peach-coloured forest of stone that so impresses visitors to-day. The arches at that time were the brutally massive round-topped kind, and the ceilings much lower and brilliantly painted and gilded. But enough of the atmosphere of the murky December afternoon in 1170 remained. We could imagine the four assassins and their followers, all rather drunk, stamping and shouting in and out of the cathedral precinct all that day, with Becket shouting back at them. Becket was certainly no tender-hearted philanthropist, and to me he seems a rather unlikeable man, a business tycoon, single-minded and inflexible. I don't suppose anyone ever called him Tom.

Sitting in front of us at the performance of the play were about twenty small boys from King's School, Canterbury. They were a grand advertisement for the school. There aren't a lot of laughs in *Murder in the Cathedral*, and sitting silent during the play must have been almost unendurable, but they uttered no sound, even when they fidgeted desperately on the hard chairs. As the four knights clanked and hollered up the aisle through the audience (it was that kind of production) Anne and I nearly lost an ear each, removed by somebody's sword as he swept by. In the confusion Anne dropped her briefcase through the scaffolding supporting our seats, and this proved a godsend to the young gentlemen of King's School. Like small grey-flannelled monkeys they swung noiselessly down through the bars and retrieved the case, handing it up with a flourish and a grin, then subsided back to silent twitching through the play, which unfolded with all dialogue sounding, thanks to the architects' and builders' grand disregard for acoustics, like the noise made by someone yelling in Japanese with his head in a zinc bucket. The lady who played the chorus leader (it's one of those plays where choruses speak in unison) declaimed her part valiantly, but looked a dead ringer for Senna, the lady soothsayer in *Up Pompeii*. A fine and worthy effort, but almost entirely inaudible from where we sat. Nobody's fault, maybe just old William of Sens getting his own back. God knows what foreign tourists made of it all. I wanted to call the whole item: 'Uncle Tom's Stabbin', but was very properly thwarted.

Our hoped-for alterations to our Welsh cottage showed absolutely no signs of being started. It would have been very difficult to keep an eye on the work anyway, hundreds of miles away as we were, so reluctantly we sold it. It took just a week – there's a moral there somewhere. Cancerian instinct must have been at work, for during the events of the next few years it would be essential to live in or near London, but in the early 1970s there seemed no prospect of any interesting jobs coming my way. I used to read glowing accounts of how women were being encouraged more and more in broadcasting, and how sundry young ladies had 'decided to work for the B.B.C.' These manifestos filled me with admiration, for I remembered Woodrow Wyatt's clear-eyed remark: 'It's not *doing* these jobs that's difficult, it's *getting* them.'

There was always plenty to do at home though. I don't know how anyone who owns a house and a small garden can ever be bored. I'm not a 'domestic' woman, but I can always find something worth doing at home, from really fascinating jobs like gardening – a truly marvellous therapy for any brain-worker; it induces a kind of happy stupor, diminishes big worries and obliterates small ones – to more monotonous tasks like cleaning out cupboards or sorting house-linen. Those jobs can be done while you're listening to the radio, anyway. And if you are one of those gifted women who can embroider, or make toys, or cook well, or do carpentry or painting (pictures or rooms) there's no end to the time you can spend and the nice things you can make for yourself or other people. Even if you think you have no talents at all, which I don't believe – everyone has at least *one* – the most precious gift you can give other people is time. Time to listen to them, time to visit them and hear their news, time to write to them, time to talk with them, particularly with old people and children. Even if you have little or no money to spare there can be hours and hours of discovery in your own suburb. (I make absolutely no apologies for using that word, I can't understand why we have to feel squeamish about living in a suburb – most people *do* live in one anyway, and suburbs can be very pleasant places. Just *how* pleasant is up to the inhabitants.) We have a house near us which was once the home of William Hogarth. It's quite small, a large three-storey cottage really. Thanks to those new Olympians, the Planners, it now lies directly beside the A 316, with only a single very high wall shielding it from the worst of the twentieth century. Once inside the gate in the wall the screaming and roaring of the traffic coming from the Hogarth Roundabout is muffled to a throbbing hum, and the extraordinary atmosphere of the place, benign and wholesome, seeps into your mind. There can be few other places in the country that have this strange soothing effect on visitors; the time of year makes no difference, the place is as enchanting on a murky November day as it is in spring. One sleepy afternoon in August Eddie and I took Valerie (the other Speechless Handmaiden from the Covent Garden days) and her husband George to see the house. George is an artist – a calligrapher, to be exact – and was naturally interested in the house and its pictures and prints. But it was the small garden that was the setting for a tableau I remember so clearly. In the middle of the lawn stands a great mulberry tree, *morus niger* – the black mulberry. At that time of year the fruits are ripe and ready to fall, like great purplish-black loganberries, plopping down on the grass from a great height like so many tiny suicides. We had never seen mulberries before, let alone tasted them, so we asked the lady in charge if we were allowed to eat some. 'Yes' she said, 'if you like . . . there's a ladder there if you want to go up the tree, as long as you don't want *me* to climb it!' She was a rosy, comely woman; if she had worn early eighteenth-century clothes she would have looked like one of Hogarth's own portraits of his friends and servants. George climbed half-way up the ladder and picked mulberries for us. They had a mysterious smoky flavour, and if I ever taste them again, wherever I am there will be Hogarth's garden, and the great tree, and George handing down the mulberries; and the warmth and good fellowship of an hour that can never come again.

Among the small advertisements in the evening paper one day I noticed that Anglia Television were asking for people to apply to take part in a new game called *Sale of the Century*. It sounded as though it was something to do with antiques (it must have been the word century that gave me that idea) so I thought I'd try for it. I know practically nothing about antiques, but when did ignorance ever stop a fortune-hunter? 'Lovely replies' were still bringing me no good tidings from B.B.C. producers. The game turned out to be a more or less straight-foward quiz, played between three contestants at a time, with really sumptuous prizes for which points could either be 'spent' as the game proceeded, or 'saved up' until the end. I'd never taken part in a commercial quiz before, all my rewards had been books, book tokens, or just plain fees, except for *Criss-Cross Quiz*. This new one was obviously going to be highly competitive – not a bit like the quizzes where you ask somebody 'What vegetable reminds you of a European capital?' hoping for the reply 'Brussels Sprouts' and they say 'French beans' . . . and get the money. The producers were impecc-ably fair, and tried meticulously to match the three players for level chances. I was auditioned with two people who were every bit as bright as I was, but unluckier with their answer-buzzers – which are vital in a commercial quiz so that the question-master and the audience can see who is ready to answer first. As we left the audition room – the drawing-room of a delightful but lifelessly decorated house in Pimlico – I felt I had to, as it were, confess former sins, so I told the two girls who conducted the audition that I was a former 'Brain of Britain'. 'How long ago?' they asked, and when I told them they seemed to think it was too long ago to disqualify me from this game, and said they would tell the producer anyway. (After the game was over he seemed to know nothing about it, until someone wrote to tell him because they considered it was unfair. I think that's like saying that any athlete who has won an Olympic gold medal should never be allowed to compete in a race where there are money prizes to be won, but at least I hadn't tried to deceive anyone.) The game was certainly not easy, and the opposition from my two fellow-contestants was formidable. It was only by being just one-tenth of a second faster on the buzzer some of the time that I managed to win prizes which were probably worth more than I'd ever earned in a whole year. Usually there is a choice of big prizes, and I was in the bewilderingly happy position of having to turn down a car, or a smart sailing-dinghy if I wanted a diamond brooch and a fitted kitchen. The most amazing aspect of the whole game was the attitude of the audience. You'd think they'd be pea-green with envy at seeing somebody else winning such valuable things, but not so. They seem actually to *enjoy* watching other people winning, and I've noticed this in other programmes where there are prizes to be won. In *The Generation Game* where the victor has to remember as many prize-items as he can in a few seconds, the audience shouts out the ones he may have forgotten. All the people who worked in Anglia studios were delightful; maybe that was due to the fact that they live and work in what must be one of the most beautiful cities in Europe, Norwich, where there are whole streets which look as they must have done in the fifteenth century, only cleaner, and where rows of old shops smile at each other across pedestrianised streets, making shopping a civilised experience. Norwich is one of those places with an ancient reason for existence, and such towns are always pleasant, particularly when they have a fine cathedral too. Chester, Salisbury, Norwich, Worcester . . . all the right size for human beings to live in, all with a centre of their own, and existing as a centre for the surrounding countryside with its smaller towns. Look at a map of East Anglia, Norwich appears like a fixed star, with roads radiating from it like beams flashing out to the bleak Norfolk coast. Citizens of Norwich tend to longevity. On one of the great pillars in the cathedral is a verse-epitaph to one Osberto Parsley, a member of the cathedral choir in the days of Elizabeth the First . . .

Here lies the Man whose name in spight of Death,
Renownèd lives by Blast of Golden Fame
. . . . who here a Singing-Man did spend his Days,
Full Fifty Years in our Church Melody.

This artless panegyric was, so unkind people say, composed by Mr Parsley himself. I don't want to believe it.

Even the two glamorous girls who acted as hostesses on the programme were the best of their kind, and both deliciously pretty. Jennifer and Carol – I wonder how their careers prospered, for that kind of work is not easy to get into or out of, you are half-way between being an actress and being a model.

Mention the name Nicholas Parsons, *Sale of the Century's* question-master, in some circles and you'll see some elements go beetroot-faced; and bare their teeth. Being well-dressed, well-bred and efficient seems such a crime in their eyes that they completely forget the cool professional nerve that's needed for *Sale of the Century*. They also forget that Nicholas Parsons acted as straight man to Arthur Haynes's disreputable wide-boy tramp for years, and being a 'comedian's labourer' is never as easy as it may seem. Nicholas reminded me a bit of Bob Dyer, the arch-professional host of the *Pick-a-Box* quiz, although his style is different. Ask either of them to fill in an extra ninety seconds and they'll do it, or *cut* ninety seconds for that matter, but Nicholas would know the answers to most of the questions that could turn up in the quiz, while Bob would cheerfully admit that he might not. The only perplexing incident during my visit was when I dashed into the offices of the Norwich Union Insurance organisation to try to insure my brooch on the way home to its lodging in the bank. Without some formalities, for which there was no time, they couldn't do it at such short notice.

In the foyer of Anglia Television studios in Norwich there stands the original Silver Knight which is the company's emblem, and every time I see him on the television screen I remember the happy excitement of that quiz. Maybe the stars were favourably aspected, I thought, so I'd take advantage of their favour, and write yet another letter to Anthony Whitby, asking if he had any more thoughts about a possible return of *Round Britain Quiz*. His reply not only brought me the greatest of pleasure by saying that another series might indeed be imminent, but acknowledged that my letter of the previous year had partly been the cause of his further thought about the programme. This kind of recognition that a reminder had come from outside the B.B.C. is almost unheard of among senior executives, and the tone of the rest of his letter was equally kindly. The probable producer chosen for the series was now to be Trevor Hill, a senior producer then acting as Network Editor (Radio) in Manchester, and Anthony Whitby added: 'I will make sure that the change of producers has not led to your name being forgotten.' This, too, showed great consideration towards a minor broadcaster like me, but I learned later that he had been amused by my previous letters, and if they made him smile I am thankful; for although few people knew it, least of all me, he was mortally ill at the time. Apparently, throughout his long illness he behaved with a sweet and stoic serenity which matched the courteous manner of his letter, and although we never met, I keep that note – with the name 'Whitby' in the signature falling downwards as though the writer were very tired – to remind me of the man who called forth so much admiration and affection from so many people.

The pilot games for the proposed new series were held in Broadcasting House, on the revered Third Floor – 'where the young star-captains glow', where carpets are thick and windows are double-glazed. I know they are double-glazed because, being too early, as always, I was shown into an empty conference-room to wait. I went to the window, and as I tried to see down into the street below, thumped my head smartly on the crystal-clean glass. Thus I went to meet my future colleagues with a truly egg-shaped head.

The room seemed full of huge men, all talking as though they knew each other well. One of the most elegantly-dressed of them came over to meet me and said 'I'm Trevor Hill.' I knew immediately that he was the sort of man I could have told about thumping my head on the double-glazing and he would have laughed, but sympathetically. There wasn't time for that, though, because a large, handsome man came over and Trevor said 'This is Anthony Quinton.' Tony was to be the London question-master, and I've watched him greeting many other people since that night. He excels in the delicate art of ensuring that newcomers are happy; he talks to them amusingly, and, even more important, he listens. More important still, he remembers. He must be one of the most distinguished academics in the country, but he can also reduce us to helpless laughter with his astonishing vocabulary which never lets him down. I listen to him amazed, and think 'He'll never get out of this sentence', but he always does, and with a fine sense of the ridiculous. From the moment we met we have had a kind of understanding, rather like that between the lion resting in the shade and the sparrow tweeting and hopping round his lair. This is because we both laugh at dreadful old jokes like 'J'y suis, j'y reste' which he swears means: 'I'm Swiss, and I'm staying the night.' (And 'Chateaubriand,' as everyone knows, means 'Your hat's on fire.') During idle moments between recordings we throw names of old musical ensembles back and forth to each other like tennis-balls: 'The Gershom-Parkington Quintet' . . . 'Fred Hartley and his Novelty Sextet' . . . 'Mantovani and his Tipica Orchestra' . . . 'The Big Ben Banjo Band' . . . 'Troise and his Mandoliers', until one of us is 'out'.

All good, crazy stuff, and show me another President of Trinity College, Oxford, and Fellow of All Souls, who could do it with such glee and expertise.

After some thought and a few trial-runs with various other eminent players my London-team partner was chosen, the brilliant and kindly Professor John Barron Mays. John is a highly-respected sociologist whose writings are text-books for other professors, and he has a great gift for making beautiful poetry of an unusually haunting and melancholy kind.

The question-master for the visitors' teams from the various regions was Sir 'Jack' Longland, one of the few men entitled to wear a 'Mount Everest' tie, and perhaps the best-known broadcaster of us all at that time.

For people who may be puzzled, perhaps I should explain that the game is played between the London team and teams from all the different regions of the British Isles and the Republic of Ireland, one each week. It really doesn't matter who wins or loses, although we do keep a scoreboard for those listeners – and players – who care about such things as marks. Three marks can be earned for a full answer; less than three if many clues are given by the question-masters. The question-masters have to be even more cunning than the players; they must know whether you are thinking on the right lines even before you really know it yourself.

Sometimes questions are sent in by listeners, sometimes devised by the question-masters, but whoever thinks them up they are all the finest examples of the devilish ingenuity of the educated human mind. The ones we use nowadays are perhaps not as 'literary' as those in the old *Round Britain Quiz*, and rather more topical, but they are every bit as tortuous and difficult to unravel. The game so enthralls me that I find myself listening to the questions aimed at the opposing team and trying to solve theirs, too. At first hearing some of these questions sound totally incomprehensible. What can you make of: 'The Scots have them in threes, the Irish in fours, and the Welsh in fives. What are they – and who has them singly?' Most old soldiers among our listeners would know that the question refers to the way buttons are grouped on guardsmen's tunics, and it's the Grenadier Guards whose buttons are in 'single file'. Another question asked us to say how St Andrew, through the name of a Russian musician, might worry St Francis and St Ferdinand. This one, taken to pieces, was a reference to the San Andreas Fault, which could cause earthquakes in San

Francisco and the San Fernando Valley – earthquakes being measured on the Richter Scale, and Richter being the name of a famous Russian pianist. (The word 'musician' in the question warns you off *composers'* names, if you are wary enough.) Our question-master for the regional teams nowadays is Gordon Clough, journalist, broadcaster and former head of the B.B.C.'s Russian section. Gordon is in the great tradition of *Round Britain Quiz* question-masters, and besides being academically brilliant he has one of the most beautiful voices in radio. Like Tony Quinton he has the cat-like sense of which way other people's minds are going to jump, and the ability to steer them towards the answer without helping too much.

We played a series of games with an American team, and then, after our fifth British series, we played another tournament with teams from France, Spain, Germany, Poland, Austria, Italy, Denmark and Switzerland. All the games were played in English, and the visiting teams' English was so shamingly good that we had to ask some of them to adopt a slight accent, otherwise our listeners would never have believed that they were foreigners. In the interests of fair play the questions for the British team were even more difficult than for the European teams, and all had a reference to whichever country we were playing at the time. My partner for *Round Europe Quiz* was Lord Norwich – John Julius Norwich, scholar, historian, traveller, writer, broadcaster, diplomat . . . and bass E-flat bombardon-player . . . which he threatens to demonstrate one day if we are not careful. John Julius, like Tony Quinton, combines scholarship with wit, and takes delight in tiny treasures like the little verse that Queen Alexandra – an enthusiastic amateur poetess – wrote to attach to a wreath she sent to the funeral of one of her ladies-in-waiting who had been blessed with a pleasant talent for sculpture. The verse on the card read:

'For dear "Feo" Gleichen –
Who was always so dear to our heart –
Oh, how we shall miss her
Nor her wonderful works of art.'
Alexandra.

Somehow it's the 'Nor' that is so touching, and John Julius tells the tale with becoming gravity. He excels in the collection of gems such as the fact that 'No cycling in the park' in Dutch sounds like: 'Nit twit tweedlies in de bush.'

This whole pot-pourri of professors, lawyers, journalists, lords, clergymen and scholars is managed and controlled by Trevor Hill, with a level-headed coolness seldom met with in broadcasting. The mere mechanics of getting us in the right place at the right time with the right sort and number of questions are difficult enough, and the setting-up of the European quiz must have been a hair-whitening business. Trevor remains calm in the most trying circumstances, rather like one of the war-time 'Two types' characters in 'Jon's' cartoons. He has great technical experience too, and this, combined with his own wide general knowledge, makes the programme run smoothly always. He is extremely kind, has a marvellous and hilarious talent for vocal mimicry, and is much tougher than he appears to be – a vital quality when you are dealing with so many high-octane characters all at once.

One part of the programme which is never heard by listeners is the talk during the dinner before the recordings. I call it a part of the programme because it can help create a relaxed and informal atmosphere which will contribute warmth to the game and give it the friendly and un-pedantic air that pleases our listeners. I often wish that preliminary mealtime conversation could be recorded – it would make a fine quirky programme in itself, full of jokes, bizarre, ancient or scholarly, according to who is telling them, and with all the normal aspects of our everyday lives, families, holidays, pets, gardening, theatre-going, enlivened and coloured by our individual styles of speech. But when microphones appear, so often does constraint – or affectation, which is worse, and concealed microphones are unethical and probably illegal too. Only among very unsophisticated or very conceited people is complete naturalness before a microphone possible, and the number of unsophisticated people diminishes daily.

CHAPTER ELEVEN

Allargando

THERE SEEMED to be a ready-made audience of listeners who were waiting for the resurgence of *Round Britain Quiz*. From our first few programmes letters poured in to the production office with comments, praise, blame, enquiries – and scores of possible questions for the game. The most baffling of these forgot to include the answers, and so the sources of the question could not be checked. Our listening public has never been analysed, but it would be an interesting exercise. We get letters from actors, academics, clergymen, children, and there seems no upper or lower age-limit. Whenever we get a question from somebody whose age is given as 'twelve' or 'thirteen' my hair stands on end, for I can imagine the lad at the other end, sitting grinning by his radio, waiting gleefully for us to fall flat on our faces. One delightful old lady is such a devotee that she listens to the 'repeat' as well. For my part I am completely happy during our recording sessions, and I hope this atmosphere of amiable rivalry shows in our performances. All my colleagues are distinguished and highly respected in their various professions, and I have no academic qualifications at all, but no one has ever made me feel inferior. I have the very greatest respect and affection for all of them, and in the case of the academics, I envy their pupils.

In 1974 one of *Woman's Hour's* most starry producers, Kay Evans, gave me the chance to *ask* questions for a change. We devised a fifteen-minute quiz, with me as question-master, using quotations and recorded voices of well-known people, living or dead. No marks were awarded, but the chief joy of the game lay in the information and anecdotes the players added to their answers, making the quiz rather like a conversation between three friends. We called it 'Who Said That?', and tried to arrange for the two players each week to be one journalist or writer and one 'show-business' personality. The ideal examples were the glamorous Kennedys – Ludovic Kennedy and Moira Shearer. Russell Harty and Barbara Castle, both from Blackburn, were two other expert players who enjoyed the quiz so much that they would cheerfully have played on all afternoon, but we ran out of recorded extracts. Robin Ray, son of the late Ted Ray, Valerie Jenkins of the *Evening Standard*, author and journalist Olga Franklin, and the engaging actor-comedian Roy Hudd were all lured into our quiz-net. We even quizzed Anthony Quinton and Sir Jack Longland. I was especially looking forward to that game, and armed myself with what I thought were diabolical questions, but on that very day I woke up with almost no voice, and what little there was faded away by mid-morning. It was too late to stop Jack and Tony from arriving at the studio, so the Show Had To Go On. On my way to the recording I had darted into every chemist's mouthing wildly at startled assistants and flourishing a note which said: 'I have lost my voice. Have you any Sanderson's Specific?'. Sanderson's Specific was an awesome potion once guaranteed to restore your voice *for a few hours*, probably through some kind of traumatic shock at the evil taste of it. Afterwards you were speechless for some days. Of course no one had heard of it, and I collected a laboratory of vivid bottles and pill-boxes, desperately sampling them all in a kind of reverse Russian roulette – surely *one* would cure me. The total affect was to make me nauseous, and in the end the B.B.C. engineers saved me with their usual calm expertise. They gave me a special microphone, and we all wore headphones. My voice was a husky whisper, and Jack and Tony manfully undertook most of the talking, and with Kay's delicate editing the programme turned out to be one of the best of the series.

A few weeks later I had a telephone call from B.B.C. Televisions's Further Education department asking if I would like to be interviewed as a possible presenter on a new television series for retired people. I've never been bold enough to ask what made them think of me, but I believe it must have been a suggestion by Roy Hudd, who turned out to be the chief presenter on the programme. When Roy had taken part in *Who Said That?* we were able to talk to each other as though we had been lifelong friends. We come from the same working-class background, and we are both Londoners, Roy from south-east London and I from the western edge. Even though I am many years older we share the same style of comic appreciation – in fact at our first meeting on that radio programme we were 'working' ancient jokes like: 'Heard the one about the old maid? She went for a tramp in the woods . . . but he got away.' Roy was brought up by his granny whom he loved dearly. I wish she could have lived to see him now, happy, successful, hard-working and a credit to her care and teaching during his childhood. After a spell as a commercial artist, and some R.A.F. service he became a Butlin's 'redcoat' and then a professional comedian. His versatility is astonishing, he can act, sing, play the guitar, do impressions and tell jokes. (I shouldn't be surprised if he also undertakes 'light removals with horse and van'!) His memory for gags is equal to Ted Ray's, and he must be a godsend to any producer; enthusiastic, industrious, and one of the most intelligent people I've ever met. He has made a special study of nineteenth and early twentieth-century music-hall, and his mind is an Aladdin's cave of information about the songs and the performers of that time. But quite apart from all this, his good-humour is amazing, and his professional manners impeccable. Every single letter from the public is answered, every shy approach from people in the street, or in trains or in hotels is responded to with warmth and kindly interest.

After my interview and a camera-test I was delighted to hear that I would be a co-presenter with Roy on the new show. The executive producer in charge of the programme was Sheila Innes (now Head of Further Education, Television) a small, chic lady with an incisive mind, a very highly-developed sense of humour and a rare gift for devastatingly exact mimicry of a certain Royal personage, all done with loving and respectful precision. Our own producer was Brigit Barry, a tall, elegant young woman who has packed more professional experience into her life than any other two people I can think of – for instance her training in film production was done in France . . . and in French, which, even though she seems utterly fearless, must have been bewildering, to say the least.

Brigit is typical of the young producers of the B.B.C.'s Further Education television programmes. They care a very great deal about their work, and their enthusiasm and conscientiousness are like champagne to the performers who work for them. Their programmes are produced on a frugal budget that any self-respecting church mouse would disdain, but their integrity and ingenuity are boundless. In Brigit's case you can add a kind heart and the most ladylike (what a fine unusual word that has become!) self-restraint, which ensures that she gets her own way without raising her voice.

The new series was to be called the 'Six-O-Seven-O-Eight-O Show', because it was originally designed as a magazine-programme for people of sixty and over. In the event we have had, for the past four years, an audience which seems to be a mixture of the over-sixties and anyone else who is able to watch the show either on Sunday mornings or on its repeat showing on a week-day afternoon. Children, young mothers, disabled or housebound people, hospital patients, shift-workers, we've had letters from them all, for many of our items, films, information about crafts and new ideas for recreation, are suitable for people of any age. We try to mix information and entertainment in equal amounts, and to balance serious and amusing items in each programme. One shrewd comment made about the programme was that it was difficult to know whether to class it as 'Further Entertainment' or 'Light Education'. We have studio guests nearly every week who take part in our discussions, as experts, or as people who have some experience of a particular subject, for we talk about literally everything – money, health, hobbies, holidays, work, ideas, art, exercise, new gadgets to help people who are either temporarily or permanently disabled, and, perhaps most important of all, what retired people can contribute to the community, by giving their skill and their time.

Roy proved an ideal 'host' for this programme, a merry Sam Weller when jokes were needed, and his own serious and kindly self when the grimmer side of life was under discussion. He is sure-footed as a cat in these matters – just saucy enough to make our guests laugh, but ready to listen intently to their opinions and ideas. We have evolved a kind of working relationship rather like that of an older sister and much younger brother, or an irrepressible nephew and well-preserved aunt. We have one disadvantage in common, both of us are appallingly short-sighted. Our programme doesn't use an autocue (the machine that most television presenters read their script from) but even if it did neither of us could see that far, so we have to learn our scripts by heart. This is not nearly as easy as it sounds; somehow the simplest sentence seems to consist of a jumble of interchangeable phrases waiting to become chaotic nonsense. Of course at one time *all* television presenters had to learn their lines, but not much learning is done nowadays, except in drama.

The *607080 Show* has been a revelation to me because of the people I have met during each series. I can remember many years ago when I was touring seaside towns we sometimes had our fortunes told by a lady who called herself Madame Rosalie. She sat in a little red-and-white wooden hut on the promenade and after the usual predictions of futures full of modest success, money, a handsome and faithful husband and healthy and intelligent children she always ended with the same words: 'You'll live to a great old age, dear, and you'll never be a trouble to anyone.' I realise now what a good psychologist Madame Rosalie was, for when most of us think of old age it is with some apprehension, if not dread, and most of that fear is of having to be dependent on the goodwill of other people, and worse still, the fear of loneliness. By loneliness I don't mean that happy solitude that so many older people really enjoy; the time to read, to garden, to listen to the radio, or just to sit and think in the comfort and peace of home. The enemy is the loneliness that means bleak greyness and endless silence that kills the spirit and drains the stoutest heart of all courage. But the older people we met during the series have proved that there is no need to dread old age, and that all the enemies, poverty, ill-health, and loneliness, can be faced and overcome. Only death defeats us all, but even he can be met with composure, according to one of our studio guests, a retired nursing sister who had seen many people die. She told us that most old people, whether they had any religious faith or not, 'die well'. (Incidentally, I wonder why death is always 'he' and not 'she'?)

The older generation is very tough. The last sixty years have made them so. They can teach those of us who are willing to learn many lessons of thrift, and unselfishness and cheerfulness in adversity. Some can be cussed and cantankerous, but young people are cussed and cantankerous too, sometimes with far less reason. The way people regard their retirement depends upon their attitude to their work. If you worked to live, then you will greet the first day of your retirement as 'Liberation Day', as one lady called it. If you lived to work, then you'll need reassurance and encouragement to realise that all your new-found time can be filled with new ideas. Many of our viewers found fresh interests when there was no longer any need to spend time and energy on a career. Some began to help with the adult literacy campaign, and their patience and experience made them excellent teachers. Twenty-four brave souls, men and women, fairly strong and not-so-strong, helped us with a really important and fascinating project designed to show that physical health could actually *improve* in older people. The two architects of the scheme were Dr Malcolm Carruthers, then of St Mary's Hospital Paddington, and Al Murray, the Olympic coach and fitness expert. They worked out a programme of exercises specially designed to suit almost everyone, of whatever age. The whole course could be done taking not more than forty minutes each week, and the results were astonishing. Our volunteers found their health improving with the minimum of effort – and some of them had taken practically no exercise before. At the other end of the health-scale we had a viewer who although partly paralysed ran a telephone message-service from her home. As she remarked with dry humour 'I'm very reliable. . . . I'm always *there*.'

Our studio guests were people whose lives had been very different from one another's – in fact the only thing they all had in common was their age. There was a retired hospital matron; a newspaper-seller; a former B.B.C. foreign correspondent; a carpenter who makes viols; and a retired naval captain who had been a fifteen-year-old midshipman during the Gallipoli landings in 1915. Captain Eric Bush must have been seventy-five when we told part of his story in an item drawing on his book about the campaign, but his coolness would have been remarkable in a man half his age. He sat all day under studio lights – which can feel like a hammer-blow to the head if you are not used to them – with a ramrod back and unfailingly courteous manner. Some of our other guests could have written books too, full of tales about their truly dreadful childhood in the poorer parts of London, when mothers would seek refuge in the workhouse at week-ends – it was the only place where they could protect themselves and their children from drunken, violent husbands. These tales were told to us without a shred of self-pity or bitterness.

Even viewers we never met sent us cards, and sometimes presents they had made. Dolls, woolly hats, hot-water bottle covers, paper roses, velvet-covered boxes of sweets, a brooch made from piano-wire, books, a corn-dolly, a splendid Welsh dragon made of wool, and an exquisite decorated egg. I treasure them all, as I do the hundreds of letters we received, personal notes quite separate from the many thousands of letters sent to the programme requesting information, addresses or leaflets about some unusual handicraft or new project. There must have been thousands of viewers who watched the programme every week in silent rooms, with no relatives or neighbours to talk to or visit. To these people a television set is like a friend sitting in a corner of their home, giving interest and companionship when needed, and if we coloured a grey half-hour for them each week we are truly proud and delighted, and we thumb our noses happily at disdainful critics who pontificate about television being 'a drug'.

Later in 1974 I took part in a hilarious and nerve-racking radio game called *The Year in Question*. The four players were given a date – 1926, 1938, 1962 . . . and then asked questions about the news of that particular year. It was a rough, every-man-for-himself affair, and luckily my partner was Paul Barnes, a cheerfully sardonic young journalist with a mind like a newspaper library and a lightning response to the questions. This game was the setting for the melodrama that all producers dread – one of the players did not turn up. The reason for Terry Wogan's absence was the same as that given by Woodstock for not flying south with the other birds . . . he forgot. Geoffrey Hamilton, former B.B.C. Far East correspondent, happened to be visiting the studio and was corralled into the game as a replacement. He is an expert on all things Japanese – the language and the martial arts too – and on that occasion he showed both inscrutability and courage worthy of a *samurai*. Helen Fry, the producer, had an idea that my mountebank career would make a short programme on its own, and Paul Barnes and I, with Janet Thomas producing, compiled a half-hour which could, with a bit of judicious editing, serve as my obituary when the time comes, called: 'She lived on her wits – and other people's' or, like Alexander Woollcott's house: 'Wit's End'.

Quiz-games, thank goodness, seem to become increasingly intriguing to listeners and viewers, for everyone, performers and people at home, can 'compete', and it's a great thrill for Dad when he knows the answer that nobody else in the family does, or for a younger child who can shine for a few minutes among older brothers or sisters simply by knowing the names of planets, or the habits of animals. The happiest animal quiz I know of is *Two by Two*, where two famous naturalists and I answer questions about animals, and then talk about them afterwards. I meet these distinguished chaps with apprehension, for natural history is not my forte, but they are unfailingly polite and sometimes highly amusing. Johnny Morris, Percy Edwards and Tony Soper all amaze me with their knowledge, and there are surprising contributors like the irrepressible Rolf Harris, a comedian and a fine artist too, and the distinguished actor Esmond Knight. Jeffrey Boswall, who leads B.B.C. natural history filming expeditions to places where butter is always liquid and you really could fry an egg on the pavement if there were any pavements, is not only a highly respected naturalist but a comedian as well, with a tenacious memory for goon-like jokes. Henry Douglas-Home sometimes journeyed down from Scotland to take part, wearing a noble and venerable tweed jacket; and showed the countryman's impassive view of the excitements of London by taking the first train back to Scotland after the recording. Phyllis Robinson, who produced the quiz, also takes my Award For Best Sound of any programme I've done. It was a collection of amateur musicians' and singers' efforts (I wanted to call it 'That will do extremely well, child, you have delighted us long enough', like Mr Bennet in *Pride and Prejudice* but the *Radio Times* columns aren't wide enough), and it was almost the only radio programme I've done where my voice sounds practically the same as it does in my head. Usually your voice sounds either better or worse than you think it is, but that time the sounds were Thomas-like.

One of my favourite quiz-games only occurs once a year. It's a gentle, scholarly game played with a New Zealand team, and Radio New Zealand call it *Stump The Brains Trust*. The two New Zealanders and I are really playing against the New Zealand listeners who send in *Round Britain Quiz*-type questions to try to mystify us all. At the end of the programme we say which question we found the most interesting and whoever sent it gets a small prize. It's a charming, civilised game, and one of the chief delights to a simple 'Pom' like me is in hearing addresses like 'Waratah Avenue, Wanganui' and 'Raratonga Drive, Timaru', with the sound of the South Pacific mixing with the English Channel. You don't have to leave London to hear the world's far-off breathing though. The B.B.C.'s World Service at Bush House in the Strand has an atmosphere as exotic as frangipani, and directly you enter the building you see photographs of people who are unknown to British listeners but household words in Singapore or Tokyo. The World Service still seems to keep the traditional B.B.C. reputation for clarity and integrity, and when the rest of London is silent in the single-digit night hours, Bush House's voices fly over the world, trying to tell the truth in Urdu or Swahili. Even the canteen serves exotic food. There's a B.B.C. folk-tale of a man who once *lived* in Bush House; he slept in an empty studio and ate in the canteen for years until his cover was blown, and it's a credible story. The atmosphere of the place is quite different from Broadcasting House. You feel that the next person to step out of the Rank-Odeon-1930s lift may be a veiled lady dressed in black velvet, wearing a fur toque, with violets pinned to her muff. She'll glide by, leaving a scent of heliotrope on the air, bound for some far-off Balkan kingdom. (You can get horribly lost there, too. On your way to General Features you may end up in the Czech Film Unit.)

Being a kind of semi-celebrity brings bizarre experiences one's way. In the winter of 1976 Bill Wright, the producer of *Mastermind*, had the bright idea of putting on an extra programme in Cambridge as a 'friendly' game between the 1976 Mastermind, the Brain of Britain, and the MENSA champion for that year, and me as a representative of *Round Britain Quiz*. The game was good fun and the MENSA champion deserved his win, but it was an illustration of how very minutely such games are followed by viewers, for there were letters to the newspapers afterwards saying that I had been asked fewer questions than the other contestants, and so had been given a diminished chance of winning. I was grateful to the writers for their sharp-eyed partisanship, but I hadn't noticed the number of questions at the time, it was just a very enjoyable game. Incidentally I have to report that the famous Black Chair is not nearly as frightening as it appears, all one's concentration is by then on Magnus Magnusson's questions, and the chair, the lights and the audience are almost irrelevant. Far more worrying is the walk to and from the chair, over slippery sisal matting – especially to the short-sighted contestant! A walk by the river next morning proved to me that King's College Chapel is even more lovely and ethereal seen through flurries of snow than it is when it gleams among its daffodils in spring.

My 'special subject' in the quiz had been the songs of the American Civil War. It had been quite hard to choose a special category, for I'm not really expert enough at any one subject, but thanks to Charles Chilton's *The Blue and the Gray* radio programme all those years before, those songs, sentimental and even mawkish at times, have haunted me ever since, not so much for their own merit as for the atmosphere of the time in which they were first sung and played. Usually I can pick my way through most quiz programmes without much extra study, but I had to pay special attention to my subject for the *Supermind* game, and it occurred to me that this might be the reason why so many women have been *Mastermind* champions. Men tend to think they will know enough about their special subject anyway, but women are nearly always less confident and 'revise' assiduously. The general knowledge marks are fairly evenly balanced between men and women. In the radio *Brain of Britain* contest only three women have ever won the title. There is no special category of questions here, and to pick up extra marks it is necessary to have a combination of boldness and sheer cheek which fewer women than men seem to possess. This could be the reason why there have been very few women stand-up comics. There are plenty of excellent character-actresses who can superbly deliver funny lines within a play or situation-comedy, but the lone comedian's art requires a masculine pugnacity and the skin of a rhinoceros.

Every year I go to the 'Women of the Year' luncheon at the Savoy. This is a very pleasant way of raising money for the Greater London Fund for the Blind. Those of us who are invited feel flattered, our contributions are useful in many small ways, and it's a grand opportunity to see famous women and their hats. The after-lunch speeches are an illustration of one of the differences between men and women. At an equivalent lunch for men the speeches would be more assertive and jokey, and sometimes boastful and swaggering. The ladies, with few exceptions, speak seriously, without much intentional humour, and lack the force and assurance of the men in similar circumstances. The audience is generous, though; women are rather nicer than men, I think – softer, and more easily impressed.

There are some women, of course, who will never admit to there being any difference between men and women. I used to think that the difference was confined to whatever went on below the nose. From there upwards, I thought, we're all the same. Now I don't think we are. Men and women can talk about the same subjects but women's attitudes and opinions will be subtly different from men's in many ways. In most radio discussions women are used in the proportion one-to-three, consequently they are easily shouted down, overpowered by the sheer loudness of men's voices and all those midnight-oil jokes, and the trumpeting about their latest book. If they shout back they sound shrill and strident. So it was pleasant to be asked to act as a kind of hostess to three other women in a weekly Radio 4 discussion in 1977. We called it *The Better Half*, a tongue-in-cheek title, and each week we dealt with a different subject; advertising, money, death, conservation, broadcasting, travel. We were very gratified when so many distinguished women agreed to take part, and many more were ready to if they were needed, but the programme must have been a disappointment to those listeners who were waiting for the kind of show where the word 'knickers' is followed by copious cackling, while for the deadly serious feminists we were not belligerent enough.

There were several critics whose indignation was extreme. Mainly they were the people who mistake gentleness and good humour for weakness, or else they may have been earnest young chaps with stern liberationist girl-friends breathing down their necks, or the die-hards who would abolish Ladies Bars in old-fashioned pubs. One incensed listener threatened to report us all to the Equal Opportunities Commission on the grounds that we were discriminating against men. I wish he had done so – the publicity would have been highly gratifying.

I have a good deal of sympathy for women who feel that they are being oppressed by a male-dominated society; after all, I have experienced a fair amount of anti-female prejudice myself, sometimes, sadly, from women. But in all the commotion and disputation engendered by the Women's Movement (a strange title, I think, it sounds like a step in a country dance) one woman is gradually becoming an endangered species as much in need of conservation as any rare animal. That is the professional housewife (and if that word brings a disdainful curl to the lip of staunch feminists I am unrepentant.) There are some progressive lady journalists who see 'housewife' as a word to describe a pear-shaped drudge carrying a string-bag. One even went so far as to write, after a glowing description of some expensive household gadget: 'So now there's really no excuse for not going out to work', as though 'work' always had to be carried on outside the home to be at all satisfying. Certainly most interviewers have stopped asking 'Do you work, or are you just a housewife?', but even now, when confronted with a happily un-neurotic full-time homemaker they look incredulous for a few seconds and then say, very kindly: 'Oh well, if that's what you really *want* . . .' So beware, all hard-working and expert ladies who manage households, there are a few querulous harpies who are trying, for some Byzantine reason, to make you feel inferior. A figurative two-fingered gesture, though rather unladylike, is all that is necessary in reply, for ultimately it is on women, and their attitudes and influence as girl-friends, wives and mothers, that civilisation depends. Your power is enormous, and certainly it can affect men's response to the rest of womankind. If you mutter a curt refusal when offered a seat in a train you chip away a man's chivalrous instinct. You may genuinely not need that seat, but the next woman he might have offered it to may be tired, or old, or pregnant, and thanks to your ungraciousness she'll have to stand. And I humbly suggest that to go round dressed as for the stage rather than for the street and then to be huffy when the local lads become a nuisance is rather like dangling a toy in front of a child and then scolding him when he snatches at it. There is another school of feminist couture which decrees that all clothes must look as though they had been made with a knife and fork and then dropped on the wearer from a great height. The face to go with this outfit must be devoid of make-up, as though the owner had just risen from a hospital bed. This can either express the 'Look how marvellous I am without makeup so think what I'd be like with it' outlook, or just the 'I can't be bothered dressing-up for the likes of *you*' creed; both are tiresome and discourteous.

The 1960s, with the growth of the permissive society – or the Age of the Toddler, when society went soft in the head, whichever way you express it – left behind certain superstitions which die hard. One is that The Pill is liberating. Maybe. Or maybe it merely transfers another responsibility from the already irresponsible man to the gullible girl. Another myth is that marriage is 'just a piece of paper' and irrelevant, and meaningless. The difference between marriage and cohabitation is almost impossible to explain, but it is like comparing astronauts in a simulator and astronauts actually in orbit. Another myth is that marriage and 'a career' can be easily combined. Again, maybe, but not easily. Whether you are the chatelaine of a two-roomed flat or of a vast Palladian mansion, for some atavistic reason the running of it will eventually devolve on you, or on a deputy of yours if you can afford one. You can be a Cabinet Minister, but only *you* can decide what to send to a jumble sale when cupboards are turned out, and Barbara Castle has recalled sitting down to a committee meeting and silently cursing because she had forgotten to make out the laundry list. If you have children then it gets more difficult still to have a career. ('Career' should be defined more clearly, especially by the kind of feminist writers who seem to spend most of their time figuratively gazing glumly up the collective crotch of womankind . . . do they mean sewing buttons on a card, or being a concert pianist? Buttons on a card can be attended to without undue worry or preparation, but being a concert pianist demands emotionally more than most *men*, let alone women, are prepared to give.) Marriage is difficult enough without added complications, and has to be worked at, like polishing and softening harness for a pair of horses. Unlike the horses, human beings harnessed together don't always trot together, generally one loves more than the other – you've seen newspaper photographs where the bride gazes adoringly at the bridegroom and the bridegroom gazes with love at the camera, an illustration of the cynical maxim 'It should be a very happy marriage – they are both so much in love with *him*.'

But one of the most powerful superstitions left over from the sick sixties is the one which has made our present child-centred society.

This violent shift from the extreme 'seen-and-not-heard' philosophy has produced a quite repulsive race of tiny consumers, fostered by advertisers and nurtured by armies of well-meaning educationalists. Every supermarket has its quota of Spock-marked young mothers, their necks and ears going crimson with suppressed rage, trying to reason with a three-year-old thug. Mamma is convinced that she must not damage Junior's personality by such a dreadful thing as a sharp smack, but judging by the way she will hiss at him through clenched teeth she is likely to be among the most fervent advocates of nursery-schools for the under-fives . . . just so that he can 'learn to integrate with his peers' of course. When you observe Junior's face shrinking to a rim of purple surrounding a square bawling mouth you wonder if King Herod was quite such a bad chap after all. This 'kicking-and-screaming-until-I-get-what-I-want' persists through adolescence and sometimes into manhood, when apparently mature men are referred to by their spokesmen as 'the lads', and there is much talk of 'demands' and 'rights', and none about duties and obligations.

One of the most painful aspects of late-twentieth-century life to my mind is the degeneration of the working-class, the class I was born in and was once so proud of. Most of the deterioration has been caused by the quite appalling sentimentality of middle-class socialists. These earnest heirs of the tweed-knickerbockered reformers of the late-nineteenth century imagined that the working-class, given lovely new flats with bathrooms and central heating, would be happily dancing round the maypole in no time. The working-class, who are not daft, seized gleefully on this opportunity, and learned the language too. When their unadmonished children chopped down the maypole it was 'a cry for help'. Pestilential nuisances were not shiftless, vicious or stupid, they were 'disturbed' or 'inadequate'. Social workers (surely enough of them now for us all to have one each) put all juvenile nastiness down to 'boredom', and politicos looking for a headline-catching cause to shine in took up the chant. Will somebody explain how in God's name any youngster nowadays can be *bored*? Boredom is a self-inflicted wound, and children have never had so many chances and interests as at present. Even the non-academic youngster can go dancing, or camping, or do gardening – someone else's if not his own – study carpentry, gymnastics, calligraphy, acting, cycling, natural history of his locality, trace his ancestry, do voluntary work, walk, play chess, or read. With this miasma of theories swirling round their heads it is small wonder that many working-class parents – and middle-class parents too – threw in the towel and let the educational psychologists romp unconfined through a complete generation. Now in the 1970s the garlands are withering and we are clearing up the mess after the party. There are still 'reformers' full of passionate intensity but their audience is drifting away.

One last myth remains, the theory that children mature so much earlier these days. Physically perhaps – but even that is only six months for every ten years, in other words your daughter is about a year or so more 'mature' than her mother was at the same age. Emotionally most youngsters are as bewildered as they ever were, although outwardly they may appear to be confident; like a cake baked in a too-hot oven they are hard on the outside while the inside is still mushy and uncooked. The too-hot oven has been provided by over-frantic advertising on the part of the ingenious fellows who stand to profit most from the Youth Industry.

When I was a child, confidence was hard to achieve, and we were considered to be apprentice adults, probationary members of society, until we had learned poise and discretion. This was taught by a mixture of love, discipline, and, best of all, example from parents and teachers. We *knew* we were ignorant, but some of today's children have the confidence of true ignorance . . . they don't know how much they don't know. Being young is *not* the best time of your life, and growing up is as painful and puzzling as it always was. I don't suppose it will ever change, but while the wretched uncertainty of youth lasts it is up to the older generation to provide security, and a few temporary guide-lines. Maybe I'll be accused of having a 'lower-middle-class work ethic', or of being simplistic, or of wanting the standard of values of a Norman Rockwell illustration, as though that were evidence of reaction. But I believe that most working-class families would like to regain those values, and a world where father worked hard and protected his family, mother kept them clean, happy and free of debt, whether she worked outside the home or not, and children had fun, respected their elders and cared for their younger brothers and sisters. Alas, it all takes a very great deal of effort, and effort has become unfashionable.

Many years ago there was a girl viola-player in the orchestra at Covent Garden whose hobby was palmistry, and during the gaps which occur in rehearsals, full of sudden changes of lighting, shuddering thumps and muffled cries of: 'From you, to me, up-end it, Bert', she read our palms. Fortune-telling is eternally fascinating. The most sophisticated television executive will want to know what his newspaper 'stars' say if you begin reading out other people's, and young women are as fascinated by the future as when Horace reprimanded his girl-friend for her obsession with signs and portents. The viola-player prophesied that my most interesting years would arrive after I was forty. Now when you are young, forty is light-years away, and time to play the Last Post and haul down the flag anyway. As it happened, the viola-player was dead right. I'll go even further and say that I truly wouldn't wish to be less than fifty for anything – unless I could know all that I know now. There really is no substitute for experience, and I've come to the time when I can sit down in the early evening of my day of life and think about what's past and what's to come. For now I know that there are certain fundamental truths which are eternal, like the fact, that no matter how you have searched, there will always be one teaspoon left at the bottom of the washing-up water; and that there is no known method of extracting grated cheese from coconut matting or raw egg from the back of the washing-machine (don't ask me how it got there, it would entail writing a whole thesis). Some more great truths are worthy of record, like the fact that nice people, unless they happen to have been born rich, generally stay poor; and that there are two kinds of music, good and bad, and that you should sometimes realise when you are licked – 'If at first you don't succeed, give up.' But it's not always easy to judge when to give up . . . except in the case of my driving-lessons. I took a short course of these, tutored by a patient and increasingly perplexed Irishman. I started and stopped with admirable smoothness, never crashed the gears, and remembered all signals and checked all dials. The only trouble seemed to be that I was utterly incapable of driving at more than ten miles an hour because almost everyone else on the roads appeared to be raving mad, and when I got out of the car my knees had turned to jelly. It's a case of 'you name it and I can't drive it', whether bicycle, skateboard or wheelbarrow. I remain a devout pedestrian and coward. It's just as well, I suppose, there are certainly enough accidents as it is without any help from me. So there's another fundamental truth; that there are certain people who are natural non-drivers.

One of the greatest truths, it seems to me is that ninety per cent of people live in a state of constant anxiety (Thoreau's 'quiet desperation') about some aspect of their lives, and are therefore in constant need of reassurance, no matter how confident they seem. This is particularly the case with very young men – it's harder to be an apprentice man than an apprentice woman, everyone expects you to be so sure of yourself, and so brave in the face of a head-waiter's scorn.

But in the world of entertainment the percentage rises to ninety-nine per cent, no matter how brash the ego. The noisy conceit is like the banging of gongs to frighten away devils, the devils being fear of failure, fear of ageing, fear of being snubbed, fear of making a fool of oneself and feeling small. Hence the often-fatal reliance on those two instant fear-quellers, drink and drugs, and the comforting pretences, the dyed hair, the face-lifts, the too-low necklines, the over-bright eye-shadow; or perhaps the reverse affectations, scruffy jeans and grubby nails. The only sure way to gain complete confidence in the entertainment profession is to be absolutely certain of your technique, whether it's in singing or dancing or acting. 'Nerves' are ninety per cent bad conscience; knowing that you haven't worked quite hard enough at your job. The other ten per cent is honest apprehension, and cannot – perhaps should not – be dispelled. There can be days when you are feeling fragile as a politician's promise, and things may go fearfully wrong when your evil genie gets to know about it. These disasters can happen in the most distinguished circles. There's a heart-stopping story of how Claudio Arrau arrived at a concert hall without rehearsal, all ready to play a Brahms piano concerto. He acknowledged the welcoming applause, bowed to the conductor and orchestra, and sat down to await the lengthy and stormy orchestral introduction to Brahms Number One. To his consternation, out flowed the introduction to Brahms Number *Two*, only a couple of bars long, and entailing a blood-chilling change of concentration. Needless to say, he coped with it.

The longer I live the more I have learned to mistrust any form of entertainment with the word 'workshop' in the title – 'Dance workshop' or 'Theatre workshop'. Generally it means a great many actors or dancers improvising lines and movements, and entails a lot of rolling about on a dusty stage and shouting in poorly-projected voices. Improvised dialogue always sounds far more self-conscious than lines that have been learned and practised after being written down, and half the audience's concentration is gnawed away by a vague worry as to whether the actors will finally 'dry'. So I have admitted to myself that what I really want to see or hear are the skills that have taken twenty years to perfect, performed by professionals in whatever sphere of the entertainment world they may have chosen. These professionals must include all ballet dancers (you really can't get away with improvisation there!) opera singers and concert instrumentalists, and the B.B.C.'s Northern Dance Orchestra or indeed any big brassy band, all accompanists, like Johnny Franz who used to play for Anne Shelton (and as far as I'm concerned was wasting his talent being a record company executive; he had such sensitivity to Anne's singing and a technique that made keyboard arabesques like the ringing of bluebells). And crack dance-ensembles like the Tiller Girls who were once the first act on every Palladium show. No matter how often I saw them it was a sheer delight to watch their routine, right up to the moment when they finish on one knee and the line of lovely feather-decked heads snaps up to smile at the audience. They were, I suppose, the feminine equivalent of the Brigade of Guards, achieving their effect with sequins and smiles instead of swords and bearskins.

Some people are born professionals, like Ivor Novello and Irving Berlin. Even if they cannot read or write music they have a steely instinct for the right formula to please the ear of the audience.

It's the creeping spread of semi-skilled performances that makes me less than enthusiastic about theatre-going, particularly to those musicals where everyone does everything, sings a bit, dances a bit, acts a bit, and none of it all that well. I like shows where singers sing, dancers dance, actors speak clearly, and where everybody has obviously worked hard at the job. Alas, managements insist on staging some musicals with rambling and unmemorable songs, and then are amazed and hurt when the show fails, no matter how hard the cast have worked. No wonder television is such an attraction, at least you can switch over – or off – to something better. (There can be some 'mauvais quarts d'heure' in opera, too. Parts of Richard Strauss's *Elektra* do go on a bit . . . There aren't a lot of laughs in it, either, but it's mercifully short, so short that Eddie says there ought to be a newsreel with it, or at least a *Tom and Jerry*.) Performers of all kinds can be grateful to television and radio. New professions have sprung fully-armed out of the air. Disc-jockeys quacking frantically to an unseen seraglio of admiring ladies, anchor-men performing their ritual threatening dances round sleek politicians who've heard it all before – and newsreaders. A great fuss is made about those, but, so far as I can see, the qualifications are minimal – an unremarkable appearance, standard English, good eyesight (to read the Autocue) and about one O-Level. And the day I'll really believe in sex equality is the day I see the news being read by a grey-haired fifty-year-old lady wearing glasses – a female equivalent of Kenneth Kendall – and nobody making any comment about it.

To be quite candid, I don't miss musical shows all that much – certainly not the 'smell of greasepaint'. There are things I do miss though. The principal one is the sense of being part of a company, as I was when I was one of the Mitchells. I miss some of the minor bonuses, like the unrepeatable 'warm-up' jokes told at rehearsals to get the audience in the right mood before television recordings of variety shows. I miss the gossip and the mild scandal of the who-is-sleeping-with-whom variety, and the cheerful vulgarity of the shows where girls are not so much auditioned as measured, and the in-jokes about personalities like the comment made when a flamboyant producer was startlingly promoted . . . 'He began his career as an effects-boy' . . . 'He still is.' And the time-honoured catch-phrases like 'Art for art's sake, cash for God's sake', and 'It'll be all right when it's lit'. This last stems from the tale of the two elderly men, one a scene-painter, the other an electrician, glumly contemplating an ill-constructed stage set. The electrician says: 'It'll be all right when it's lit'. And after a while his friend says: 'And if it's not, we'll *paint* t'boogger.' I miss the costume-fittings in tiny Soho workrooms where two elderly sisters would, if I had time to spare, use me as a clothes-horse to fit dancers' costumes while they told me tales of the 1920s and '30s, in between sips of gin to ease the coughing caused by their dangling cigarettes. I miss the entirely spontaneous parties that grew out of conversations between four or five touring actors in the bar of some grimy provincial hotel. You couldn't organise such events . . . you could collect the same people in the same bar another evening and nothing would sparkle. I miss the weird theatrical folk-tales, like the tradition that Max Jaffa was able to play a piece called 'The Canary' with his violin *behind his head*, and the legend of the famous horn-player ploughing manfully through a noisy *avant-garde* concerto conducted by the composer. After some minutes of ear-splitting cacophony the soloist gave up, and played phrases from one of the Richard Strauss horn concertos instead. At the end of if all, the composer-conductor shook his hand warmly, evidently much moved by the performance. There were truly eerie tales too, like the one about the chorus-girl who went out from her digs in a northern town to post a letter and was never seen again.

I suppose the secret of serene living is to know your own faults and accept adversity with as good a grace as possible. My chief faults, I think, are an over-emphasis on saving money (less pronounced since an American-Jewish friend reminded me that there are no pockets in a shroud), an increasing reluctance to go out to parties or even to entertain people at home ('We shall be at home between seven and eight on Thursday and we hope you will be, too'). This unsociable outlook may be due to my certainty after all these years that there's nothing all that fascinating going on anywhere else, and it's all so much nicer at home, where I can sit in the garden for hours doing absolutely nothing – sometimes not even thinking. I'm increasingly intolerant of bad manners and grubby habits – people resting their dirty boots on the opposite seat in railway carriages, people who sneeze and cough without using their handkerchiefs, as though their germs were a sort of divine confetti that we should all be pleased to receive. My chief fault remains a lack of singlemindedness. Other people stride purposefully on, their eyes fixed determinedly on the horizon, and there am I, dawdling along, kicking pebbles, distracted by the flowers in the hedgerows, and beguiled by passing cats. I've tried to be more positive, honest I have, judge, but I know that even though I want to speak Chinese I don't want to *learn* to speak Chinese. I suppose, no matter how you may strive, you have a fundamental character that won't change, rather like one of those bead-curtains hanging in a doorway, disturbed by the movement of people passing through and then settling back and showing its original pattern of shadowy flowers and birds. I should perhaps talk a lot more, but I find it exhausting, and I like listening. I sometimes think it might have been very pleasant to have been born rich, all my small talents are ones that needed watering with cash to bring them into an early flowering. But there, if I'd been to Oxford what would I have become? . . . perhaps a history professor, or an expert on Elizabethan music, and I doubt very much if I would have had as much fun. But these are only vague, rueful excuses, and from here on there are comparatively few things I crave. A small Regency house in Richmond perhaps; to have a flower named for me . . . an iris, maybe; to find out who on earth my paternal grandfather was . . . quite impossible; an honorary degree . . . highly unlikely; . . . to sing with a group of 'Sweet Adelines', those cheerful and enthusiastic American ladies who are the female equivalent of the barber-shop quartets . . . now *there's* a possibility, but it would take a great deal of practice, and I'm one of nature's sprinters, not really a long-distance runner.

During one of my browsings through a delightfully time-wasting reference book I discovered that Eddie and I will soon be celebrating our 'pearl' wedding . . . thirty years. Wedding anniversaries get more valuable names as the years go on, starting at one year, merely 'cotton'. The couple who survive the matrimonial steeplechase for forty years are entitled to a 'ruby' wedding, then gold, then diamonds. Is it because after sixty years they *deserve* diamonds, or is it that only after all that time can they afford them?

After so many years I can honestly say that, even though we know so much about each other that we can answer each other's questions half-way through ('Where's the. . . .? Right-hand kitchen cupboard, top shelf,'), I am continually amused and delighted by my husband's company. Infuriating he often is, boring never. He understands me better than I understand myself, and remains my dearest friend and counsellor. His presence is a constant joy to me, and the mere sight of him, whether he's planting out petunia seedlings, listening to opera records while watching television rugby with the sound turned down, reading his Italian books or walking beside me along the towpath to Kew, always gives me pleasure.

One of us will inevitably die first, and the other will be left alone again (as every human being essentially is, for no one, however loving, can know another person's innermost thoughts or feel someone else's pain, but can only try to imagine those things).

'The secret of love is greater than the secret of death' sings Richard Strauss's Salome, and so it has always seemed to me, whether the love is that between husband and wife, or between two friends, or between parent and child. Love is certainly stronger than death. People you love die, but your love for them does not. It is as if they were in another room, not visible, but still not far away.

All that can be said about love between two people – in this case husband and wife – was said two thousand years ago in a poem written by a Chinese general to his wife, and translated by Arthur Waley.

Since my hair was plaited and we became man and wife
The love between us was never broken by doubt.
So let us be merry this night together,
Feasting and playing while the good time lasts.
I suddenly remember the distance that I must travel;
I spring from bed and look out to see the time.
The stars and planets are all grown dim in the sky;
Long, long is the road; I cannot stay.

I am going on service, away to the battle-ground,
And I do not know when I shall come back.
I hold your hand with only a deep sigh;
Afterwards, tears – in the days when we are parted.
With all your might enjoy the spring flowers,
But do not forget the time of our love and pride.
Know that if I live, I will come back again,
And if I die, we will go on thinking of each other.

No one can be conscious of deep love all day, every day. But it is there, sometimes hardly noticed, underlying everything, like the strong canvas underlying the colours and shapes in a painting. That poem holds both the sureness of loving and the uncertainty of living.

As I grow older my appreciation of small pleasures gets much sharper, because I measure them against past grimness, and one of my five senses becomes more acute day by day, my sense of smell. Not always a blessing, but it helps memory and adds piquancy to living. Some monumental odours recall places – like the smell of the old Cardiff buses, an overpowering mixture of tobacco-smoke, urine and stale chips – some recall times, like the smell of paraffin reminding me of the rosy pattern the ornamental top of our old oil-stove made on my bedroom ceiling when I was a child. The dank earthy smell of seldom-used country churches is saddening, the smell of tar reminds me of the hot summer roads in the nineteen-thirties. But where are the old perfumes . . . Atkinson's White Rose, reputed to have been Queen Alexandra's favourite . . . and Coty's flowers of the thirties and forties: Jasmine de Corse, Rose Jacqueminot, Lilas Pourpre, Nouveau Gardénia? How charming it would be to live in a halcyon world full of lilies-of-the-valley and lilac, cats, and Earl Grey tea, and expensive stationery, and teddy-bears and the songs of Fauré and Reynaldo Hahn. I must plant some more rosemary, not only for remembrance, but for its own sweet aroma. Billy Rose of the 'Diamond Horseshoe' began his memoirs with: 'What I don't know would fill a book and, dear reader, it's going to.' Dante ended one of his works because he ran out of paper '. . . ma piene son tutte le carte.' Who'll lend me an ending for mine? At the end of television scripts the instruction is 'Fade Sound and Vision', but I'll borrow from Lady Mary Wortley-Montagu who concluded: 'Well, it's all been very interesting.' It still is, Lady Mary, it still is.

Index